Locating the Field

ASA Monographs

ISSN 0066-9679

Locating the Field

Space, Place and Context in Anthropology

Edited by Simon Coleman and Peter Collins

Oxford • New York

First published in 2006 by
Berg
Editorial offices:
1st Floor, Angel Court, 81 St Clements Street, Oxford, OX4 1AW, UK
175 Fifth Avenue, New York, NY 10010, USA

Berg is the imprint of Oxford International Publishers Ltd.

Library of Congress Cataloguing-in-Publication Data
Locating the field : space, place and context in anthropology / edited by
Simon Coleman and Peter Collins.
    p. cm. — (ASA monographs, ISSN 0066-9679 ; 42)
  Includes bibliographical references and index.
  ISBN-13: 978-1-84520-403-7 (pbk.)
  ISBN-10: 1-84520-403-4 (pbk.)
  ISBN-13: 978-1-84520-402-0 (hardback)
  ISBN-10: 1-84520-402-6 (hardback)
  1. Anthropology—Field work. I. Coleman, Simon, 1963- II. Collins,
Peter (Peter Jeffrey) III. Series: A.S.A. monographs ; 42.

  GN34.3.F53L63 2006
  301.072'3—dc22   2006010298

British Library Cataloguing-in-Publication Data
A catalogue record for this book is available from the British Library.

ISBN-13 978 1 84520 402 0 (Cloth)
ISBN-10 1 84520 402 6 (Cloth)

ISBN-13 978 1 84520 403 7 (Paper)
ISBN-10 1 84520 403 4 (Paper)

Typeset by Avocet Typeset, Chilton, Aylesbury, Bucks
Printed in the United Kingdom by Biddles Ltd, King's Lynn

www.bergpublishers.com

Contents

Acknowledgements

When and where was this book born? The easy answer is that it began its life at the ASA annual conference held in Grey College, Durham, from 29 March to 1 April 2004. At that conference Simon Coleman and Peter Collins were merely the nominal organizers. A great debt is owed to Rohan Jackson and his band of helpers, without whose efficient work the conference would have been far less convivial. We should also thank our three plenary speakers, Ulf Hannerz, Webb Keane and Nigel Rapport – and especially the latter, who agreed to cover a colleague's withdrawal at the last minute. Valuable funding was obtained from the British Academy and from the Department of Anthropology at Durham. Richard Fardon, Chair of the ASA, proved an admirable support and speaker, as did Alan Bilsborough, biological anthropologist and Pro Vice Chancellor of the University of Durham. Hannah Shakespeare of Berg Publishers has been a patient and helpful presence during the preparation of the manuscript, and Trevor Marchand an excellent adviser on the ASA series. However, there is a more complicated answer to our opening question. The book, or at least parts of it, has been gestating in the minds (and bodies) of a group of authors who have worked in Africa, Asia, Europe and the Americas. They have observed, talked, listened and written in a multitude of places and in wildly varying contexts. Locating the book, like locating the field, is hardly a straightforward matter, but here it is: the material product of a partially material and thoroughly co-operative process.

Simon Coleman
Peter Collins

List of Contributors

Leslie Bank is the Director of the Institute for Social and Economic Research at the University of Fort Hare in South Africa and is a Research Fellow of the Centre for African Studies at the University of Cambridge. He is a Ph.D. in Social Anthropology from the University of Cape Town and has conducted considerable research in urban and rural communities in different parts of South Africa over the past two decades. He has published widely in Africa-related journals and is the author of a forthcoming book for Pluto, *Home Spaces, Street Styles: Contesting Power and Identity in a South African City.* He has also recently edited a special issue of *Social Dynamics* (31 (1), 2005), *Land Reform and Rural Development in South Africa's Eastern Cape.*

Simon Coleman is Professor of Anthropology at the University of Sussex. Previously he was Reader in Anthropology and Deputy Dean of Social Sciences and Health at the University of Durham. Publications include *The Globalisation of Charismatic Christianity: Spreading the Gospel of Prosperity* (2000, Cambridge University Press), *Reframing Pilgrimage: Cultures in Motion* (co-edited with John Eade, 2004, Routledge) and *Religion, Identity and Change* (co-edited with Peter Collins, 2004, Ashgate).

Peter Collins is Lecturer in Anthropology at the University of Durham. He has conducted fieldwork among Quakers, local government employees and in National Health Service hospitals, all in the UK. His interests include religion and ritual, space and place, aesthetics, qualitative methodology and, increasingly, death. Recent publications include *Religion, Identity and Change* (co-edited with Simon Coleman 2004, Ashgate) and *Reading Religion in Text and Context* (co-edited with Elisabeth Arweck, 2006, Ashgate).

Susan Frohlick is Assistant Professor in the Anthropology Department at the University of Manitoba, Winnipeg, Canada. Her key research interests are gender and sexuality, transnationalism and globalization, travel and tourism, and multi-sited ethnography. A current project focuses on transnational intimate relations between tourists and locals in the Caribbean Costa Rica and questions of mobility, 'travelling sexuality', imagination and place. Recent publications include (2004)

'Who is Lakpa Sherpa? Circulating Subjectivities in the Local/Global Terrains of Himalayan Mountaineering', *Journal of Social and Cultural Geography* 5 (2): 195–212; and (2003) 'Negotiating the Global Playground: Shifting Contours of Everest as a Transnational Workplace', *Canadian Review of Sociology and Anthropology* 40 (5): 525–42.

Ulf Hannerz is Professor of Social Anthropology, Stockholm University, Sweden, and has taught at several American, European, Asian and Australian universities. He is a member of the Royal Swedish Academy of Sciences and the American Academy of Arts and Sciences, an honorary fellow of the Royal Anthropological Institute of Great Britain and Ireland, and a former Chair of the European Association of Social Anthropologists. His research has been especially in urban anthropology, media anthropology and transnational cultural processes. Among his books are *Soulside* (1969, Columbia University Press; 2004, University of Chicago Press), *Exploring the City* (1980, Columbia University Press), *Cultural Complexity* (1992, Columbia University Press), *Transnational Connections* (1996, Routledge) and *Foreign News* (2004, University of Chicago Press).

Tim Ingold is Professor of Social Anthropology at the University of Aberdeen. He has carried out ethnographic fieldwork among Saami and Finnish people in Lapland, and has written extensively on comparative questions of environment, technology and social organization in the circumpolar North, as well as on evolutionary theory in anthropology, biology and history, on the role of animals in human society, and on issues in human ecology. His recent research interests are in the anthropology of technology and in aspects of environmental perception. His major publications include *Evolution and Social Life* (1986, Cambridge University Press), *The Appropriation of Nature* (1986, Manchester University Press), *Tools, Language and Cognition in Human Evolution* (co-edited with Kathleen Gibson, 1993, Cambridge University Press) and *Key Debates in Anthropology* (1996, Routledge). His latest book, *The Perception of the Environment*, was published by Routledge in 2000. He is currently writing and teaching on the comparative anthropology of the line, and on issues on the interface between anthropology, archaeology, art and architecture.

Sigridur Duna Kristmundsdottir is Professor of Anthropology at the Department of Anthropology, University of Iceland. Her research interests include gender, political anthropology, biography, method and applied anthropology. Among her publications are '"Father Did Not Answer That Question": Power, Gender and Globalization in Europe', in Angela Cheater (ed.), *The Anthropology of Power: Empowerment and Disempowerment in Changing Structures*, ASA Monograph 36 (1999, Routledge) and 'Women's Movements and the

Contradictory Forces of Globalization', in Hilda Romer Christensen, Beatrice Halsaa and Aino Saarinen (eds), *Crossing Borders: Re-mapping Women's Movements at the Turn of the 21st Century* (2004, University Press of Southern Denmark).

James Leach is Research Fellow and Director of Studies in Anthropology, King's College Cambridge, and an Associate Lecturer in the Department of Social Anthropology at the University of Cambridge. He has carried fieldwork in Madang Province, Papua New Guinea and in the UK. His research interests include kinship and place, creativity, artistic production, ownership and cultural/intellectual property. Recent publications include *Creative Land: Place and Procreation on the Rai Coast of Papua New Guinea* (2003, Berghahn Books) and *Rationales of Ownership: Transactions and Claims to Ownership in Contemporary Papua New Guinea* (co-edited with Lawrence Kalinoe, 2004, Sean Kingston Publishing).

Jo Lee is an Academic Fellow in the Department of Anthropology at the University of Aberdeen, where he has been carrying out an ESRC project entitled 'Culture from the Ground: Walking, Movement and Placemaking' with Tim Ingold. He is also working on publications from his Ph.D. on landscape and social change in Orkney, Scotland, and on European rural development.

Sharmina Mawani is currently a Ph.D. student in the Department for the Study of Religion at SOAS, University of London. Sharmina's research interests focus on the role of language in the transmission of religious knowledge amongst young Ismailis in Canada and India. She is particularly interested in the manner in which traditional religious practices are adapted to suit the personal needs of individuals living in contemporary societies.

Anjoom Mukadam completed her Ph.D. in Sociolinguistics from the University of Reading in 2003. Anjoom's research interests are inter-disciplinary and include issues of identity, language, culture, religion and gender, with respect to post-diasporic Indians in the West. She coined the term 'Indobrit'® in 1999 to reflect the fused ethnic and national identities of young South Asians living in Britain. At present she is a research associate at Lancaster University's Centre for Excellence in Leadership.

Nicholas Nisbett's doctoral research was primarily concerned with the impacts of internet use and IT-related employment amongst middle-class men in Bangalore. Research interests to emerge from this work include: gender, class and consumption in urban India; social mobility within the outsourcing industry; the 'knowledge society'; and development discourse and the middle-class narrative of

IT-driven progress. He is currently employed as an ESRC Postdoctoral Research Fellow in the Department of Anthropology at the University of Sussex, UK.

Nigel Rapport holds a Canada Research Chair in Globalization, Citizenship and Justice at Concordia University of Montreal, where he is Director of the Concordia Centre for Cosmopolitan Studies. He is also a Professor at the Norwegian University of Science and Technology, Trondheim. His research interests include: social theory, phenomenology, identity, individuality, consciousness, literary anthropology, humanism and cosmopolitanism. Among his recent publications are: *I am Dynamite: An Alternative Anthropology of Power* (2003, Routledge); (as editor) *Democracy, Science and the Open Society: A European Legacy?* (2005, Lit); and *The Trouble with Community: Anthropological Reflections on Movement, Identity and Collectivity* (co-edited with Vered Amit, 2002, Pluto).

Introduction: 'Being ... Where?' Performing Fields on Shifting Grounds

Simon Coleman and Peter Collins

Pick up a copy of Evans-Pritchard's *The Nuer* (1940). Ignore the text and look at the maps. Opposite the first page we find Africa, with a small, shaded area indicating the part of the continent that E.P. will describe. A couple of sides later we gaze at a specific region in the Sudan that is punctuated by the White and Blue Nile. Finally, four pages further along[1] there is a sketch-map of the place where the larger Nuer tribes are to be found. In a book that so brilliantly describes 'local' understandings of landscape, time and space, Evans-Pritchard brings us into the field not only with text but also with images that successively sharpen and frame our focus on the ground. It is as if we were on a plane from another continent, watching the ground and its people hurtle towards us as we come in to land after hours of distanced contemplation (cf. Coleman 2002).

In his analysis of the ethnographic state of 'being there', Geertz (1988) has famously argued that Evans-Pritchard presents the anthropologist as both pilgrim and cartographer, inserted into place by ethnographic artifice. Certainly, landscape has provided a powerful tool of framing description in classic monographs of the British school and beyond (Hirsch 1995): tropes of place, constructing the sense of a 'there' to 'be' in, simultaneously describe and constitute an epistemological attitude often perceived to be central to our discipline. If in subsequent years the self-effacing authorial signature of an E.P. or a Firth – establishing the identity of the writer before disappearing into scientific omniscience (Shore 1999: 29) – has been replaced by a more self-conscious and fretful presence of the ethnographer throughout the work, the process of demonstrating the physical connection of researcher and text with place has remained of prime importance. Even Rabinow's *Reflections on Fieldwork in Morocco,* published nearly four decades after *The Nuer* and with a very different ethnographic sensibility, displays some familiar framing techniques. Interposed between an account of the callow ethnographer setting off from Paris and his encounter with the deceptive 'field' of the Hôtel de Oliveraie in Sefrou, there is a verbal sketch of 'The Said plain which stretches over lightly rolling countryside' (1977: 8).

Schwarz and Ryan (2003: 4) have referred to the specific practices of visualization through which geographical knowledge is conceived, and in anthropology also we see significant links between the visual and the spatial – in both methodological and, as we shall explore, metaphorical terms. Of course the grounds and the perspectives of our discipline have shifted since the 1940s or even the 1970s, and are still moving.[2] This volume, derived from the ASA conference of 2004, provides a good overview of where anthropology is at the beginning of its second century as a professional discipline. If the 1980s began to see a deconstructive lens applied to the writing of ethnography (e.g. Marcus and Fischer 1986), so in the 1990s a more 'dislocating' perspective was applied to constructions of the field, and not least to the sense that sites could still be seen as autonomous units of practice and analysis in contexts of increasingly obvious mobility (e.g. Marcus 1995). At issue now must be the possible connections between the concerns of these two past decades, between epistemological (and political) challenges to the anthropologist as producer of text, and to place as container of culture. Some contributors to this volume take up the challenge of reflecting on these conjoined questions, most notably Frohlick in revealing her originally misguided assumptions about 'local' informants in Nepal, Kristmunsdottir in discussions of biography as ethnography, and Hannerz as he traces his autobiographical and ethnographic path through the multiple sites that have constituted his fieldworking career.

These and other anthropologists are responding to what we might think of as the simultaneous prominence and disappearance of place in contemporary ethnography. On the one hand, concerns over how we understand the role of place, space and locality have become ever more evident.[3] Thus while Appadurai refers to the way most ethnographic descriptions have taken locality as ground rather than figure, 'recognizing neither its fragility nor its ethos as a property of social life' (1995: 207), he does so in a text that reverses the hierarchy between the two precisely by looking at politically and analytically charged constructions of locality and neighbourhood. On the other hand, we might argue that, if authors have become more prominent in ethnography (as the construction of texts also takes the foreground of analysis), in a curious sense places have disappeared – or at least the boundaries around them have become deeply problematized as connections between culture and territory, identity and fixed community, are challenged. It may be a sign of the times that a recent textbook on 'key concepts' in social and cultural anthropology by Rapport and Overing (2000) lacks an entry on the concept of place, but does have one on *non*-places (see Augé 1995), zones of transit such as airports and supermarkets where organic social life is supposedly deprived of sustenance.[4]

Admittedly, writing about non-place is a way of giving it back a presence, but Rapport and Overing are pointing to what seems like a collapse of one particular vision of place in anthropology. For them the concept of non-places serves the purpose of exploding the normative singularity of place; so that place and non-place represent contrastive modalities, the first never wholly constituted, the second never completely arrived at. The possibility and experience of non-place is never absent from any place, with the result that no place is completely itself and separate, and no place is completely other. (2000: 293–4)

It might seem that, under assault from the causes and consequences of globalization, anthropology is now engaged in a transposed echo of its origins: instead of telling ourselves that we are salvaging people from modernity, we are now salvaging organically conceived places from 'super-' or post-modernity, and in both cases the rescue operation can be construed as directed towards our own discipline as well as the cultures we study. The reassertion of 'depth' appears to be necessary to resist a McDonaldization of fieldwork, constituting an academic reassertion of authenticity in the face of more superficial or commoditized forms of work.

However, such assumptions of disciplinary self-defence provide too pessimistic and one-dimensional a view, as this volume seeks to demonstrate. We cannot assume that naïive suppositions concerning the autonomy of place should be replaced by knowing, if gloomy, assertions of the creeping ubiquity of non-place; or that it is our duty to assert the ethnographic charisma of one in opposition to the (sociological? economic?) rationality of the other. Both orientations express demonstrably partial positions. Similarly, of course, the totalizing concept of 'the global' cannot be ignored but must be deconstructed and *re*located within its numerous spatial and ideological sources. Here, it is useful to reflect on Edward Casey's (1996)[5] examination of assumptions that our informants nobly transform pre-existing, empty and absolute space into meaningful place. Casey's assertion is that in fact place is general and includes space, in other words that space is particular and derived from place, rather than constituting 'some empty and innocent spatial spread, waiting, as it were, for cultural configurations to render it placeful' (ibid.: 14). We might say something similar of global/local dichotomies where the small-scale is often seen to defer to a somehow pre-existing larger realm. After all, neither space nor the global can be seen as a homogeneous, culture-free entity, as if embodying an unproblematic genericization and neutralization of the grounds of social life.

In this volume, we examine various means through which the global is brought down to earth, but in such a way that does not involve a knee-jerk reassertion of the determining power of the autonomous and taken-for-granted local (and, by implication, of the agency of the ethnographer as traditionally conceived). Indeed, various forms of strategic *dislocation* permeate contributions: for instance, Kristmundsdottir focuses on a single life rather than a grounded people; Lee and Ingold analyse the construction of locality through movement – not of the globe-trotting, cosmopolitan variety, but through walking (there is an echo here of Casey's discussion of how the living-moving body is essential to the process of emplacement [1996: 24]); Nisbett provides a compelling juxtaposition of the sociality of a male-dominated internet café with the social, if virtual, relations formed with (presumed) women over the Net; Mukadam and Mawani attack a concept – that of diaspora – that has itself been used to suggest and cement the supposedly 'in-between' status of many so-called 'migrants'; Bank, in similarly iconoclastic mode, explores the effectiveness or otherwise of different styles of exploring urban fields in South Africa. If it can be stated that 'border fetishisms' tend to occur in contexts of anxiety-provoking and fissured spaces (cf. Spyer 1998). then we are attempting to defetishize concepts of the field that posit either the unproblematic existence of cultural boundaries or the need for their blanket removal in contexts of so-called 'globalization'. Furthermore, part of our argument is that 'fields' themselves include but are about much more than space or place, and to that end we will suggest a multi-dimensional approach to understanding – and 'locating' – the changing disciplinary practices of anthropological fieldwork.

Grounds of Knowing: Genealogies and Grammars of the Field

Anthropology's understanding of its disciplinary uniqueness has rested in good measure on the appropriation of a particular vision of fieldwork, but the method itself was hardly invented by ethnographers.[6] Kuklick (1997: 49–50) notes that, in order to gain credibility, nineteenth-century naturalists were required to go out and gather the data on which their generalizations rested – a model followed by figures such as Darwin, Wallace and von Humboldt. In biology, organized fieldwork emerged in the 1870s, involving the synchronic observation of living creatures in their natural habitats (ibid.: 50).[7] Nor can we assume that ethnographic fieldwork was created for purely disinterested motives. According to Young (2004: 158), Haddon's early efforts were motivated not only by scientific curiosity but also by political instinct, since he felt that the best way to found a school of anthropology at Cambridge was visibly to promote field research.

A little later, Malinowski's sojourn in the Trobriands was as much an unanticipated confinement as it was a planned period of study. Indeed, Malinowski's role in the emergence of the anthropological field is interesting not only for his self-mythologizations (as supposedly isolated hero of a personal odyssey), but also for his strategic exclusions at various levels. At the same time as he was grounding his academic persona methodologically and textually in the Trobriand Islands, he was helping to move anthropology away from an alternative paradigm, that represented by Sir James Frazer, author of *The Golden Bough* – a kind of scholarly pilgrimage through the mythologies of world cultures in search of a thread of intellectual progress. Malinowski travelled far away but focused his analytical gaze primarily on one region; Frazer's focus flitted restlessly between places, cultures, Western and non-Western, creating no connection between ethnographic persona and particular place. Furthermore, quite apart from 'discovering' a method that already existed,[8] Malinowski's relative lack of interest in physical anthropology or material culture studies helped to promote a vision of the discipline in Britain as more 'primitive sociology' than ethnology (Young 2004: 398). Yet even Malinowksian efforts at creating a field science were hardly definitive in themselves: Gupta and Ferguson (1997: 7) note that many of his own students did library dissertations before ever going into the field, as did their Boasian contemporaries. Indeed, the Boasian tradition provided a more eclectic, less doctrinaire position on encountering a supposedly pristine and isolate field (ibid.: 21).

More could be said of the emergence of the idea of participant observation in self-contained contexts, but enough has been stated already to indicate the fuzziness of the field as a disciplinary leitmotif: not confined to anthropology in its conception,[9] not properly (*pace* Malinowski) associated with a single founding figure, and not in practice gaining a methodological hegemony for some time, if ever. What is therefore fascinating is the continued strength of the idea of the field and its reinforcement through forms of disciplinary amnesia that have reduced the 'cognitive dissonance' associated with the lack of clarity in its emergence and continued implementation. Even today, it can sometimes be hard for postgraduate researchers to defend proposals that aim to transcend single, seemingly well-defined contexts, though of course Malinowski himself explored different sites within the Trobriand Islands in his iconic, yet movable, tent.

Rather than simply existing 'out there' (and 'there', and 'there'...), the ethnographic field can therefore be seen as emergent from, and a 'localized' expression of, a distinct institutional apparatus – that shifting 'anthropological field' identified by Bourdieu (2003: 283) as the professional universe of the ethnographer, constituted by her social origins, affiliations, dispositions, gender, and above all her position within a microcosm of fellow anthropologists. The point here is more than that, in a world of interconnections, we never leave the field (cf. Appadurai 1988: 35; Gardner 1999), even though that is true; it is also that anthropology as discipline maps certain understandings of culture and theoretical concern on to regions, thus naturalizing their subsequent 'discovery' or elucidation by the ethnographer. Such processes of cultural cartography have reflected and reinforced the colonial legacies of the discipline. More generally, however, there has been the continued micro-political positioning of anthropology as a 'field' of study in relation to allied disciplines that have maintained methodologies sometimes uncomfortably overlapping with our own, such as sociology and cultural geography (see also Gupta and Ferguson 1997: 2). In the face of competition from proximate parts of the academy, promotion of immersion in remote and bounded fields has had a considerable advantage as totem of disciplinary identity, shifting data collection to contexts sufficiently remote to avoid the gaze of all but the most determined colleague, either from within anthropology or without, while also distinguishing us from tourists and other more casual travellers.

What happens when the ethnographer 'reaches' the field can be equally mysterious, in part because the site and its boundaries may actually be determined *post hoc* through processes of analysis and writing (as we shall discuss later). However, some broadly common if frequently implicit assumptions have pervaded much of (at least Anglo-Saxon) ethnography throughout the discipline's post-Malinowskian history. We attempt to characterize them in the following, while also indicating some of the ways in which they have been seen to be challenged in recent times:

Metaphors to Work By: Spatiality and the Field

If fields have often been perceived as bounded spaces, spatial metaphors have formed a good portion of the 'grounds' on which ethnographic descriptions and theoretical assumptions have been based – starting of course with the notion of 'the field' itself.[10] Architectural notions of 'structure' (Harris 1996: 6), lending at times spurious stability to our understandings of culture, may be increasingly mistrusted, but notions of site, field, landscape, ground, prevail. The anthropological tendency to rely on spatial tropes in conceptualizing the theoretical 'landscape' (Hastrup and Olwig 1997: 4) is even implicated in the apparent fragmentation of such metaphors, since notions of 'diaspora' and 'mobility' imply the existence of pre-existing, fixed states from which social groups have become newly liberated.

Spatial metaphors also reinforce a wider, more naturalizing apparatus of thought. If the 'native' has been frozen in place by virtue of birth,[11] so Appadurai (1988) has pointed to more subtle forms of descriptive confinement associated with languages of 'niche' and 'adaptation' in relation to environments. Malkki (1992: 29) highlights the depiction of links between people and place through specifically botanical metaphors – terms such as native, indigenous and autochthonous have served to 'root' cultures in soils, while the word 'culture' itself derives from the Latin for cultivation. Furthermore, to pursue Appadurai's confinement metaphor, one can argue that incarceration of natives in place has led to the ideal of a form of ethnographic panopticism, based on the assumption that the fieldworker should aim to gain a privileged and totalizing view of those being observed (see also Frohlick, this volume).

Fardon (1995: 2) points to the sensitivity displayed by anthropologists in relation to thinking through spatial metaphors. Such awareness can now be seen partially as a product of the seeming vulnerability of the linguistic apparatus of the field. While spatiality has sometimes implied stasis in the cultures or categories explored, newer disciplinary metaphors have emphasized forms of flow. It is as if the waters previously lapping the shores of Malinowskian islands have begun to overflow, bringing with them metaphorical and analytical sea-changes. Bauman

(2000) explicitly refers to 'liquid' modernity, alongside his promotion of mobile metaphors of pilgrimage and tourism in describing contemporary forms of identity (cf. Coleman and Eade 2004: 5). Clifford's (1997) depiction of the ethnographer studying 'dwelling in movement' and 'travelling cultures' has been influential, though it has been argued that some earlier work, such as Rabinow's *Reflections* (1977), was already 'saturated with the language of movement' (Buroway 2000: 36). Appadurai's (1996) multiple 'scapes' interestingly combine a visual metaphor with a sense of the sometimes mutually contradictory appropriations of the global; mobile (if map-like) senses of perspective perhaps challenge more fixed images of the ethnographic gaze.

In methodological as well as theoretical terms, Marcus's concept of 'multi-sited' ethnography (1995) has proved a source of considerable debate and inspiration over the past decade, though – in common with many such concepts – it has undergone a fate of multiple interpretation. Marcus's phrase interestingly fragments the sense of a single field but retains the spatial imagery of 'site'. He writes: 'The distinction between lifeworlds of subjects and the system does not hold, and the point of ethnography within the purview of its always local, close-up perspective is to discover new paths of connection and association by which traditional ethnographic concerns with agency, symbols, and everyday practices can continue to be expressed on a differently configured spatial canvas' (ibid.: 98). The emphasis placed here on sites has perhaps prompted a tendency to see Marcus's proposal as simply linking otherwise bounded locations across global space, but it is important to note the first part of the quotation – the desire to develop an ethnography that collapses lifeworld/system, indeed local/global, oppositions. The traditional aim of fieldwork as seeking serendipity, or at least the unpredictable, is retained in a limited sense given that the object of study is 'emergent', but the agency and organizing power of the ethnographer is made explicit through strategic decisions to 'follow' people, things, metaphors, and so on. Such 'following' echoes the mobiliary metaphors of Clifford's travelling cultures or Bauman's tourists, and to it is added the language of 'circulation', 'connection' and 'association'. Thus Marcus's work mediates between images of fixity and flow, accepting the contingency of the ethnographic object but retaining emphasis on the need to explore everyday consciousness of informants, including indeed their 'system awareness' and knowledge of other sites and agents.

The Synecdoche of Place

Reliance on the alleged autonomy of place – what Clarke refers to as the 'geography of subjects within-self-contained spaces' (2004: 1-2) – has not of course prevented ethnographers from making 'larger' claims for their work. For instance, the Malinowskian assumption that the part (a village) could stand for the whole (a culture) has pervaded much anthropological thought. It might seem that such a view has been balanced by a powerful countervailing tendency against generalization and a sense that the fieldworker's village, seen up close, possesses a uniqueness that is part of its claim to ethnographic authenticity. In practice, however, these positions have proved to be largely compatible, both largely containable within a discourse of area studies that maintains the importance of drawing boundaries of difference between regions, wherever that boundary happens to be placed at any given analytical moment. Both positions have helped to sustain what Hannerz (1992: 219) has referred to the sense of cultures as discrete pieces of a mosaic, as well as drawing on romantic assumptions of holistic, bounded culture as existing *sui generis*.

Spatial encapsulation and bounding of culture have been key to two central, analytical practices within anthropology. First, they have helped to reinforce assumptions of internal consistency and external difference that can permit, even encourage, comparison. Thus holism has combined with strategically placed rupture, and in ethnographic texts has been bolstered by tropes of departure and return to the geographically and/or culturally distant field. Second, they have helped to constitute the 'problem' of context (Dilley 1999; see also Strathern 1995) – the key epistemological weapon in anthropology's conventional defence of its methods. As Dilley puts it: 'Stress on context in interpretation is a distinguishing feature of social anthropology' (1999: ix), with all the connections and disconnections that follow. Yet contextualization is itself a performative act (ibid.: xi and 5), embedded in some of the spatial metaphors we have discussed earlier – environment, background, and so on.

In the light of such disciplinary assumptions, forms of mobility and globalization have appeared to create 'matter out of ethnographic place', confounding contexts by colonizing spaces between 'wholes', and indeed fragmenting such 'wholes' irrevocably. The ethnographic gaze may sometimes disturbingly turn into a glance, and a partial and unfocused one at that. Crucially, the often-invoked couplet of local:global, while expressing another figure/ground relationship, does not correspond exactly to the synecdochic juxtaposition of village:wider culture, since in much anthropological thought the local is presented as preferably resisting rather than reflecting the global (the latter often embodied in Westernization or Americanization). To the extent that the local is seen simply to embody globality, it may be dismissed (or lamented) by anthropologists as a form of failure, a submission to the characteristics of non-place. However, despite the frequently expressed desire to celebrate the local – perceiving it as form of heroic persistence rather than backward survival – the shattering of anthropological contexts constitutes a key problem of interpretation, and moreover one where distinctions between informants and ethnographers become problematic.

The Indexicality of Presence

A metaphysics of presence has obviously been a significant dimension of ethno-graphic practice and self-understanding. Since the early part of the twentieth century, cultural knowledge has ideally been obtained through face-to-face, *in situ* encounters. But 'presence' cannot be taken for granted as a concept or technique, and in practice has contained within its rubric a huge range of activities and degrees of success in gaining access to social groupings.[12] However, Pinney notes that in the Malinowskian model the afar is a special place to which the anthropol-ogist is to be 'indexically exposed' (1992: 82). The hint of the photographic metaphor is important here, with Pinney arguing that, post-Malinowski: 'Whereas once it had been the camera which had recorded the refraction of light off objects, now the fieldworker-anthropologist came into what was articulated as an unmedi-ated relationship with the people he studied. Participant observation transcribed in monographic text now captured the soul of a people' (ibid.).

Such use of the self as tool is significant and distinctive (providing, to deploy another kind of language, a kind of contagious cultural magic conjured up in the encounter between ethnographer and informants), but one might argue that any camera metaphor should also expose the degree to which the observer 'filters' information in the very process of gathering it. In addition, 'presence' has histori-cally been complemented by a variety of unacknowledged absences on the part of the anthropologist. We have already seen how the textualization of ethnographic experience in classic monographs has displayed a tendency to establish the authority of the self before disappearing into authorial omniscience. Furthermore, Okely claims that: 'It is no accident that the geographic space which has been obliterated or defined as the ethnographic periphery for orthodox anthropology is the very same which is occupied by a centre of academic power' (1996: 3).

Of course, reflexivity in writing is now an important part of our intellectual armoury, as Okely's own work illustrates. In addition, anthropology 'at home' has also become an increasingly significant dimension to ethnographic practices. However, it is worthwhile briefly reflecting on some of the ambiguities of the notion of 'home' as field (cf. Rapport and Dawson 1998). While often taken to refer to the specifically Western contexts in which many anthropologists live (Jackson 1986), it should properly refer to the context studied by any ethnographer when working on his or her 'own' culture. Yet both of these forms of domesticated ethnography contain further opacities. How close to home is 'home', for example? For example, it is notable (despite the work of a scholar such as Danny Miller, e.g. 2001) that anthropologists based in the West have been keener to work on inner-city diasporas than they have on middle-class suburbs.

All forms of fieldwork are challenged by yet another assault on presence: the increasing virtualization and distanciation of social life through electronic communications. Thompson asks: 'What is it like to live in a world where the capacity to experience events is no longer determined by the possibility of encountering them on the time-space paths of daily life?' (1995:6). For anthropologists, at least, the disruption of such time-space paths has demonstrated the need to comprehend new forms of public, constituted by forms of interaction and communication inevitably remote from our purview, and thus at first sight resistant to ethnographic 'immersion'.

Temporalities of Rupture and Repetition

The depiction of 'presence' in classic ethnographic models has depended on constructing a presentist frame (Fabian 1983) that adds a temporal rupture to the spatial disjuncture already 'surrounding' and helping to constitute the field. Both forms of boundary-marking can be seen as contributing to a scientific move in anthropology that often severed 'tribal' societies from colonial and capitalist determinations' (Buroway 2000: 7); and both, as we have seen, contribute to the comparative move in ethnography, the ability to juxtapose one cultural 'whole' with another. Alongside such rupture has been a valorization of a complementary way of perceiving time: through detecting the presence of repetition and maintaining the assumption that the ethnographic gaze is able to detect the stabilities of social and cultural life. In another context but a similar vein, Robbins (2003: 221) has talked of anthropology as a 'science of continuity', a discipline with the tendency to argue that symbols, meanings, logics, have an enduring quality that is not subject to change, and which can be detected in conceptions of 'localization', 'indigenization' and syncretism.

If spatial flows have disrupted Malinowskian islands,[13] so currents of history have challenged functionalist assumptions of stability as a foundation of cultural understanding. Malkki thus documents her struggle to 'foreground not just historical structures but accidents of history, not just functioning systems but emergency measures' (1997: 86) in her work on refugee camps. It is as if such camps display the wrong kind of ethnographic uniqueness: not the allure of the 'exotic local' but the confusions of a context that cannot fully be perceived and delineated through ethnographic frames.

There is a further important way in which ethnographic temporality has been increasingly challenged in recent years. The search for a graspable cultural order in fieldwork has co-existed with an assumption that the field, as initially encountered, will be an unpredictable place – one that is elucidated through long-term physical presence. However, the impact of 'audit cultures' on research cultures, and what some have seen as the adoption of natural science models of practice by ethics committees (e.g. Coleman and Simpson 2001), have increasingly required ethnographers to present hypotheses about what will be encountered and even 'tested' in the field. Such governmentality is thus taken to stretch across national and cultural borders, while ethnographers are required to take a proleptic view of their fieldwork encounters, anticipating what will be discovered in the field.

'Becoming There': Performing the Field

Recent developments therefore suggest the emergence of fields where both 'rupture' and 'repetition', as we have described them, are difficult to retain as tropes of practice. Fields cannot be seen as disconnected – spatially, temporally or ethically – from the academy, while the field can no longer be seen as an oasis of stability in opposition to the vagaries of modernity. One tempting way of summarizing the current condition of the four 'grounds of knowing' that we have identified is to see it through a metaphor of decline – constituting a story (with apologies to Benjamin) of 'The Work of Ethnography in an Age of Postmodern Production'. If Benjamin famously noted the decline of the aura surrounding the work of art that had lost its unique presence in time and space, our image may seem to describe the troubled place of ethnography in a globalized era when the auratic distance between field and home, ethnography and other forms of writing, has become deeply problematic. In such terms, the ethnographic aura can be seen as a kind of sacralization of cultural difference rooted in place, a celebration of the particular methodologies as well as of the particular geographical regions appropriated by ethnographers.

However, we must bear in mind our previous comments about the fuzziness of the field and the ambiguities of ethnographic history. Rhetorics of globalization often seem rather like those of secularization, in that both have the tendency to exaggerate the uniqueness of the present through a hyperbolic creation of the past as other. Current developments are hardly without precedent, and the story we have to tell is neither a linear nor a simple one. Eriksen (2003: 6ff.) points to diffusionism and cultural evolutionism as providing two potential lineages for globalization or at least transnationalism, even if both fell out of favour as anthropology emerged as a discipline. More seriously, analytical engagements with the state, urban networks, systems theory and even capitalist formations have encouraged anthropological efforts to consider cultural flows and mobilities over more than just the last two decades.[14] For instance, the post-war Manchester School under Gluckman focused on social process, conflict and forms of tribal 'integration' into wider social structures (Buroway 2000: 17).[15] Indeed, Wright (1994: 10) shows that Manchester shop-floor studies of the 1950s and 1960s can be seen as attempts to test out social theories developed in Africa.

We argue further that the anthropological tendency to argue and think through spatial metaphors has concealed the degree to which fieldwork has never been dependent on fixed places as such. In this volume, Hannerz refers to his belief that in conceptual terms social anthropology is primarily about social relationships, and therefore only derivatively about places. This is a far from trivial point. As implied for instance by Marcus's metaphors of 'following' the field, depth in analysis can be achieved through strategic lateral movement through cultural frameworks, rather than simply remaining in one spot. This type of movement should ideally retain the ethnographic 'habitus' of remaining as open as possible to the unpredictable and the informal in social life – a point made by Frohlick in this volume. Furthermore, if the ethnographer by necessity encounters increasing numbers of short-term relationships in such fields, such an experience is likely to be replicating that of informants.

Perceived in these terms, a metaphor of performance can be deployed to describe the construction of the field, sometimes replacing more purely spatial modes of description (cf. Coleman and Crang 2003: 6ff.). Here, we refer to the sense that a field is constructed through a play of social relationships established between ethnographers and informants that may extend across physical sites, comprehending embodied as well as visual and verbal interactions. 'Performance' not only has the advantage of suggesting dynamic, mutual implication in constructing the field (even if actors have very different motives, resources and mutual understandings), it can also contain a performative element (see also Dilley 1999), a sense that something is being constructed out of social action.[16]

Unlike conventional notions of fixed places, performances can be seen as repeated or transformed over time, and we think that such a characteristic captures the sense that fields (and associated relevant 'contexts') are created anew each time the ethnographer, with or without informants being physically present, invokes the field in the process of research or writing. Thus the field as event is constantly in a process of becoming, rather than being understood as fixed ('being') in space and time, just as the audience for the performance can shift between academic and research locations, and just as the specific meanings of 'presence', synechdoche and scales of comparison may vary according to ethnographic strategy and contingency.

Although they do not themselves deploy a metaphor of performance to describe their work, some of the contributors to this volume hint at its relevance to understanding means of 'locating' the field. We see, for instance, how Hannerz's 'diversified engagements' involve a concern to maintain his ability to engage in the contingencies of research firsthand, rather than drawing on the ethnographic experiences of hired assistants. It is as if a degree of commitment to engaging in the performance, and not just observing from the seats (or from the verandah), is the key to his ethnographic commitment. Or we might look to Lee and Ingold's 'beating of the bounds' of the field through walking with informants, reconstituting a field each time they choose a path through Aberdeen. Or again, there are Nisbett's observations on how his informants create numerous spaces (and places) of interaction before his very eyes, as the sociality of the internet café expands or contracts along with the face-to-face and virtual conversations of the young men and women he describes.

The Chapters

Our volume begins with Ulf Hannerz considering past ethnographic experiences in the context of a discussion of current 'field worries'. Hannerz locates himself as operating predominantly within a post-classical period of the discipline, and certainly one where the orientations of research – up?, down?, at home?, and so on – have been up for debate. The chapter illustrates the varieties of approach containable within the broad methodological rubric of fieldwork, and Hannerz points out that his research on an urban community in Nigeria carried out some decades ago can now be seen as covering a 'multi-site' field. However, he also traces a gradual shift in the scale of his interests, moving from an American ghetto to the seemingly global interactions of newsmedia foreign correspondents.

Here, we wish to highlight two important themes emerging from Hannerz's combination of intellectual autobiography and field report. First, his assertion (in line with that of Marcus) that multi-site field studies are usually not a matter of squeezing several local fields into one ethnographic package: the point is that such studies may not involve the same kind of social units and social relations as classic single-site projects, and so we must be prepared to adapt our understandings of field methodologies and scales of operation accordingly (cf. Tsing 2000). Second, Hannerz's diagnosis of some of the causes behind anthropology's collective anxieties includes the argument that the field can be seen as a multivalent symbol of tensions in the discipline as community, reflecting a concern with its entry points and boundaries. Here we see again how 'the field' maps institutional concerns on to often distant cultural arenas.

Hannerz reveals the influences of the Manchester School in his discussions of the complexities and internal diversities within an African urban context, and such themes are taken up by Leslie Bank in his discussion of differing ways in which knowledge has been produced in the coastal South African city of East London. Hannerz traces numerous sites examined in a single career, whereas Bank's historical trajectory is longer, and comprehends the attempts by various anthropologists to understand broadly the same urban context. In part a critique of the *Xhosa in Town* trilogy, Bank's contribution focuses on methodological rather than more commonly adduced political problems with the work. A central plank of his argument is that as fieldworkers the Mayers failed to notice the forms of 'popular modernism' forming in the streets, tearooms, dancehalls and beaches located beyond the 'verandahs' of the domestic urban sphere. Just as Hannerz takes note of the numerous sites within a site that he encountered in Nigeria, so Bank argues that a more varied fieldwork strategy on the part of the Mayers would have generated a very different understanding of the location's cultural dynamics. We see here how certain kinds of seeming immersion can actually provide an ethnographic trap, prompting an inability to comprehend – or even notice – cosmopolitan cultural forms.

Interestingly, Bank invokes metaphors of spatial circulation in seeking to define the kind of flexible, mobile fieldwork strategy that would have provided a more satisfactory account of the public spheres of urban life in East London. Jo Lee and Tim Ingold's chapter also seeks pathways through the city, albeit for a rather different theoretical purpose. Their account of 'fieldwork on foot' draws parallels between ethnography and pedestrian movement. While both Hannerz and Bank indicate the value of perceiving single sites as containing multiple social and cultural arenas, Lee and Ingold show how a single, apparently fixed place – Aberdeen – can be seen as constituted by numerous pathways that become known through varieties of walking styles. This chapter therefore provides a further dimension to the concept of 'being there', going beyond a Geertzean textual emphasis through exploring dimensions of physical co-presence in the field.

These three opening chapters all explore 'fields' that are predominantly urban in form. Susan Frohlick's contribution apparently takes us into very different cultural arenas since her focus is ostensibly on mountaineering in Nepal. However, cross-cutting themes exist. One of the most powerful points that Frohlick makes relates to her original 'misrecognition' of the forms of mobility or otherwise of her Nepali informants, and her gradual understanding of the limitations of a conventionally 'local' mode of ethnography has parallels with Bank's discussion of his problems with the Mayers' work. While Lee and Ingold focus on one form of mobility, Frohlick's chapter is constituted by a variety of sometimes intersecting forms – the journeys paid by tourists to Nepal, the movements up and down Everest by 'locals' and visitors, but also, and crucially, the trips taken by female and male Nepali mountaineers into Western contexts that afford a further link with circuits of transnational relations. Frohlick agrees with Hannerz that we need to rethink our methods in order to comprehend the complexities of moving populations, but she adds that a key problem is that we have a knee-jerk tendency to see informants' mobility as separate from ours, thus providing us with new means of shoring up local–global, travel–location dichotomies. Revelation comes to Frohlick through serendipity: rather than her simply following mobile informants, the latter follow (or bump into) her in contexts away from her conventional field. She uses such experience to challenge notions of multi-sited methodology as a matter of *systematically* following the circulation of people, objects or practices within globalized worlds (cf. Marcus 1995). She also offers some thoughts on 'immersion', and the sense that it need not be achieved in a single locale but can be realized by placing oneself in the circuits of social relations and exchanges striven for by our research subjects.

Frohlick's chapter indicates some of the politically loaded ways in which anthropologists represent the movement of others, often seeing it as 'natural' and enclaved, in contrast to the cosmopolitan mobilities of the ethnographer. Anjoom Mukadam and Sharmina Mawani take this argument further in an analysis not only of post-diasporic Indian communities in the UK and Canada, but also of how such communities have been represented in the social sciences and the media. Their central argument is that terms such as 'immigrant' and 'diaspora' are still deployed in references to individuals who have been born and brought up in the West, and who have not actually made the journey from a supposed 'homeland'. Thus while Frohlick explores the politics of denying the mobility of informants, Mukadam and Mawani problematize the tendency to retain politically inappropriate metaphors of mobility and deterritorialization in describing populations such as second-generation Nizari Ismaili Muslims of Gujarati ancestry in London and Toronto. These Muslims are faced with the challenge of constructing a 'homeland' in a social situation containing others who would – inadvertently or otherwise – deny them their understandings of self-identity. Although its approach is not conventionally ethnographic in itself, Mukadam and Mawan's contribution suggests that ethnography has an important role to play in the study of apparently single-sited contexts created by emergent communities that are now self-consciously located in fixed geographic locations.

Observations on the troubled relations between transnational mobilities, anthropological categories and forms of self-identification are also provided in Nick Nisbett's account of a manifestation of the new informational economy in Bangalore. Nisbett observes the social relations fostered in a cybercafé occupied by middle-class youth. While some of what he discusses involves the development of gendered identities, he also shows how place identities remain important even in the context of invoking cyberspace, as certain parts of the world are particularly valorized in chatrooms that encourage the presentation of idealized selves. On the one hand, Nisbett is careful to show how his work must be 'grounded' in locality: he notes, for instance, that the cybercafé 'Networld' is situated in a suburb forming a border between the old British cantonment and new areas that have grown up in post-independence decades; and he traces the ways in which a demand for greater embodiment emerges as the relationship between potential couples progresses. However, Nisbett is also describing a way to conduct fieldwork in a new form of social location, constituted by informants' own tropes of place and globalized identity as well as by both mediated and face-to-face relations.

Frohlick, Mukadam and Mawani, and Nisbett all provide us with examples of how informants' perceptions of space and place in relation to 'the global' need to inform our understandings of the field. In line with most other chapters in this volume, they implicitly introduce the issue of scale as a key problem in defining the field. This latter question is central to Leach's striking discussion of how to understand and describe questions of power, regeneration, personhood and scale on the Rai Coast of Papua New Guinea. Leach begins with the problem that, while we are keen as ethnographers to show how our work reveals informants seeing the world in surprising ways, we still deploy a descriptive logic that is a product of our own 'rational', hierarchical, forms of scaling. Thus we locate the geographic and material conditions of a context before moving into 'higher' levels of interpretive work; aesthetic moments or single images are forced to nestle within 'wider' social and material domains. Again, there is a political dimension to such description, since it tends to avoid the problem of meeting informants and their thought systems on equal terms.

Leach wants to reveal and challenge the scaling effects of conventional ethnographic forms of description. He therefore shows how in his 'field' a complex spatiality is evident: land is seen as contained within persons as shared substance, knowledge and power. 'Situatedness' in this context becomes placement in a human, temporal and spatial relational matrix, inseparable from particular generative relations between persons and spirits. Given that persons are in effect places made mobile, then the logical 'scaling' of persons *in* places that encompass them must be challenged. Leach goes on to describe the making of a carving by his friend Yamui, showing how for Yamui there is no natural scaling of the carving and the world it brings forth: in other words, they are not seen as proportional to one another in order of magnitude. A carving does not 'stand for' a power, acting as a token event substituting for a larger realm of myth and magic; it *is* that power. Scale becomes something fluid, and place is scaleable in the sense that it can be singular and contained in a person or carving or it can encompass others and ultimately act as an image of world-generation. In one sense, therefore, Leach appears to be providing conventional ethnography in a bounded and 'distant' place; in another, he is presenting a radical challenge to some of our most deep-seated assumptions about context. Through doing so, he is asking the key question of the extent to which informants' own understandings of 'scale' and 'context' should inform our own.

In his chapter, Leach questions conventional ideas of scale in part through a description of the activities of a single person, Yamui. Sigridur Duna Kristmundsdottir actively deploys the notion of biography as field in order to expand our understanding of what 'location' might mean. She describes some of the methodological and epistemological issues she faced in writing an anthropological account of Björg C. Thorlaksson, a woman born into an agricultural Icelandic society in the latter half of the nineteenth century, who completed a Ph.D. at the Sorbonne. Scale here becomes subject to particular forms of expansion (across countries) and introversion (contained within a single life), as Kristmundsdottir is faced with the problem of whether to consider her biography as offering a 'mirror' on to wider culture. She decides that her field is constituted by the events of the life she describes, so that it is not a single physical place but a location defined by the life being followed. In effect, the researcher enters the field whenever she is researching, a process that may involve extensive travel as well as exploring written documents, reminiscences, and so on. If Leach talks of the location of place in the person, Kristmundsdottir talks of the researcher *as* location.

Bringing the volume to its close, Nigel Rapport takes ethnographic locality into contexts yet more remote than the cyberspace described by Nisbett, the shifting scales presented by Leach or the biographical field that Kristmundsdottir discusses. He combines ethnography with advocacy in laying out three 'voices' of a proposed supranational city. So while the volume begins with three chapters displaying the complexities of cities as sites, it ends with a vision of the city not fixed on 'a hill' but as a location for a new kind of social order. In common with Mukadam and Mawani, Rapport addresses the concept of diaspora with some scepticism, worrying that essentialized peripheries are becoming the new centre. He is also concerned to find a way to understand the diverse manifestations of movement that can be accommodated within a cosmopolitan social order. A key trope for Rapport is that of mutual guest-hood, seen as a means of accommodating multicultural and transcultural travellers through which the state of being 'at home' is a matter of the nature and purpose of particular exchanges rather than of absolute identities. Rapport's vision appears to be neither place nor Augéan 'non-place', but then neither is it presented as pure utopia.

Our book, then, is intended not to banish spatial considerations from concepts of the field but rather to put them in their place, as significant but not absolutely primary dimensions of ethnographic practice. Current debate within anthropology revolves around the extent to which fields can remain distant, autonomous containers of culture; but in fact they have never been so, not only because no culture is truly an island but also because 'the field' has always been a shifting product of the interactions between institutions and assumptions stretched across colonial and then post-colonial realms. Our argument here is that fields are as much 'performed' as 'discovered', framed by boundaries that shift according to the analytical and rhetorical preferences of the ethnographer and, more rarely, the informant. The image on the front of this book, of hands reaching out towards a globe, is meant to capture this troubled and sometimes disturbing, yet also occasionally hopeful, vision of our discipline.

Notes

1. And past a photograph between pages 4 and 5 of 'Youth [Eastern Gaajok] fastening giraffe-hair necklace on friend'.

2. One might argue that, as anthropological concepts of place have started to shift ground, so some anthropologists are beginning to take a new interest in

geography. At a recent American Anthropological Conference (2001 in Washington, DC), a panel was entitled 'Anthropologies and Geographies: Re-examining Culture, Space and Time'.

3. See, e.g., Feld and Basso (1996); Gupta and Ferguson (1997); Hastrup and Olwig (1997); Hirsch (1995); Lovell (1998); Low and Lawrence-Zúñiga (2003).

4. Rapport and Overing claim, 'No anthropologist could ever have been unaware of the contingency of socio-cultural "places"; the image of a closed and self-sufficient world (of relations, identity and history) was never more than an instrumental semi-fantasy, a provisional myth' (2000:293).

5. See Low and Lawrence-Zúñiga (2003: 17); cf. Tuan (1977).

6. We can point to the emergence of anthropology during a time in European history when appreciation of an explicit idea of landscape was emerging (Hirsch 1995). Featherstone (1997: 241) notes that the increasing valuation of travel as experience, as in the case of educative, self-formative projects, can be found, for instance, in the Grand Tour of the eighteenth century. In due course some forms of travel would also partake of a masculine, Victorian valorization of physical danger and toil, promoting a broadly Protestant ethic of travel as travail.

7. Haddon originally intended to work as a marine biologist.

8. Young (2004: 162) argues that Rivers's study of *The Todas*, based on field-work in 1902, was one of the first attempts by a British anthropologist to apply the principle of intensive study of a restricted area.

9. Not to mention the use of the term in, for example, physics.

10. The significance of metaphors in constructing the field is notable, given the ambiguities of the word 'ethnography' itself – mediating between practice *in* the field and writing *of* the field.

11. A sentiment shared with, among other influences, nineteenth-century German Romanticism.

12. Fieldwork itself can include 'joining in', 'hanging around', overt observation, interviews, surveys, and so on.

13. And sometimes of course linked with temporal processes through talk of space-time compression.

14. Yet other examples of transcendence of locality might be produced, ranging from French structuralism to an example provided by Hannerz in this volume, that of Ruth Benedict's *The Chrysanthemum and the Sword* (1946), based on a wartime study at a distance of the culture of an enemy nation.

15. Buroway (2000: 7) also discusses Thomas and Znaniecki's sociological work, *The Polish Peasant in Europe and America* (1927), originally published in five volumes between 1918 and 1920, which depicts the lives of Polish peasants in both Europe and America, thus describing communities in flux. Buroway sees the work as global in scope but broadly ethnographic in method.

16. Providing what one might call a variety of 'performative observation'.

References

Appadurai, A. (1986), 'Theory in Anthropology: Center and Periphery', *Comparative Studies in Society and History* 28 (2): 356–61.

Appadurai, A. (1988), 'Putting Hierarchy in its Place', *Cultural Anthropology* 3 (1): 36–49.

Appadurai, A. (1995), 'The Production of Locality', in R. Fardon (ed.) *Counterworks: Managing the Diversity of Knowledge*, London: Routledge.

Appadurai, A. (1996), *Modernity at Large*, Minneapolis: Minnesota University Press.

Augé, M. (1995), *Non-places: Introduction to an Anthropology of Super-modernity*, London: Verso.

Bauman, Z. (2000), *Liquid Modernity*, Cambridge: Polity.

Benedict, R. (1946), *The Chrysanthemum and the Sword*. Cleveland: Meridian Books.

Bourdieu, P. (2003), 'Participant Objectivation', *Journal of the Royal Anthropological Association* 9 (2): 281–94.

Buroway, M. (2000), 'Introduction: Reaching for the Global', in M. Buroway (ed.), *Global Ethnography: Forces, Connections, and Imaginations in a Postmodern World,* Berkeley: University of California Press.

Casey, E. (1996), 'How to Get from Space to Place in a Fairly Short Stretch of Time: Phenomenological Prolegomena', in S. Feld and K. Basso (eds), *Senses of Place*, Santa Fe, NM: School of American Research Press.

Clarke, K. (2004), *Mapping Yorùbá Networks: Power and Agency in the Making of Transnational Communities,* Durham, NC, and London: Duke University Press.

Clifford, J. (1997), *Routes: Travel and Translation in the Late Twentieth Century,* Cambridge, MA: Harvard University Press.

Coleman, S. (2002) 'From the Sublime to the Meticulous: Art, Anthropology and Victorian Pilgrimage to Palestine', *History and Anthropology* 13 (4): 275–90.

Coleman, S. and Crang, M. (eds) (2003), *Tourism: Between Place and Perform-ance*, Oxford: Berghahn.

Coleman, S. and Eade, J. (eds) (2004), *Reframing Pilgrimage: Cultures in Motion*, London: Routledge.

Coleman, S. and Simpson, R. (2001), 'Anthropology Inside Out: Identity and Agency in the (Re-)production of a Discipline', *Anthropology in Action* 8 (1): 1–5.

Dilley, R. (1999), *The Problem of Context*, Oxford: Berghahn.

Eriksen, T. (2003), 'Introduction', in T. Eriksen (ed.), *Globalisation: Studies in Anthropology*, London: Pluto Press.

Evans-Pritchard, E. (1940), *The Nuer: A Description of the Modes of Livelihood and Political Institutions of a Nilotic People*, Oxford: Oxford University Press.

Fabian, J. (1983), *Time and the Other: How Anthropology Makes Its Object*, New York: Columbia University Press.

Fardon, R. (1995), *Counterworks: Managing the Diversity of Knowledge*, London: Routledge.

Featherstone, M. (1997), 'Travel, Migration, and Images of Social Life', in W. Gungwu (ed.), *Global History and Migrations*, Boulder, CO: Westview Press.

Feld, S. and Basso, K. (eds) (1996), *Senses of Place*, Santa Fe, NM: School of American Research Press.

Gardner, K. (1999), 'Location and Relocation: Home, "the Field" and Anthropological Ethics (Sylhet, Bangladesh)', in C. Watson (ed.), *Being There: Fieldwork in Anthropology*, London: Pluto Press.

Geertz, C. (1988), *Works and Lives: The Anthropologist as Author*, Cambridge: Polity.

Gupta, A. and Ferguson, J. (1997), 'Discipline and Practice: "The Field" as Site, Method, and Location in Anthropology', in A. Gupta and J. Ferguson (eds), *Anthropological Locations: Boundaries and Grounds of a Field Science*, Berkeley: University of California Press.

Hannerz, U. (1992), *Cultural Complexity: Studies in the Social Organization of Meaning* New York: Columbia University Press.

Harris, O. (1996), 'The Temporalities of Tradition: Reflections on an Changing Anthropology', in V. Hubinger (ed.), *Grasping the Changing World: Anthropological Concepts in the Postmodern Era*, London: Routledge.

Hastrup, K. and Olwig, K. (1997), 'Introduction', in K. Olwig and K. Hastrup (eds), *Siting Culture: The Shifting Anthropological Object*, London: Routledge.

Hirsch, E. (1995), 'Introduction: Landscape: Between Place and Space', in E. Hirsch and M. O'Hanlon (eds), *The Anthropology of Landscape: Perspectives on Place and Space* Clarendon: Oxford.

Jackson, A. (ed.) (1986), *Anthropology at Home*, London: Tavistock.

Kuklick, H. (1997), 'After Ishmael: The Fieldwork Tradition and Its Future', in A. Gupta and J. Ferguson (eds), *Anthropological Locations: Boundaries and Grounds of a Field Science*, Berkeley: University of California Press.

Lovell, N. (1998), 'Introduction: Belonging in Need of Emplacement?' in N. Lovell (ed.), *Locality and Belonging*, London: Routledge.

Low, S. and Lawrence-Zúñiga, D. (2003), 'Locating Culture', in S. Low and D. Lawrence-Zúñiga (eds), *The Anthropology of Space and Place: Locating Culture*, Oxford: Blackwell.

Malkki, L. (1992), 'National Geographic: The Rooting of Peoples and the Territorialization of National Identity among Scholars and Refugees', *Cultural Anthropology* 7 (1): 24–44.

Malkki, L. (1997), 'News and Culture: Transitory Phenomena and the Fieldwork Tradition', in A. Gupta and J. Ferguson (eds), *Anthropological Locations:*

Boundaries and the Grounds of a Field Science, Berkeley: University of California Press.

Marcus, G. (1995), 'Ethnography in/of the World System: The Emergence of Multi-sited Ethnography', *Annual Review of Anthropology* 24: 95-117.

Marcus, G. and Fischer, M. (1986), *Anthropology as Cultural Critique: An Experimental Moment in the Human Sciences*, Chicago: University of Chicago Press.

Miller, D. (2001), *The Dialectics of Shopping*, Chicago: University of Chicago Press.

Okely, J. (1996), *Own or Other Culture*, London: Routledge.

Pinney, C. (1992), 'The Parallel Histories of Anthropology and Photography', in E. Edwards (ed.) *Anthropology and Photography 1860–1920*, New Haven and London: Yale University Press.

Rabinow, P. (1977), *Reflections on Fieldwork in Morocco*, Berkeley: University of California Press.

Rapport, N. and Dawson, A. (1998), *Migrants of Identity: Perceptions of Home in a World of Movement*, Oxford: Berg.

Rapport, N. and Overing, J. (2000), *Social and Cultural Anthropology: The Key Concepts*, London: Routledge.

Robbins, J. (2003), 'On the Paradoxes of Global Pentecostalism and the Perils of Continuity Thinking', *Religion* 33: 221–31.

Schwarz, J. and Ryan, J. (2003), 'Introduction: Photography and the Geographical Imagination', in J. Schwarz and J. Ryan (eds), *Picturing Place: Photography and the Geographical Imagination*, London: I.B. Tauris.

Shore, C. (1999), 'Fictions of Fieldwork: Depicting the "Self" in Ethnographic Writing', in C. Watson (ed.), *Being There: Fieldwork in Anthropology*, London: Pluto Press.

Spyer, P. (1998), 'Introduction', in P. Spyer (ed,), *Border Fetishisms: Material Objects in Unstable Spaces*, London: Routledge.

Strathern, M. (1995), 'Foreword: Shifting Contexts', in M. Strathern (ed.), *Shifting Contexts: Transformations in Anthropological Knowledge*, London: Routledge.

Thomas, W. and Znaniecki, F. (1927), *The Polish Peasant in Europe and America*, New York: Alfred Knopf.

Thompson, J. (1995), *The Media and Modernity: A Social Theory of the Media*, Cambridge: Polity.

Tsing, A. (2000), 'The Global Situation', *Cultural Anthropology* 15 (3): 327–60.

Tuan, Y.-F. (1977), *Space and Place: The Perspective of Experience*, Minneapolis: University of Minnesota Press.

Wright, S. (1994), *Anthropology of Organizations*, London: Routledge.

Young, M. (2004), *Malinowski: Odyssey of an Anthropologist 1884–1920*, New Haven: Yale University Press.

Studying Down, Up, Sideways, Through, Backwards, Forwards, Away and at Home: Reflections on the Field Worries of an Expansive Discipline

Ulf Hannerz

We seem to worry about 'the field' these days. Perhaps anthropologists always did, in a more private way, even in the past when elders tended to be secretive or at least vague about the field experience, and when first fieldwork was thus indeed like a rite of passage into professional maturity. But that field was probably a rather fixed entity to worry about, a 'tribe', a village, some place you could get to know by covering it on foot and engaging with its people face to face. And it used to be self-evidently a matter of 'being there' – *away*, rather than 'here'. Now we do not seem to know what the field is, or where it should be, if it is real or perhaps virtual, and even if there has to be one at all.

Yet there may still be limits, or at any rate proclaimed limits. When some colleague, not least a young one, or a youngish one beginning to stake a claim to seniority, now comes up with what he or she sees as a new kind of field, or a new way of approaching a field, the elders might curtly say, 'It's already been done', but they could also snap, 'That's not anthropology'. And that would mean that it would not serve as a rite of passage.

I will try here to look at some understandings of fields and fieldwork as they have developed in the last few decades, in the post-classical period of social anthropology. This will be in large part my own story, partly perhaps to show my credentials, partly because I am reaching the stage where one's point of view becomes increasingly retrospective and where one is quick to grasp occasions for nostalgia – but mostly, I hope, because my field experiences, basically four of them, can illustrate reasonably instructively some of our shifting notions of, and arguments about, proper locations.

It seems that most of the time that I have been in anthropology, there have been key terms of direction, mostly of expansion, suggesting important ways in which the discipline has continuously reinvented itself. Classic anthropology was a matter of 'being there', away, an expatriate anthropology; thus calls for an 'anthropology at home', fieldwork without malaria pills, already signalled an expansive innovation. As on reflection it was soon understood that much of that anthropology 'at home' had become a matter of 'studying down', it was proposed that we should do more 'studying up'. But then as some anthropologists focused their ethnographic curiosity on people with practices not so unlike their own, this could readily enough be labelled as 'studying sideways'. And when it was understood that the construction of fields could involve tracing webs of relations between actors, institutions and discourses, a notion of 'studying through' was close at hand.[1] Recently, moreover, the field has sometimes been 'here and there', in many sites, 'trans-' or 'multi-' something or other. If we bring time in as well, to complicate things yet more, the classics may have tended towards the construct of an 'ethnographic present', but even when Radcliffe-Brownean strictures on conjectural history were still a reigning orthodoxy, there were those who quietly went on with their ethnographic excavations of the past. Later on historical anthropology indeed became a growth area, but it was also understood to include a 'history of the present'. And if anthropologists have tended to be mostly sceptical about predictions, one can spot here and there an interest in the future, and in people's ideas about the future: in terms of hope or despair, or in terms of scenarios.[2] So anthropologists now study not only here or there, and up, down, through or sideways, but also backwards and forward.

Assuming, as I do, that the overall agenda of anthropology involves the mapping of a continuously changing human diversity, that is all fine. It is an agenda where most of us can fit in somewhere, with all the particularities of our interests, temperaments and situations. Our paths through this expanded terrain of anthropology may be very personal, revealing themselves only cumulatively, depending on practical circumstances and experiences as well as on debates within the discipline. At that level we may mostly take a few steps at a time, dealing with problems pragmatically as we encounter them, less concerned with what these individual moves in their aggregate mean to anthropology. In large part that is the kind of story I will tell.

But then to the extent that the discipline is also some sort of community, perhaps as some of these particular moves are added up, and as they combine with more general conjunctures, they may lead towards more collective worries. And then the practical and technical issues may turn out to have become mixed with moral matters having to do with the coherence of the community. I will suggest that we have seen this happening recently, with 'the field' serving as a symbol of tensions which also have other dimensions. And I will end by pointing to some circumstances affecting our relationships to 'the field' that we perhaps need to think more about.

From Ghetto to Global

I have always been an expatriate ethnographer, in the routine sense of not being in the field, in any organized way, in my own country. I went into anthropology because of an early engagement with Africa, at about the time Harold Macmillan, British prime minister, was proclaiming that a 'wind of change' was blowing through the continent; a wind of independence. We might describe it as a period of Afro-optimism. I had already done a little travelling in West Africa before, but by the time I was ready for serious fieldwork, in the mid-1960s, the country I had in mind, Nigeria, descended into civil war, and it seemed wisest to think of something else. I was offered a position as staff anthropologist in an applied socio-linguistic project concerned with Afro-American dialect in Washington, DC, and so I spent two years in the latter half of the 1960s hanging out in a black neighbourhood in that city; a ghetto neighbourhood, as one would say (Hannerz 1969).

At that point in time, the location may have been rather unconventional for an anthropologist, but the fieldwork was mostly according to the rules. The social and political climate was not such that I wanted to have a high profile as a researcher, doing more or less formal interviews or even surveys. Instead this was participant observation in a quite strict sense, mostly within one city block and its immediate surroundings. Above all, in the eyes of neighbourhood people, I was a young white foreigner, and a student of some sort; no doubt noticeable enough, although I tried to be unobtrusive. Since then, as anthropologists have become more self-conscious about their ways of being in the field, the notion of the observer as a 'fly on the wall' has come in for much ridicule. Indeed we could seldom be so inconspicuous, and it would have been entirely unnatural to be somehow present but not engaged in human interactions. None the less, in the field in my Washington neighbourhood, I preferred to let people walk their walk and talk their talk, to have everyday events as far as possible take the course I believed they would have taken without me; in that sense surrendering to the field. This seemed least risky in terms of my personal acceptability, and, moreover, since it was a central purpose of the study to understand how the modes of thought and action of black ghetto-dwellers differed from those of mainstream America, indeed whether they differed, more active interference on my part would have seemed quite counterproductive. In summary, then, my Washington experience seems to me to have been a case of fieldwork by immersion, of the classical type or even in certain ways a somewhat extreme version of it.

If anything worried me about my Washington field, then, it was hardly the general nature of my endeavour. I was aware of questions of personal safety, but less because I was a conspicuous outsider than because people in the neighbourhood were themselves a bit preoccupied with the threat of violence – the management of danger indeed became one research topic (cf. Hannerz 1981). Moreover,

I occasionally felt some dismay, especially early in fieldwork, about the hours I seemed to be wasting in semi-darkness, watching bad TV programmes with neigh-bourhood friends. Standard ethnographic practice in the 1960s was not yet about media use.

Two developments in the growing self-consciousness and intensifying debate among anthropologists about their fields occurred about the time of my work in Washington, or soon after. One was the emergence of that notion of 'anthropology at home' – there had perhaps always been some, but now it became increasingly recognized as a tendency, and professionally legitimized. But what was 'at home'? I was rather amused when I received an invitation to an ASA conference on that topic on the basis of my Washington experience – I had hardly thought of my Afro-American ghetto neighbourhood in that way. But since I did not attend the confer-ence, I did not get to voice my doubts. The underlying assumption may still have been that any fieldwork in an urban Western setting was not quite 'away', at least unless you were a non-Occidental anthropologist yourself – other ethnographers, other Bongo Bongos.

The second development could be readily identified with one particular anthro-pologist, and one particular chapter in a book criticizing established anthropology. In her contribution to *Reinventing Anthropology,* Laura Nader (1972) argued that it was time for anthropologists to 'study up' – for various reasons they had been 'studying down', observing people rather less powerful and privileged than them-selves; but to understand how powerlessness and poverty were shaped, one must scrutinize the activities of the people at the top. And so, in these terms, what I had done in Washington was merely one more case of studying down.

As things turned out, in my next field, after a fashion, I did study up. After com-pleting my Ph.D. I spent the next year doing Swedish military service, and just after I got out of that, I had an invitation to a conference at the University of the West Indies in Jamaica. Since I was not due back in Stockholm until the next aca-demic year, I had time to spare, and decided to stay on in the Caribbean for that period. Where I went was in large part a matter of accident. When I had made a brief excursion from Washington to Jamaica a few years earlier, the airline booking agent had regretted that I could not get on a non-stop flight from Jamaica back to the USA, but had to have a brief stop on the Cayman Islands. That way, at least, I became aware of their existence, in the late 1960s, when this small lin-gering outpost of the Empire had not yet earned a reputation for either tourism or more or less shady offshore banking. I found that little anthropological work had been done there. So to the Cayman Islands I returned, in 1970, for a slightly longer stay (Hannerz 1974).

I had a very modest research grant which at least allowed me to rent a bicycle, although after having found that one stretch of road was inhabited by some mean dogs, I began to rent a car for selected excursions instead. At any rate, the grant had not required very precisely identified research goals, so when just about a week after my arrival a local political crisis erupted, I could quickly focus my attention on that. The British colonial administration had announced plans for regulating land sales and construction more strictly than in the past. The growth of tourism, the rise of new hotels on the sea front, and the perceived interest in plots for foreigner-owned second homes appeared to require such planning. Various local entrepreneurs, however, probably with expatriate interests in the background, much preferred to continue their less constrained style of business, and they mobilized local opinion. There was heated agitation, and a protest march unique in the history of the islands. Then one morning a British gunboat was seen anchored off the small harbour, and rumours were flying that soldiers were hiding in the bushes inland. Eventually there was a dramatic all-day meeting of the Legislative Assembly, some kind of compromise was hammered out, and the Islands could return to their ordinary tranquillity.

While the crisis lasted, I had had a close-up view of local-level politics and of the styles of populist leadership exhibited by some of the prominent agents of protest. During the remainder of my stay in the Cayman Islands, much of my time was taken up by trying to grasp the character of recent political history in the territory, after an administrative link to Jamaica had been cut as that larger island moved towards its own independence, through a short-lived attempt at party politics, to the current state of personalized flux. After a period of intense observation followed a phase where I did extensive interviews with the politicians involved, with people in the administration, and with various other observer-commentators. Some of the politicians had had their egos or their reputations bruised and were eager to talk. Apart from these encounters, I sought out various written materials – what little there had been of a Caymanian press, official documents, old manifestoes, and the like, which some politicians could retrieve from half-forgotten personal collections. Working my way from the present into the past, then, I was studying backwards. But to repeat, I was also studying up, insofar as I was dealing in large part with the Caymanian political élite. Yet such things are relative. These leaders were mostly petty entrepreneurs in a small-scale society, struggling to rise a little above the level where one merely makes ends meet. One could insert here that much anthropology from the classic early or mid-twentieth-century period is indeed ambiguously placed in terms of studying up or down. Certainly it was often about kingship, chieftaincy and rule, thus 'up'. Yet entangled in the power relationships of colonialism, anthropologists may have found themselves almost inevitably studying 'down'.

For my next field engagement, beginning in the mid-1970s, I was back in West Africa, where I had intended to start my career as an ethnographer, in a Nigerian town which had grown around a new railway junction in the colonial era. But by now my plans had been influenced not least by my Washington field experience. If the latter, like much urban ethnography, had involved a smaller unit within a city, in this case a neighbourhood, in Nigeria I wanted to try to deal with an entire urban community, even if not a particularly large one. (In this case, if I took a couple of hours, I could in fact walk around all of it.) While ethnicity and occupational structure were the main dimensions of my study, in a way I tried to maximize ethnographic diversity. I should add that it was also in a period when I was strongly influenced by the work of the 'Manchester School' in Central Africa, and while my Nigerian town was of a different kind than the urban communities which the Mancunians had dealt with on the Copperbelt, I found their conceptual innovations and methodological expansiveness appealing.

The result was that I tried to combine more conventional participant observation and informant work with a wider methodological battery, some of it invented on the spot, and for the first time I worked with field assistants.[3] In this diverse and segmented community, I found myself juggling with several mini-fields. Conceptually, that might be a matter of keeping them together, placing them in a coherent structure. Practically, it was sometimes a challenge of keeping them apart, as their inhabitants would not always mix well. When the hard-working, well-mannered Ibo Methodist minister would come to the guest inn where I was staying – 'in order to greet me', as the saying went – and found the funny, outspoken but often not so sober Camerounian tailor already there, there was some possibility of embarrassment. At one or two points when such salutational visiting seemed to become just too intense and too varied to handle, I escaped to the old regional capital to spend some time in the archives while things cooled down a little. The materials in the archives were from the colonial period, and included documents like the handwritten or typed reports that had been sent to superiors in the colonial hierarchy from the young, eager British district officers who had been stationed in my town in the 1930s, 1940s and 1950s. Returning to the town, I enjoyed confronting my archival notes with the oral history I could still retrieve from local veterans.

By the time I started my project in the Nigerian town, I was in a phase in my academic career which would not so easily allow full-length single field stays. So I expected to do what many anthropologists do in that situation – you view the field as an on-and-off thing, expecting to continue work over many shorter stays, perhaps even building that time dimension into the research design. Indeed I came back to the town a number of times. Meanwhile, however, the economy and politics of Nigeria again took a turn for the worse. I had started my project during the oil boom. In 1983, when I came on what turned out to be my last visit, the prevailing mood among townspeople was not so upbeat. The elected, civilian government was seen as incompetent and corrupt. 'Our best hope now', said one of my friends, a petty trader with a stall in the market place, 'is that the the military will take over again – but why would they want to take on this mess?' Yet about a month later the soldiers did indeed return to power. And for almost the next two decades they stayed on, and the mess just got worse and worse.

By then, however, my interests were again going through a shift in scale. If moving from the Washington neighbourhood to the Nigerian town entailed a turn from an urban part to an urban whole, while I was in that town I became increasingly drawn to yet wider issues. It was a time when, back in the debates of 'the First World', terms like 'cultural imperialism' were in the air, while in academia 'world-system theory' was increasingly influential across several disciplines; but neither of these views seemed really to illuminate the contemporary Nigerian culture I had around me. Consequently I began to cast about for ways of dealing with the latter, ethnographically and conceptually.[4] Thus I was on my way to a focus on what, a decade or two later, would be summarized as 'globalization'. While not being in the field much for an extended period, and not particularly attracted by the prospect of a return to a Nigeria under the haphazard domination of soldier thugs, I kept working away, mostly at my desk, on the implications of global interconnectedness for anthropological thought and practice (Hannerz 1996).

Yet as more absences from the office, and more presences in some sort of 'field', again became a real possibility, I also felt free to think about what kind of entity that might be in the context of a global ecumene. In retrospect, what I had drifted into doing in the Nigerian town could be seen as a variation on the theme of 'the global and the local', a kind of story increasingly often told in late twentieth-century anthropology. No doubt it has been worth telling, but perhaps it soon became a little predictable. And it seemed to me a rather intellectually and methodologically conservative reaction of anthropologists to globalization, insofar as it allowed them to continue with their cherished local field research practices with only rather limited adjustments.

Perhaps that is conservative, too, but I believe I have been reasonably consistent over time in sticking to the idea that social anthropology, conceptually, is primarily about social relationships, and only derivatively, and not necessarily, about places. And if globalization involves a new balance in the combination of local and long-distance relationships, it makes sense to seek out field entities that illustrate that development, and which are not in themselves defined in territorial terms. By the time I got that far in thinking about more field research, several of my colleagues and students in Stockholm had already proceeded to take literally the expression 'globalization at work' – they were doing ethnographies of transnational occupations, and distributing their field studies over several sites.[5] So in the mid-1990s I embarked on my most recently completed project, a study of the work of newsmedia foreign correspondents (Hannerz 2004). Not only was this a project involving a group dispersed across the world, it also examined an occupation with a major influence on public understandings of the world and its parts. And the foreign correspondents drew my curiosity because while the circumstances of their work are quite different, it is somewhat like that of many anthropologists: it entails reporting over distances which may be not only spatial but also social and cultural. Consequently, this has been a project involving, in my own invented term, 'studying sideways'.[6]

In large part, fieldwork in this study consisted of extended, rather freeflowing interviews, of a kind I prefer to think of as conversations, with foreign correspondents especially in Jerusalem, Johannesburg and Tokyo. I had meetings with correspondents or ex-correspondents in other places as well, but my preference was to get together with them where they were currently practising, because in that way the conversations could go most concretely into the day-to-day vicissitudes of the craft. I also preferred talking to correspondents in postings sufficiently exotic to their audiences that their reporting would be likely to involve some amount of cultural interpretation, of representation of otherness. Thus I was more interested in 'Africa correspondents', 'Asia correspondents' and 'Middle East correspondents', and less so in those many correspondents reporting, say, between New York and London, or between Brussels and Stockholm.

This, then, was multi-site field work – as I have put it elsewhere, a matter of 'being there...and there...and there!' (Hannerz 2003b). I also talked to some foreign news editors in New York, Los Angeles, London, Frankfurt and Stockholm to get the view from headquarters. Moreover, I followed the foreign news reporting itself in the media, although scrutinizing the end product was not as dominant a component in this study as it tends to be in most media research. The sizeable body of autobiographical writings by the foreign correspondents themselves was another noteworthy source of understandings.[7]

Chance and Risk

So these are my four fields, ghetto to global – and now what can I say on the basis of these experiences? First of all I would note the part that chance or unforeseen circumstances played, repeatedly, in the choice of fields and field problems. The first field I had had in mind, in Nigeria, I did not get to, at least not then; I went to an urban neighbourhood in another continent instead because somebody in Washington remembered me. I went to the Cayman Islands not because of any particular commitment to Caribbean studies but because it seemed at one particular moment to be an optimal use of time and limited resources. And going there had something to do with an unintended airline stopover a few years earlier. If that grey gunboat had not then appeared on the horizon, and if that protest march had not occurred, I would probably not have turned my attention to local politics, of which, most of the time, there was little of any very noticeable kind.

Then when I did go to Nigeria, it was indeed a matter of research which had involved much planning and preparation, but the choice of that particular town was again a matter of coincidence. On an early, non-anthropological journey through Nigeria I had been on a train that stood still at that railway junction for a long time, and I had been curious about the great many people milling about, seemingly in the middle of nowhere, on the savannah. Soon after, I came across what amounted to a brief ethnography of the town in an early Nigerian novel, by an author who I surmise had grown up there (Nzekwu 1962). Thus when I had a notion of what kind of town I wanted for this project, I thought I would go and look at this one first, and that was where I stayed. I returned several times, but not as many times as I might have if what in Nigeria has passed for politics had not intervened. When I began thinking seriously about the foreign correspondent study, it helped that a couple of American colleagues had kinship connections in the business that gave me a favourable start in some pilot interviews in New York. As I got to the stage of thinking about the selection of the more central sites for the study, the one I was quite sure of from the beginning was in South Africa, whether it would be Johannesburg or Cape Town, because that would be where 'Africa correspondents' would primarily be located, and I was still an Africanist at heart. Yet it also had to do with the fact that, interested as I was in South African society in itself, I belonged to a generation who had mostly chosen not to go there during the apartheid period; so this was a chance to make up for that loss to some degree.[8] Beside South Africa, there were some other possibilities for field sites. I decided on Jerusalem quite early, in part because when I planned the project I had recently been on a lecture tour in Israel, and had realized that Jerusalem had a sizeable number of correspondents covering a mostly quite compact Israeli–Palestinian beat. But then, after the timing of one national election campaign (during which correspondents would probably not have had time to spare for me) and one minor ailment had twice upset my plans for a period in Delhi, I went to Tokyo instead, partly because it could be combined with an invitation to an academic workshop.

I enumerate these circumstances not because I think they are particularly unusual, and certainly not to claim that I have been to any unique degree either a victim or a hero, but rather to suggest that anthropology is often like that. We seize on experiences and openings which somehow come our way, and are vulnerable to happenings in the world over which we have no control. If we can draw any lessons from this, one might be that we try to manage risk, long-term and short-term, in our selection of fields, and point out to those at the beginning of their professional lives that they might be wise to do the same. It may seem brave to go out there and confront risks, and at times it may be worth doing, but it can also turn out to be costly. On a more positive note, I would conclude that it might help to be well prepared, which means broadly prepared, for the serendipities of the field experience. With an internet café in every town, and academic libraries going electronic, we can perhaps now more often quickly read up on the kinds of things we were not prepared for, wherever we find ourselves when they confront us. I still think it is important to cultivate a certain willingness to seize unforeseen opportunities, a general sensibility towards ways of making anthropology out of realities which might otherwise remain mere distractions. And that also entails some readiness to depart from research plans and research designs that we carry into the field when we run into opportunities that simply should not be missed.

Diversified Engagements

Looking back at these field experiences, too, I see a fair amount of diversity. They have involved studying down, up (to a degree) and sideways. More importantly, perhaps, I have worked in rather different ways, ranging from the fairly strict participant observation approach in the Washington neighbourhood to the foreign correspondent study, where there was little of that, and much more interviewing. Usually, however, combinations of approaches and materials have been involved. In both the Cayman Islands and the Nigerian town, I got myself into studying backwards to some degree, looking up relatively recent historical materials (from about a decade earlier in the former and about fifty years earlier in the latter) to see what light they could throw on the present. I began the Washington study being somewhat uneasy about time spent watching TV, until I realized that the commentary of my co-viewers was quite revealing, and I still did fairly little with current media in the Cayman Islands (where there were at the time only a weekly newspaper, a magazine, and no local radio or television). By the time I got to the Nigerian town, however, I just could not disregard the role of the technologies of culture in making imagined worlds a great deal larger than the town itself – and this included the global dumping of old American TV sitcoms as well as the teacher and his students in a dusty hole-in-the-wall commercial school together studying a torn copy of *Macbeth*. I suspect that it may now indeed be difficult to do an ethnography of any way of life, just about anywhere, without paying at least some attention to media habits, as if everything happened in a face-to-face world. Yet then, of course, in my foreign correspondent study, following newsmedia reporting was itself central.

One might also say that this latter study was different from the others in being multi-local or trans-local rather than single-site. In fact, however, one could argue that the Nigerian town in its complexity, with its varied groups, institutions and settings, became a little like a multi-site field in a limited space. Furthermore, that study had one more multi-local aspect to it methodologically insofar as I also did a couple of interviews in London with elderly ex-colonial officers whose mid-century reports on the town I had read in the Nigerian archives. These, too, contributed to the oral history.

Probably, however, the increasing diversity, and lack of orthodoxy, in the ways I have been going about fieldwork myself in large part mirror more general developments in the discipline. About this I am not too worried. Participant observation is often a good way of finding out about things, but fieldworkers have always done a lot of other activities as well. If Hugh Gusterson's (1997: 116) term 'polymorphous engagements' sums up the way we do ethnography now, I think the difference over time is mostly one of degree. Moreover, it is not that fieldwork now *has* to be done, in every instance, in these more complicated, combinatory ways, but rather that this frequently goes with those expansive ambitions of studying upwards, sideways, backwards or whatever. Again, we have our different priorities in what we want to do with our anthropology. I have heard one colleague describe anthropology as 'the study of intimacy' – perhaps you can then stay in one place and derive your ethnography entirely from face-to-face encounters. But I doubt that everybody will agree that this is what all anthropology should be about, and what would worry me rather more would be if we insisted on defining the discipline in terms of a methodological standard operating procedure, and thereby painted ourselves into a corner from which we could not reach out to much of contemporary human life.

If I do not seem too unhappy about the more varied current ways of demarcating and approaching fields, and also to some extent of reporting on them, it may have a little to do with the fact that I happen to have been thinking about my topic here while spending several months at the University of Tokyo. Thus I have pondered the fact that the most famous anthropological study of Japan remains Ruth Benedict's *The Chrysanthemum and the Sword* (1946), based on the extremely unconventional approach of a wartime study at a distance of the culture of an enemy nation. And probably the next-best known study of the country is Chie Nakane's *Japanese Society* (1970), a somewhat similarly broadly interpretive study which is an example of 'anthropology at home'. Neither of the two have escaped sharp criticisms, and yet they have achieved the status of classics.[9] In fact, it may be that many of the books by anthropologists which have been most widely read, and are most vividly remembered, by their colleagues and a wider public, are like these two – not field monographs of a more traditional type. Despite all that has been said in recent times about 'writing culture', I am not sure we have yet adequately faced up to the problematic of diversifying anthropological genres.

The Field and the Divisions of the Anthropological Community

If anthropologists have recently been inclined to worry about fields and fieldwork, however, I wonder if we should not look for some of the sources of unease in circumstances which have less to do with field technique as such. They may have to do with the discipline as not merely a professional but a moral community, and with its divisions and its wider environment. 'The field' has stood for a rich and at the same time demanding experience, and a central question underlying our worries may be whether some of the membership of the community now miss out on that experience, or cheat by circumventing it.

The term 'polymorphous engagements' may point to the current, ever-shifting diversity of the fieldworker's craft, but if that suggests more of a continuum of assemblages of approach and experience, let me identify a couple of terms pointing towards greater discontinuity, even polarity. We may think of the classic ideal of participant observation as 'anthropology by immersion', an involvement so deep that the supposed risk was one of 'going native'. (Hardly anybody did.) In contrast, we now hear of 'anthropology by appointment' – with some irony or self-irony no doubt intended, yet referring to the reality that often enough in modern life generally, although not least in studying up or sideways, there may be less to participate in and observe fruitfully even if we had total access, but also that access to people, to informants, is in fact often limited, regulated and timed.[10]

Anthropologists, it has been observed, are not inclined towards hired-hand research. They want to be 'out there' themselves, involved with all their senses. During the period in the Nigerian town when I had several local assistants doing interviews and observations for me, I did not particularly enjoy having a fair amount of my own time occupied by interpreting their notes, and organizing and typing these, instead of wandering through the streets, or talking to traders in their market stalls. Fieldwork of the immersion type can be an intellectual, emotional and aesthetic pleasure, the kind of experience we feel makes both our minds and our hearts grow. It may involve memorable personal encounters: I am not likely to forget Sonny and Beejay, streetcorner intellectuals in my Washington neighbourhood, World War II veterans, probably drinking themselves to death much too early, bringing a *bricolage* of unexpected references into our exchanges, reminding me in a way of Victor Turner's (1960) key Ndembu informant, Muchona, whom the ethnographer could imagine as an eloquent, incisive, agitated Oxbridge don. If deep personal sympathy may not always grow out of these relationships, they may still give some special insight into how circumstances shape human beings, at the same time as these themselves try to shape their circumstances.

If there are moral overtones to the debates over what anthropologists now make their fields, it may not just be a matter of proper field technique, but also of a suspicion that if one does something more like anthropology by appointment, one misses out on some of that deeper personal experience, and also fails to face up to whatever kinds of tangible or intangible hardships tend to accompany such experience. And so, to those who feel that they have come through all that, such a person may seem not quite a real anthropologist, not a full member of the community, not a peer. That sort of suspicion may be difficult enough to deal with, around the seminar table or in corridor talk, if it appears on its own. But then the suggested difference may have been aligning itself with other large or small irritations in and around the community. As I have hinted already, it could appear as a conflict between generations as the espousal of other kinds of fields, other ways of doing fieldwork, seems to devalue the symbolic capital of elders, who in their turn hint that their juniors make it easy on themselves. In the discipline as a transnational community, too, controversy over understandings of the field could also, in a rather stereotypical fashion, set Europeans against Americans. Much of the critical scrutiny of old assumptions about the field, and many of the innovations in defining it, have come out of American anthropology, but then on the other side of the Atlantic divide their reception may be mixed with some resentment of a hype of newness in an academic market system which creates stars and fashions, and whose denizens often seem ignorant of the work of colleagues elsewhere, at a time when Europeans feel themselves unhappily caught up in the spread of a constraining and intellectually distracting academic audit culture.[11] The preoccupation with what should count as fieldwork has likewise seemed to show up in the concern with policing the border towards cultural studies, where practitioners, it is fairly widely held, too often get away with 'ethnography lite'. If such boundary maintenance activity would normally be expected to result in heightened in-group solidarity, perhaps it has not quite worked this time because the in-group has its own internal differences of opinion.

What, if anything, might we now want to do about these differences? Personally I am perhaps not ready to stand up and be counted as an entirely reliable partisan. Rooted on the European side of the Atlantic, I may still see some of the benefits of an academic market system in generating innovation; and I can even sense that it has been somewhat useful if cultural studies, mostly without knowing it, has challenged an anthropology rather too set in its ways. Perhaps what we could do, however, would be to try to spell out more explicitly our assumptions about different kinds of fields and fieldwork, and try to keep these separate from moral overtones and animosities. That may not always be easy; perhaps I have not been entirely successful myself here. But I think it would help if we could find a conceptual apparatus that bridges the gap between types of fields, allows us to compare them more precisely, and renders similarities and differences identifiable and literally debatable. For one thing, we might try to cultivate an understanding of the connections between the kinds of relationships we study and the relationships we ourselves have in the field.[12] If anthropology by immersion and anthropology by appointment are actually often about different kinds of relationships between other people, what sort of depths of experience and inter-personal closeness we reach in them ourselves is perhaps a little beside the point. To take another example, I have elsewhere tried to show why multi-site field studies are mostly not, as it is apparently sometimes misunderstood, a matter of somehow squeezing several conventionally defined local field studies into one single ethnographic package (Hannerz 2003b).[13] They tend not to involve the same kind of social units and relations as classic single-site fields. We should be wary of allowing the routine assumptions from established styles of fieldwork to carry over into and dominate arguments about newly emergent styles. And instead of dismissing some ways of being in the field only as deficient with regard to true field experience, we could ask what would be the long-term consequences for anthropology if conceptions of field and fieldwork were not allowed to vary and change.

Conclusion: Where Our Fields Are – Or, Away with 'Away'?

I have tried to make a case for keeping some room in fieldwork for chance, serendipity and improvisation. In broad terms, this also has something to do with my idea of what anthropology can be good for. I started out by identifying the mapping of human diversity as the agenda of anthropology. Beyond any such general formulation, I am sure we can all have our varied opinions about the particular strengths and possibilities of the discipline, but personally I still like to see anthropology as a kind of exploration. And although I have much respect and even intellectual affection for those who devote their labours to ever closer views of the cultural minutiae of the *longue durée*, or of vanishing tradition, I think exploring the emergent in culture and society goes well with both an inclination in anthropology towards openness in fieldwork and a habitual readiness to re-examine central assumptions and concepts. For me, that played a part in bending my project in the Nigerian town, originally conceived in more local terms, to something relating more to global processes. However, I think I can see a similar attraction to emergent phenomena and their organization in thought and life as anthropologists, with one twist of 'anthropology at home', turn to engaging with the nature of virtuality in society, or, when studying sideways, they make their approaches to the worlds of scientists.

Yet, in the end, we must also remind ourselves that past, present and future engagements with the field have been and will be as much determined by practical, material and organizational constraints as by our own scholarly ideals and internal debates.[14] The landscape of future fieldwork may place new risks and obstacles in our way. Could it be that we are worrying about the wrong things? It seems that at least some fields are becoming increasingly regulated. Changing conceptions of intellectual property rights can come to limit our access to, and use of, information. Ethics codes which require us to specify in advance precisely what we will do and ask about may not go well with our ideas of the reasonable way of doing ethnography.

What I want to dwell on, however, is a worry over the future geography of field experiences. We are used to thinking of anthropology as a discipline with a special relationship to global space, even as we notice that the distribution of fields in that space has kept changing. Looking at the discipline over time, we have seen streams of expatriate anthropologists moving between regions and continents. I went into anthropology, as I have said, with a particular interest in Africa; but while that interest is still with me, I have not worked there recently, except for my sojourn with the Africa correspondents in Johannesburg. As practical conditions of work changed and perhaps as Afro-optimism turned into Afro-pessimism, many other Africanists may also have become more strictly speaking ex-Africanists, at least as far as active field engagements are concerned. Perhaps we can discern that there have been other streams in and out of Papua New Guinea (related to changing conditions of law and order), out of Afghanistan and areas of the Middle East, and partly out of North American Indian reservations. In one period, it seemed, American anthropologists found themselves not very welcome in India; so they hurried to Nepal instead. And then recently anthropologists from elsewhere have headed into Eastern and Central Europe and Russia on a scale hardly conceivable as long as there was something called an Iron Curtain. In Tokyo I find a young Japanese colleague catching the Vladivostok flight to take him to the site of his study of education in Siberia.

A chapter in the history of anthropology could be written about these collective exits and entries and their implications for the discipline. Of course they have not just involved our scholarly or personal whims or fashions, but have had much to do with our particular vulnerability to political and other changes in the world. At present, however, I wonder if, rather paradoxically in what is supposed to be an era of globalization, the most marked tendency is not to head for some new, accessible region out there, 'away', but to find one's field 'at home'. To reiterate, what is 'at home' is not entirely obvious, but let us for the moment again accept the simple assumption that it is in one's country of residence.

There may be various reasons for a tendency towards more anthropology 'at home'. It may have to do with limited funding for fieldwork, or with other personal commitments such as family life, or with a feeling that it is generally less risky than going anywhere abroad. I suspect, however, that it is also a tendency which has to do with widespread changes in the structuring of European academic life. Current official pressures towards accelerated passages through doctoral degree programmes make fieldwork of the classical type difficult. It is hard to fit the intellectual preparations for working in an alien culture, including learning another language quite possibly from scratch, into that very limited time frame which, according to principles of academic mainstreaming, is likely to be uniform for all disciplines.

I have never been among those who would argue that all 'real anthropology' must be 'away', expatriate anthropology. I have not seen any convincing intellectual arguments for that, and I have been happy enough with a situation where expatriates and local scholars mingle in the same territories. That may sometimes generate tensions relating to the worth of local knowledge and to the centre–periphery relationships of international academic structures, but it can also bring new dialogues and fresh insights. I would be less happy, on the other hand, with the prospect that national anthropological communities, or local communities such as that of a university anthropology department, should come to be made up just about entirely of people who have done all their anthropology 'at home'. We could continue teaching students about the Trobrianders, and the Kwakiutl, and the Swat Pathan, but if you looked around the table of the local seminar room, you would see only the faces of people who have had their fields in Great Britain, or Sweden, or Italy, or in whatever other country that seminar room happens to be located. Perhaps it was always rare, even an anthropologist's Utopia, to have around that table a gathering of colleagues who together represented a global ethnographic experience. It may even sometimes have been fairly concentrated to some corner of an empire which had, for fieldwork purposes, become the departmental turf. Yet even that would have been, in Clifford Geertz's phrasing, 'another country heard from' (1973: 23). If, with the kind of influence that the departmental seminar supposedly represents in the reproduction of anthropological ideas (cf. Spencer 2000), all or most of what would be heard in it would be the voices from home, anthropology would seem to become much like other academic disciplines as normally constituted in European universities: sociology, history, cultural studies, political science or whatever. What has generally been an expansive discipline would for once be contracting.

Here and there this may already be the situation. In other places, perhaps, the geographical redistribution of field experiences will never reach that point. Some enthusiasts will heroically or foolhardily insist on battling with the difficulties placed in their way. It could be, too, that transnational migration and the presence of diasporas will be a factor in maintaining a degree of diversity, as for some anthropologists what colleagues will see as 'away' will in one way be 'at home', in another country. Yet even this will not quite involve anthropology as we have known it, with its personal passages into distant and alien cultures.[15]

Perhaps anthropology will continue to reinvent itself, attenuate that special relationship to global space, and make 'away' a less significant term for the orientation of its interests. The scrutiny of its central concepts might lead ethnographic explorations into yet other directions (and vice versa). But that would involve a fundamental change in the imagery with which 'the field' as an anthropological keyword has so far been associated – within the discipline, in the academic division of labour, and in public culture. Thinking forwards, whether we like it or not, it is a scenario we should not disregard.

Notes

1. Shore and Wright (1997: 14) propose 'studying through' in their mapping of an anthropology of policy, drawing this from an unpublished thesis by Susan Reinhold.

2. On the future in anthropological study, see Wallman (1992), and more

recently Malkki (2001), Hannerz (2003a), Miyazaki (2003) and Appadurai (2004).

3. On my methodological interests in this field, see Hannerz (1976).

4. The earlier anthropological literature on 'social change', 'acculturation', and so on, seemed less useful in the late twentieth-century postcolonial condition.

5. These multi-site studies were not all transnational, and there were some others which were not devoted to occupations, but the collected effort resulted in what is probably the first entire book on such research in anthropology (Hannerz 2001).

6. I used the term first in a discussion of several occupations on tracks parallel to, or crossing, those of anthropologists (Hannerz 1998). Marcus's (1997) essay on the anthropological turn to studies in 'power/knowledge' is also relevant to this terminological invention.

7. I should add here that while autobiographies of this kind concentrate on more dramatic events and experiences, my own work has dwelt at least as much on the routines of correspondent work.

8. My interest in South Africa had even resulted in a publication which was both 'studying backwards' and 'at a distance': a paper on Sophiatown, the famously culturally vibrant neighbourhood of Johannesburg torn down by the apartheid regime in the 1950s (Hannerz 1994).

9. In July 2003, one could be reminded again of the continued public standing of Benedict and her book on Japan, as a writer in the *New York Times* noted, in the context of the occupation of Iraq, that her example showed how anthropological expertise could be useful in rebuilding a defeated enemy country (Stille 2003).

10. The term 'appointment anthropology' may be Luhrmann's (1996: vii). On interviewing access to élites, see, for example, Thomas (1993).

11. This is certainly not to say that the interest in rethinking 'the field' and fieldwork has been uniquely American – see, for example, an issue of the *Anthropological Journal on European Cultures* (2002). Nor is it to suggest that the audit culture is not reaching into academic life in the United States as well; see Brenneis (2004).

12. Reading a book manuscript by Brian Moeran (2005) on his different field experiences in Japan cast more light on this issue for me.

13. In my foreign correspondent study, for example, I was not trying to deal with Jerusalem, Johannesburg and Tokyo as cities, but merely considering their characteristics as working environments for newspeople.

14. See Parkin's (2000: 107) brief comment.

15. It is also conceivable that even if the conditions of postgraduate education would not favour more exotic fields, those who have passed that hurdle could turn to them later on, less hurriedly. But this is not what has usually happened recently: more people who have gone away first have stayed at home with their fieldwork later.

References

Anthropological Journal on European Cultures (2002), Issue on 'Shifting Grounds: Experiments in Doing Ethnography', 11.

Appadurai, A. (2004), 'The Capacity to Aspire: Culture and the Terms of Recognition', in V. Rao and M. Walton (eds) *Culture and Public Action*, Stanford, CA: Stanford University Press.

Benedict, R. (1946), *The Chrysanthemum and the Sword*, Boston: Houghton Mifflin.

Brenneis, D. (2004), 'A Partial View of Contemporary Anthropology', *American Anthropologist*, 106: 580–8.

Geertz, C. (1973), *The Interpretation of Cultures*, New York: Basic Books.

Gusterson, H. (1997), 'Studying Up Revisited', *Political and Legal Anthropology Review* 20 (1): 114–19.

Hannerz, U. (1969), *Soulside: Inquiries into Ghetto Culture and Community*, New York: Columbia University Press.

Hannerz, U. (1974), *Caymanian Politics: Structure and Style in a Changing Island Society*, Stockholm Studies in Social Anthropology, no. 1.

Hannerz, U. (1976), 'Methods in an African Urban Study', *Ethnos* 41: 68–98.

Hannerz, U. (1981), 'The Management of Danger', *Ethnos* 46: 19–46.

Hannerz, U. (1994), 'Sophiatown: The View from Afar', *Journal of Southern African Studies* 20: 181–93.

Hannerz, U. (1996), *Transnational Connections: Culture, People, Places*, London: Routledge.

Hannerz, U. (1998) 'Other Transnationals: Perspectives Gained from Studying Sideways', *Paideuma* 44: 109–23.

Hannerz, U. (ed) (2001), *Flera fält i ett*, Stockholm: Carlsson.

Hannerz, U. (2003a), 'Macro-scenarios: Anthropology and the Debate over Contemporary and Future Worlds', *Social Anthropology* 11: 169–87.

Hannerz, U. (2003b), 'Being There ... and There ... and There! Reflections on Multi-site Ethnography', *Ethnography* 4: 229–44.

Hannerz, U. (2004), *Foreign News: Exploring the World of Foreign Correspondents*, Chicago: University of Chicago Press.

Luhrmann, T.M. (1996), *The Good Parsi: The Fate of a Colonial Elite in a Postcolonial Society*, Cambridge, MA: Harvard University Press.

Malkki, L.H. (2001), 'Figures of the Future: Dystopia and Subjectivity in the Social Imagination of the Future', in D. Holland and J. Lave (eds), *History in Person: Enduring Struggles, Contentious Practice, Intimate Identities*. Santa Fe, NM: School of American Research Press.

Marcus, G.E. (1997), 'Critical Cultural Studies as One Power/Knowledge Like, Among, and In Engagement with Others', in E. Long (ed.), *From Sociology to*

Cultural Studies, Malden, MA: Blackwell.

Miyazaki, H. (2003), 'The Temporalities of the Market', *American Anthropologist* 105 (2): 255–65.

Moeran, B. (2005), *The Business of Ethnography: Strategic Exchanges, People and Organizations*, Oxford: Berg.

Nader, L. (1972) 'Up the Anthropologist – Perspectives Gained from Studying Up', in D. Hymes (ed.), *Reinventing Anthropology*, New York: Pantheon.

Nakane, C. (1970), *Japanese Society*, Berkeley: University of California Press.

Nzekwu, O. (1962), *Blade among the Boys*, London: Hutchinson.

Parkin, D. (2000), 'Templates, Evocations and the Long-term Fieldworker', in P. Dresch, W. James and D. Parkin (eds), *Anthropologists in a Wider World*, Oxford: Berghahn.

Shore, C. and Wright, S. (1997), 'Policy: A New Field of Anthropology', in C. Shore and S. Wright (eds), *Anthropology of Policy*, London: Routledge.

Spencer, J. (2000), 'British Social Anthropology: A Retrospective', *Annual Review of Anthropology* 29: 1–24, Mountain View, CA: Annual Reviews.

Stille, A. (2003), 'Experts Can Help Rebuild a Country', *New York Times*, 19 July.

Thomas, R.J. (1993), 'Interviewing Important People in Big Companies', *Journal of Contemporary Ethnography* 22: 80–96.

Turner, V. (1960), 'Muchona the Hornet, Interpreter of Religion', in J.B. Casagrande (ed.), *In the Company of Man*, New York: Harper & Row.

Wallman, S. (ed.) (1992), *Contemporary Futures*, London: Routledge.

–2–

Beyond the Verandah: Fieldwork, Locality and Understanding Urbanism in a South African City

Leslie Bank

Introduction

Duncan Village in the coastal South Africa city of East London is a well-worked site of knowledge production in anthropology. In the 1930s, Monica Hunter conducted fieldwork there as part of her classic study *Reaction to Conquest* (1936). Written up as part of an exploration of the cultural impact of urbanization on the Pondo people (in a broad sense a subset of Xhosa-speakers), she left it to the end of her monograph, offering a 'culture contact' perspective. Twenty years later, Philip and Iona Mayer and their colleagues from Rhodes University embarked on extended fieldwork in the old East Bank location (subsequently called Duncan Village). Their engagement with East Bank people proved to be much longer and more significant than Hunter's, and resulted in three anthropological monographs: Reader's *The Black Man's Portion* (1960), Mayer's *Townsmen or Tribesmen* (1961) and Pauw's *The Second Generation* (1963). Collectively, these studies became known as the *Xhosa in Town* Trilogy. They divided the population of East London into two distinct socio-cultural categories: the so-called 'School' people or *abantu basesikolweni*, who were seen to be receptive to European cultural influences, urbanization and Christianity, and the 'Reds', the *abantu ababomvu* or *amaqaba*, who were said to reject Western values, lifestyles and Christianity. The latter, who celebrated their rural traditions and values in the city, fascinated the Mayers, who admired the determination of the Reds in their refusal to relinquish their unique cultural identities in the face of European domination.

In the anthropological literature on urbanization and social change in southern Africa the Trilogy has thus stood out for its ethnographic account of cultural conservatism and the persistence of tradition in a changing urban context. *Townsmen or Tribesmen,* in particular, emerged as a classic anthropological study which demonstrated the capacity of poor rural migrants to resist cultural domination and to defend their pre-existing rural cultural identities and traditions in an industrializing South African city. In a context where anthropology as a discipline was starting to grapple with the impact on communities of rapid social and cultural change, the Mayers' work provided a good example of the lengths to which some people would go to resist acculturation and defend themselves against Western culture. But the initially positive reception given to the Trilogy faded in the 1970s as apartheid polices were entrenched in South Africa and social anthropology as a discipline came under close scrutiny for its political role during the colonial era (Asad 1973; Eriksen and Nielsen 2001). In the new political and intellectual climate, the Mayers' celebration of Red identities and lifestyles in East London became problematic, especially since they seemed to be suggesting that some Africans in the Eastern Cape were refusing to modernize and preferred to develop along tribal or ethnic lines. As a result, the Mayers were now accused, especially by scholars working outside of anthropology, of being apologists for apartheid (Beinart 1991: 15–17).

From within anthropology, the assessment of the Trilogy also changed in the 1970s. With the increasing influence of Marxism in anthropology, the Mayers and their colleagues were now criticized for their theoretical conservatism, for their lack of historical perspective, and for their failure to situate adequately their analysis of cultural change within the political economy of colonialism and racial capitalism. The Trilogy was found both politically and theoretically wanting and was criticized for over-emphasizing the salience of the Red–School, townsmen–tribesmen divide. It was pointed out that other divisions, such as those based on class difference, were ignored and that these studies also under-estimated the situational dynamics of identity formation. The essential critique of the *Xhosa in Town* project was that it had been theoretically over-determined and became locked into an outmoded 'two-system cultural model', which could not account for the enormous complexities of urban African identity formation in the 1950s. The critics had made some powerful points and, in 1980, Philip Mayer recast his analysis of Red and School in more politically fashionable terms. Drawing on the work of the French structuralist Marxist Louis Althusser, he argued that Red and School were, in fact, *both* long-standing rural resistance ideologies, which had their roots in the history of African dispossession, missionary activity and colonial exploitation in nineteenth-century Eastern Cape history. Significantly, while Mayer added historical depth and context to his earlier work, he did not suggest that he had originally over-estimated the salience of the Red–School divide. He pointed out that the material and social basis for this division was historically rooted, but had been progressively undermined with apartheid-driven agrarian change, first with the introduction of betterment planning in the 1950s and then bantustan development which increased rural poverty and landlessness in the 1960s and 1970s (cf. Mayer 1980).

In this chapter I want to revisit the *Xhosa in Town* project again, but this time from a methodological perspective. Between 1999 and 2002, I was given the task of researching urban land restitution claims in East London, which included the restitution claims of some 5,000 families from the old East Bank location – the site of the *Xhosa in Town* Project (cf. Bank and Maqasho 2000, 2001). As a sample of former East Bank residents, the claimant group included many more urban-born individuals than labour migrant. But, this bias notwithstanding, I was nevertheless immediately struck on meeting these claimants by how many of their accounts of cultural life in East Bank differed from the dominant 'tribesmen-in-town' narrative of the Trilogy. Many of the claimants suggested that the central cultural dynamic in the 1950s was not defined so much by a defence of tradition as by a growing infatuation with cosmopolitanism, or what Khan (2001) might call new forms of 'popular modernism'.[1] According to old East Bank residents, this engagement was forged around common interests in sport, music (especially jazz) and politics amongst the youth. In view of the evidence I collected, the central aim of this chapter is to explore why the work of the *Trilogy*, which was so detailed and ethno-graphically rich, missed the vibrancy and intensity of local engagements with cos-mopolitan styles and identities. How could urban anthropologists, who claimed that their aim was simply to 'describe and record', end up portraying such a single-stranded view of urban life in this city?

In trying to address these questions, I focus less on issues of politics and theory, which have dominated previous assessments of this work, and concentrate instead on fieldwork practice and its role in the production of anthropological knowledge. I argue that the perspective of the Mayers and their colleagues was essentially 'homemade' as it was generated largely from fieldwork and interviews conducted in the space of the house and the yard. I suggest that had these scholars been able to extend their fieldwork practice and vision 'beyond the verandah', to the spaces of the street, the tearoom, the dance-halls, and to public spaces beyond the loca-tion, such as the beach, the station and the sports tournaments, they would have probably 'read' local social and cultural dynamics slightly differently. In the chapter, I dwell on the strengths of the 'homemade' perspectives and traditions of these urban anthropologists, but also highlight the need to always connect up the cultural circuitry of the home with broader, public arenas of cultural production. I conclude by advocating that an anthropology that is able to creatively access dif-ferent scales and levels of urban experience simultaneously and can strike the sen-sitive balance between fieldwork within and beyond the home will continue to make a vital contribution to the understanding of urban life and experience.

The *Xhosa in Town* Project

As an intellectual project, the *Xhosa in Town* series emerged in the wake of bur-geoning scholarships on urbanization and social change on the Zambian Copperbelt from the Rhodes–Livingstone Institute (RLI), established by the

British government in Northern Rhodesia in 1937. Godfrey Wilson's path-breaking study of the mining community at Northern Rhodesia's Broken Hill laid the foundation for a new tradition of urbanization studies, which became the RLI's hallmark (cf. Wilson 1941/2). Within the colonial milieu there was much discussion and concern around the concept of 'stabilization' – a term used to refer to the length of stay of Africans in the city, and to the increasingly permanent urban settlement of African workers and their families. According to Ferguson (1999), RLI anthropologists aimed to challenge the prevailing wisdom in colonial government circles that a 'tribesman' in town remained a 'tribesman'. They intended to counter the assumptions of colonial administrators and mine owners that African townsmen constituted 'a very primitive population' (cf. Brown 1973; Ferguson 1999; Schumaker 2001; Werbner 1984).

It was in this political context that liberal anthropologists at the RLI argued that the colonial regime had under-estimated the capacity and speed with which Africans entering urban areas were able to adopt and absorb essential aspects of modernity, and Western values and lifestyles. They argued that Africans responded to urbanization and social change by shedding their rural 'tribesmen' identities and adopting new urban identities. This thinking was captured in Gluckman's famous phrase, 'the African townsman is a townsman' (Gluckman 1960: 55). In the multi-ethnic mining towns of what is today Zambia, the RLI's anthropologists stressed the capacity of Africans working in towns to change their identities and behaviour to fit the situations in which they found themselves. Their observations formed the basis of what became known as 'situational analysis', which emphasized the ability of individuals to shed older identities and adopt new ones as the situation demanded. However, as Ferguson (1999: 20) has argued, this emphasis on the capacity of urban workers to define themselves situationally was embedded in a wider narrative of modernization and progress, in terms of which urban Africans were inevitably *en route* to civilization and modernity.

These ideological assumptions also shaped the *Xhosa in Town* project. Philip Mayer and his colleagues were interested in showing 'how some Xhosa during the course of their East London careers undergo the transition from migrant to real townsmen and others do not' (Mayer 1963: xvii) They defined the process of urbanization as, on the one hand, a slackening of ties with the former rural home to the point where the migrant no longer felt the pull of the hinterland and, on the other, a simultaneous acquisition of Western values and cultural forms. The point at which a person's 'within-town ties' came to predominate over their 'extra-town ties' could be revealed, they suggested, by a study of their relational network, while their changing socio-cultural orientations could be explored through an assessment of changing norms and values in town (ibid.).

Philip and Iona Mayer distinguished the quantitative process of urban 'stabilization', equated with 'length of time in the city', from the qualitative process of 'urbanization', as the acquisition of a Westernised lifestyle, norms and values. They argued that there was no reason to assume, as some Copperbelt studies had, that staying for long periods in the city necessarily led to loss of tribal identity and cultural orientation. Philip Mayer's comment was that a large segment of East London's migrant labour force had become 'stabilized' without being 'urbanized' (that is, without adopting Western values) (Mayer 1961: 10–20). He suggested that this was not simply due to apartheid's enforced migrant labour, but was also a product of a deep-seated rejection by many migrants of Western culture and Christianity. In East London, *amaqaba* (Red) migrants in particular showed little interest in socializing outside a narrow group of 'home mates' (*abakhaya*) in town. Moreover, they focused their energies on saving money to send to rural homes to build up their homesteads (*imizi*) for retirement. These men, according to the Mayers, were tribesmen in town. Their strategy and orientation was to defend and maintain their tribal cultural values and identities. Rather than picking up or discarding identities at will, as suggested by the Copperbelt studies, the Mayers argued that the *amaqaba* identity was a relatively fixed, total identity that had become internalized in town through a process of 'incapsulation'.[2]

To ensure that the Trilogy focused not only on migrants, Philip Mayer commissioned a study of urban-born, second-generation families in the East Bank location. Undertaken in the late 1950s, it constituted the third volume in the series – Pauw's *The Second Generation*. Pauw extended the Mayers' insights by gauging the level of East London-born Africans' absorption of Western values and lifestyles. He worked with a series of categories or 'social types' based on a combination of criteria, including household material, culture, education, income and level of 'Westernization'. He concluded that while second-generation families were considerably more 'Westernised' than those of most migrants (for instance, they were less inclined to use witchcraft), their transition to 'full urbanization' was incomplete and disparate. He noted the continued adherence of many second-generation families to traditional Xhosa religious beliefs. Pauw thus developed a further typology to place second-generation urban households on a scale from 'semi-Red' to 'fully westernized' (Pauw 1963: 170–4). But despite his interest in broad processes of cultural change and identity, his urban research was closely focused on the domestic domain and the changing urban family structure. This notion of the domestic sphere as the primary site of cultural knowledge and social organization and the key locus of socialization and cultural transmission, in fact, underpinned the Xhosa in Town project as a whole. The failure of the Trilogy researchers to engage effectively with the dynamics of social life and cultural production in public spaces beyond the home, I argue later, created significant social and cultural 'blind spots'.

The fact, as I have suggested, that *Townsmen or Tribesmen* became an anthropological classic had much to do with how its arguments corresponded to the dominant themes and conventions of disciplinary knowledge at that time. As Clifford explains, it was common in the 1950s and 1960s for the 'cleared spaces' of scientific work in anthropology to be 'constituted through the suppression of cosmopolitan experiences, especially those of the people under study' (1997: 201–5). The complex, fluid and seemingly unbounded creolized dynamics of city life, he argues, was not exactly what anthropologists working in the dominant paradigm wished to encounter. It was an anthropologist's nightmare, as Mintz remarked of the Caribbean, to find 'houses constructed of old Coca-Cola signs, a cuisine littered with canned corned beef and imported Spanish olives, rituals shot through with the cross and the palm leaf, languages seemingly pasted together with ungrammatical Indo-European usages, all observed within the reach of radio and television' (quoted in Gupta and Ferguson 1997: 21).

But it was not the failure of the project to grasp the creolised cultural dynamics of urban life that initially attracted the attention of the critics; rather it was the absence of a thorough analysis of political economy, labour migration and colonial exploitation. In the 1970s, Bernard Mugabane, drawing on neo-Marxism and dependency theory, attacked the *Xhosa in Town* project for failure to grasp the complexities of colonial and racial capitalism. Magubane, however, also rejected the linear models of cultural development that seemed to underpin these studies, which presented European civilization and Westernization as the desired end point of African cultural development (Magubane 1971, 1973). He argued that urban Africans generally did not seek to mimic Western ways, but were constantly adapting, reinterpreting and reworking Western cultural influences through the prism of their own local cultural experiences. In subsequent critical reviews, such as those by Moore (1994: 57–62) and Mafeje (1997: 12), it has been suggested that the contrast between Red and School was overdrawn and that in reality the urban and the rural co-existed and were more intertwined and overlaid. The problem with the cultural analysis of the Trilogy, it was suggested, was that it seemed to miss the large social and cultural spaces that existed 'in-between' tradition and modernity. Yet in revisiting East London's old locations through the narratives of their former residents, it is not the complex integration of tradition and modernity that they emphasize, but the ascendancy and dominance of cosmopolitanism as a social and cultural force, especially in the post-war period. A careful reading of Monica Hunter's 1936 account of life in East Bank provides a useful starting point.

Revisiting East Bank

Monica Hunter's account of the cultural dynamics of the East London locations in the 1930s is in many ways strikingly different from that presented in the Trilogy twenty-five years later. Unlike the Mayers, who were struck by the cultural conservatism of city migrants and the desire of many to defend rural cultural values and orientations, Hunter was alarmed by the speed with which newly urbanized individuals and families were changing their outlooks and orientations in the city. She was, for instance, concerned at the enthusiasm with which location residents, some of them in the city only briefly, desired money and modern things:

> Money gives power to obtain so many of the desired things of European civilization – better clothing, housing, furnishing, food, education, gramophones, motor-cars, books, power to travel – all the paraphernalia of western civilization is coveted. Again and again old men spoke to me of how intense was the desire for money in the younger generation. (Hunter 1936: 455).

She noted that 'in town it is smart to be as europeanized as possible. In their dress men and girls follow European fashions – "Oxford bags", berets, sandal shoes. Conversation is interlarded with European slang. ... Houses, furniture, and food are as European as earnings permit' (ibid.: 437). 'Raw tribesmen' found themselves in a marginal position in the city, since

> The values in town are European, not tribal. Status depends largely on wealth and education and these entail Europeanization. ... Knowledge of tribal law, skills in talking, renown as a warrior, and even the blood of a chief's family, count for comparatively little in town. These conditions make for the speedy transference of at least the superficialities of culture. (ibid.)

Even in terms of social life and entertainment, Hunter argued, tribal influences were on the wane. She observed that tribal rituals were not held in town and that

> There is little Native dancing. ... Young people gather in private houses, particularly on Friday and Saturday evenings, for parties, but here European fox trots [*sic*] were more often performed than the old Bantu dances. And the music is European or American ragtime. About the street one more often hears ragtime hummed than an old Bantu song. (ibid.: 455)

In highlighting this appetite for Western-style entertainment, Hunter noted that by the 1930s the location had its own cinema, 'at which there are two evening performances and one matinee a week' (ibid.: 467). She also provided a detailed inventory of the wide range of social clubs, societies and churches operating in East Bank. They included dancing clubs and musical societies specializing in European and American styles, savings groups, tea clubs and a wide variety of sports clubs. Hunter's Xhosa fluency, and her close connections with the township élite, ensured her access to these associations. During her three months in East London, Dr W.B. Rubusana,[3] leader of one of the location's largest Christian churches and a founding member of the African National Congress, hosted her.

Through Rubusana, she appears to have had easy access to the location and was able to walk the streets and enter households, almost at will. Consequently she encountered a fairly broad spectrum of township life and developed a perspective, which encompassed aspects of both private and public life. Her view was framed, however, within a model of 'culture contact' and 'detribalization' that precluded her disguising her concerns about the social consequences of rapid social change.

The cosmopolitan cultural influences alluded to by Hunter in *Reaction to Conquest* seem to have deepened significantly during the 1940s and 1950s and emerged as a central theme in the narratives of former East Bank residents in their recollections of this period. Many identified the Second World War as a political and cultural watershed, a period during which location residents became more aware of their rights and were profoundly affected by popular transnational cultural forms. In the late 1940s, drought in the Ciskei pushed a new wave of rural youth to the city in search of work and the possibility of permanent urban residence. On the streets of East Bank these youth encountered local urban-born youths who exuded a new self-confidence, a fashionable look and a street-wise, cocky modern style, which was now more conspicuous than ever. On the political front this new self-confidence was reflected in the formation of a dynamic branch of the African National Congress Youth League in East London in 1949. The Youth League, led by the multi-talented triumvirate of C.J. Fazzie, A.S. Gwentshe and J. Lengisi, broke ranks with the more conservative African National Congress (ANC) old guard in the locations as they injected new life and energy into the resistance politics (Lodge 1987). With key political figures like Gwentshe and others involved in popular jazz bands, theatre and dance groups and sports clubs, there was a significant convergence during this period of struggle politics and cosmopolitan cultural orientation. This is not to suggest, as Lodge (1987) points out, that the political leadership did not try hard to bridge the divide between urban and rural youth, it is simply to note a growing infatuation amongst the East Bank youth of the 1950s with a fashion-, music- and entertainment-driven 'popular modernism'.

According to the former residents of East Bank whom I interviewed, the cultural dynamism of the late 1940s and 1950s had diverse sources. Some attributed the changes to the influence of returning Second World War servicemen. Others associated them with the opening of new factories and the growth of the local urban working class. Yet others referred to events on the Reef and the popularity of South African magazines like *Drum, Bona* and *Zonk,* which kept location residents abreast of cultural developments in larger cities and abroad. Whatever the reasons, there was consensus that the post-war period signalled 'a local cultural renaissance' that raised cosmopolitan influences in location life to new levels. It initiated an explosion of new music groups, sports clubs and dancing styles, and brought a succession of musical, sports and dance acts to the city. One former resident explained:

It felt like we had become the Sophiatown of the Eastern Cape. We had the jazz bands, the politicians, sportsmen and the style. We were up with all the new trends. Here in the location we did not have much time for tradition and tribal culture. The guys had come back from the war with a new confidence and there was a great expectation of change.[4]

In writing the history of *Drum* magazine, Michael Chapman points out that when the magazine had started in the early 1950s, it carried stories about tribal customs and dance, which attracted such negative readership response that they had to be dropped. A reader reported:

'Ag, why do you dish out this stuff, man?' said the man with the golliwog [*sic*] hair in a floppy American suit, at the Bantu Men's Centre [in Johannesburg]. 'Tribal Music! Tribal history! Chiefs! We don't care about chiefs! Give us jazz and film stars, man! We want Duke, Satchmo, and hot dames! Yes brother, anything American. You can cut out this junk about kraals and folk-tales ... – forget it! You are just trying to keep us backward, that's what! Tell us what is happening here, on the Reef!'(Chapman 2001: 187)

Such a view was common in East Bank too. Young people in particular did not want stories about tribal culture so much as to keep up with metropolitan styles, to watch American movies and engage in dynamic new urban cultural forms and styles-in-the-making. They recounted stories about the notorious shebeens (illegal taverns) on Ndende and Camp Streets; *tsotsi* gangs, including some called the Vikings and the Italians; jazz events at the Peacock Hall and political meetings on Bantu Square. They also remembered Coca-Cola fashion shows and ballroom dancing at the Social Centre, B-grade American movies at the local Springbok bio-scope and exciting sports and social events hosted at Rubusana Park.

As in Sophiatown, East London's urban youth fed on images of black America, developing a myriad of new styles and fashions, which were displayed on the streets and at the dance-halls (cf. Coplan 1985; Glaser 2000; Hannerz 1997; Mattera 1987; Themba 1985). Starting in local tearooms and on the household verandahs, where people would listen to the radio and read magazines, and at the cinema, where American movies played all week, location residents experimented with new fashions and styles. On the streets youths copied imported styles, adapted them and put them on public display, whilst at the dance-halls on Saturday night many were dressed to the nines. Mrs Mthimba recalled that:

Dressing up became a big thing. There was always talk about what was new in the shops on Oxford Street [East London's main shopping precinct]. Many of us bought outfits from 'La Continental', a fashion shop, which had good Italian gear in the North End. Some of the older men would not buy off the shelf. They preferred to have their suits made up by a tailor, of which there were many in the location and the North End.[5]

Home-made Ethnography?

How could the Mayers and their colleagues have failed to notice such seemingly obvious social and cultural dynamics? Did they not emphasize these popular cosmopolitan cultural forms because they were committed to clearing *ethno*-spaces that conformed to the dominant models in the discipline at that time? Or were there other reasons? Both Philip Mayer (1961: 319) and Pauw (1963: 230) explicitly denied that they were overly influenced by theoretical models, emphasizing rather that their main aim was 'simply to record' and to present 'first-hand factual knowledge' about the urban African society. So how in the process of 'simply recording' could they have missed so much?

Several factors seem to be important here. Firstly, it should be noted that when the *Xhosa in Town* researchers first visited East Bank in the mid-1950s, the township was in political turmoil. In 1952, the locations erupted into political violence when police and army troops were deployed to quell, violently, political protests. During the unrest several whites were killed, including a Roman Catholic nun who lived and worked in the location. The political environment in East Bank was still tense in 1954 when the Mayers and their colleagues started research on the *Xhosa in Town* project.

Unlike Monica Hunter, who came to East Bank with the blessing of one of the location's most senior political leaders, the Trilogy researchers lacked powerful local political allies within the location and had to rely heavily on the support of white clerics and officials. When I interviewed Philip Mayer in his home in Oxford in 1994 about the fieldwork methods they had employed in East Bank, he recounted their difficulties as white, non-Xhosa speakers from out of town with no local reputation, nor any significant political connections. He also reflected that his work commitments at Rhodes University in Grahamstown, 160 kilometres away, precluded a sustained presence in the field. As the research project wore on, he was increasingly forced to rely on local research assistants to stand in for him, and to administer pre-designed questionnaires aimed at gathering information about household dynamics and social attitudes. In 1994, he showed me some of the questionnaire schedules he had supplied to his assistants as a means of gauging 'urban commitment'. They included questions about issues such as clan affiliation, frequency of home visits and religious beliefs, as well as migrant views about economic resources, such as fields and livestock. The structure of certain questionnaires seemed to allow for the easy classification of respondents as either Red or School, without necessarily discovering how they classified themselves in different social contexts. Mafeje, who worked with Monica Wilson (formerly

Hunter) in the 1960s, has recently claimed that their feeling at the time was that the social categories of Red and School had been somewhat over-determined in the *Xhosa in Town* project (Mafeje 1997; Wilson and Mafeje 1963).

The use of questionnaires was also a key feature in Pauw's work. It appears that his research was based mainly on the administration of formal structured questionnaires, coupled with occasional field visits. He explains that

> Liberal use was made of the services of Bantu [*sic*] research assistants, but the author made a point of taking part in different phases of the field-work himself so as to be able to evaluate properly the information collected by assistants. Mr S. Campell Mvalo must be mentioned for having done the lion's share in collecting raw material. ... Mr Enos L. Xotyani also gave assistance at various stages and his contribution of reports rich in detail was particularly valuable. (Pauw 1963: 230)

In my interview with Philip Mayer, I was also struck by the limited extent to which he and his colleagues had engaged in what some anthropologists call 'deep hanging out' (Rosaldo 1989), simply circulating in the townships, speaking to people informally and gathering information on an *ad hoc* basis. In retrospect, it appears that the *Xhosa in Town* researchers employed a two-pronged strategy, combining structured household interviews with attitudinal surveys generally conducted by their assistants. This is clearly evident in the text of *Townsmen or Tribesmen*, where attitudinal information is often presented without close attention to biographical (life history) or situational context. The attitudes of migrants and townsmen often appear detached from their social and historical contexts, simply presented as apt illustrations of Red or School outlooks or orientations. This style of presentation also contributes to the over-determined distinction between Red and School in the Mayers' work. Consequently, *Townsmen or Tribesmen* gives the reader very little sense of the blurred and complicated nature of the Red and School cultural categories in people's varied and complex everyday interactions. Thus, rich and detailed as the Mayers' ethnography is with regard to migrant life in the city, there is nevertheless a disjuncture: a sense of distance between the cognitive maps of migrants and embedded social and cultural practice. Such a disjuncture leaves an impression that 'the cultural' and 'the social' have been separated out, and then – and only then – mapped and overlaid on to each other.[6]

While there were similarities in the research methods of the Trilogy and those of the RLI anthropologists, it is significant that the Trilogy lacks any sustained analysis of public events and occasions of the kind seen in Mitchell's 'The Kalela Dance' (1956). One of the reasons for this silence is related to the Trilogy researchers' understanding of processes of cultural transmission. The assumption that seemed to underpin the project as a whole was that the transmission of culture essentially occurred as a domestic, inter-generational process, where learned behaviour was passed on from one generation to the next in situations of social intimacy. As a result it is perhaps not surprising that domestic groups and their local equivalents – the migrants *intanga* (age-mate) domestic and *iseti* beer-drinking groups – emerged as the primary focus of analysis. This belief that the domestic domain was the critical and formative locale for the analysis of cultural transmission in East London's politically unstable locations was clearly central to the spatial strategies the Mayers and their colleagues adopted as fieldworkers. It is indicative of the extent to which the Trilogy's ethnographers confined themselves to the relative safety of people's homes and yards. Such spatial confinement blunted their sensitivity to developments beyond the house, and especially to the changing cultural dynamics on the streets, in the dance-halls and in other public spaces. By the same token, one of the main reasons for the comprehensiveness of the Mayers' own account of *amaqaba* cultural forms and for Pauw's detailed account of the social dynamics of the matrifocal household was that these forms were largely contained within the spaces of East Bank homes. In the case of the *amaqaba* migrants, the social stigma they carried in the location meant that they felt safest in their rooms and yards, where they communed with home-mates (*abakhaya*).

In the case of Pauw's account of matrifocality, the situation was a little more complicated because single mothers or *amakhazana* often exerted considerable power and influence on the streets and in their neighbourhoods (Pauw 1963: 141–65). The active involvement of these single, unmarried women in public life is seen not only in the fact that many of them ran businesses, but also in their active involvement in public and political protests during the 1950s. Minkley claims that independent women virtually 'owned the location' in the 1950s by virtue of their business acumen and influence in public affairs. He suggests that their capacity for independent social and political agency became a matter of grave concern to local Christianized location élites, who looked down on the practice of single mothering (cf. Minkley 1996). On the basis of Minkley's account it is difficult to understand why Pauw confines his discussion of matrifocality so narrowly to the home. One way of explaining his rather narrow ethnographic focus is to return to the project's evaluation of the domestic arena as the primary site of cultural production and transmission. By Pauw's own admission, he spent little time attending public events, visiting shebeens or standing around on street corners. The public roles, voices and agency of single women were therefore generally beyond the reach of his 'field'.

This contrast between the largely home-focused fieldwork strategy of the *Xhosa in Town* researchers and the RLI researchers' strong focus on the urban public and political sphere is interesting and clearly requires more careful attention than I have space for here. One of the reasons that Philip Mayer shied away from the public sphere and the political was also because he was more influenced by Meyer Fortes and Monica Wilson, with their concern with institutions, social group formation and domestic cycles, than by Max Gluckman, with his penchant for social change and 'situational analysis'. But it should also be noted that South African townships, like East Bank in East London, Cato Manor in Durban or Alexandra in Johannesburg, were very different places to mining towns on the Copperbelt, where Mitchell and Epstein worked (Schumaker 2001: 176–80). They had complex and particular internal residential ecologies in which migrants and permanently urbanized families lived cheek by jowl on the same residential sites. In many areas, like the East Bank location, the space of the yard, which usually comprised a main house and several outbuildings, appeared as a natural unit of analysis, as a fairly clearly demarcated physical and social space. The spatial layout and social syntax of old locations like East Bank drew researchers into what appeared to them to be the relatively contained world of the house and the backyard. In compounds and townships, like Luanshya on the Copperbelt, there was a different socio-spatial dynamic, and this left its mark on the way field-work was undertaken there.[7] Moreover, it was clear that Mitchell had more of a flair for statistics and sociological survey techniques on the Copperbelt than Philip Mayer ever had in East London, and this might also account for differences in approach (Hannerz 1980: 119–63).

Spatial Circuits: Beyond the Verandah

How might a different spatial strategy have led the Mayers and their colleagues to different kinds of conclusions? In this section, I explore this issue by attempting to trace the circuits of connection between the house and other more public spaces such as the street, the verandah, the dance-hall and beyond. Let me begin with the street.

The streets of the old East Bank location were created at the turn of the twentieth century as wide public thoroughfares associated with neatly fenced-off residential sites. As the population of the location increased, people spilled out of their overcrowded houses and the streets emerged as important sites of public interaction and everyday community life. They became places of recreation, sites of contested identities and reputations. The process whereby East Bank's residents claimed the streets was slow and geographically varied. As the location grew, new streets were added, some outside the original grid pattern, making them and their associated neighbourhoods relatively invisible to the purview of officials. Areas like 'Gomorrah' and 'New Brighton' became infamous for their drinking houses, *tsotsi* gangs and prostitution, as well as for the absence of any official presence, as did Camp and Ndende Streets.

But it was not just everyday occupation of the streets that occurred. In some areas, older public thoroughfares had been blocked off and the spatial layout changed with time. Ronnie Meinie recalled:

As it became very overcrowded, people had nowhere to build extensions to their properties, and this sometimes led them to build into the streets. You really had to know
your way around, because some streets just came to a dead-end because people had
built houses and rooms across them. In my case, you had to know that you couldn't get
to Coot Street from Fredrick Street, where I lived, because there were dwellings in the
way. It was like this all over.

I remember clearly during the 1952 riots when we were running away from the
police, how we would use these dead-ends and detours to trick them. We knew that they
would not be able to get vehicles through in certain places and darted for those streets
where the police would be trapped and have to turn back. This is how we played cat and
mouse with them.[8]

The state's loss of control of the streets was one of the main reasons why white
local officials increasingly insisted, from the 1930s, that the location be demol-
ished.

In connecting the space of the street to that of the house, the intermediate,
almost liminal, space of the verandah proved to be a critical conduit for transactions. The verandah constituted a sort of social membrane between street and
house: between public exterior and private interior. In many East Bank houses, the
front rooms were blocked off from the street by heavy drapes, while the front door
was left open to allow access to the house's main living rooms. One reason for
shutting off the street was that residents did not want officials surveying their
house interiors from the street. With police raids a regular occurrence and families
often harbouring 'illegals', either as tenants or visitors, it was inadvisable for a
house's interior to be visible from outside. The verandah thus became a space from
which threats of raids and official surveillance could be monitored. Shouts of
kobomvu (literally, 'it is red') hailed out from the slightly elevated verandahs
warned people of impending police patrols. The warnings were not only to assist
the queens of larger shebeens and urban 'illegals', they were also important for
ordinary townsmen and -women, travelling without one of the multitude of documents required by the state.

The verandah, usually above street level, was also a space from which women
made their presence felt. East Bank's verandahs can in some ways be likened to the
Dutch window, which, according to Cieraad (1999), allowed women, who were
expected to remain indoors and attend to domestic pursuits, to extend their gaze
and influence onto the street.[9] In the East Bank, where female domesticity was not
as spatially confined and women were generally more visible on the streets, the
verandah proved to be an important site from which women could command a
hearing on the street. One former East Bank resident explained:

Women were always on the verandahs, chatting and going about their business, but
their eyes were on the street watching everything that was happening. They were always

the first to know if a stranger was hanging around or whether something significant had happened.[10]

Other ex-residents remarked on how women would lean over the verandah and communicate with people on the street – other women or children at whom they were shouting. Washing clothes on the verandah allowed East Bank mothers and matriarchs to exercise surveillance of the street while pursuing their domestic chores. We were told that it was common practice in some areas that every morning before they had left for school the children of the house would collect two tubs of water, one for washing and one for rinsing, and leave them on the verandah for their mothers. It was also their job to dispose of the dirty water when they returned from school.

The verandah was also a space from which urban mothers and matriarchs created solidarities and extended their influence beyond the home. It was from here that independent women solicited migrants and lured men into their drinking houses. They also used the verandah as a relatively secure, albeit liminal, space from which to comment on, criticize and engage the street without having to occupy it physically. The verandah was also a space from which women could quickly disappear when threatened. It allowed them to be simultaneously on and off the street. Occupying the verandah was a statement of wanting to develop a street profile and presence. The verandah was, therefore, a critical conduit in allowing women to exert a presence on the street and to escape the confines of the house. But the verandah was also a contested space. Men and youths found they had to compete with women for the right to be there. Youths liked to sit on the verandah smoking and chatting. New musical groups even practised on the veran-dahs of houses, using them as a testing ground for artists with ambitions of making it to the Peacock Hall or the Community Centre.

Behind each house's verandah lay its more private space, not readily seen from the street. Despite the use of drapes to hide the interior of a home, the sharp distinction between the house and the street, between the private and the public (as noted by authors such as Cieraad [1999] in her account of nineteenth-century Dutch life), was not so very evident in the East Bank, where overcrowding limited the capacity of households for privacy. Many wood-and-iron houses were extended by building backrooms to accommodate tenants. In some cases backrooms were allo-cated to extended family members, but more often than not they were rented to migrants for extra cash. Township rentals were high and proved to be a good source of income. The physical location of migrants in these backrooms, with their activi-ties spilling out into the yards, created a distinction in many houses between the front and back sections. The distinction between migrants and townsmen in East Bank of the 1950s was thus often a distinction between front rooms and backrooms – house owners generally used front rooms, while migrants lived in backyards.

Backroom living was always more acceptable for migrants than living on the street fronts. As the Mayers (1963: 111–24) describe, it was in those yards where migrants gathered to socialize over weekends and drink beer in groups, known as *iseti*, of their rural home-mates (*amakhaya*) (also see Bank 1999).

The other key circuit of public power and cultural exchange was one that connected the community halls, sports grounds and other recreational areas to the street. Productions of regular musical, dance, sports and entertainment events at places like the Peacock Hall, the Community Centre and the Rubusana Sports Grounds made these important sites for cultural production and performance. They emerged as definitive spaces in the construction of cosmopolitan styles, fashions and an East Bank economy of prestige. The latest fashions and styles were displayed there and people from East Bank, West Bank and North End socialized and engaged in processes of competitive style-making. Rubusana Park and the Peacock Hall were particularly significant, the former because it was the city's major sports venue for blacks, the latter because it was the main live music venue for East Bank, West Bank and North End residents. Given the limited access that location residents had to public space in the white city, they made the most of their segregated public facilities by hosting a wide range of events that drew massive popular support. One former East Bank resident remarked, 'If you wanted to hire the Peacock Hall you would often have to wait more than a year for a booking.'[11] The venues' annual calendars were full of public events and carnivals: Santa Day, the Bat Fair, the Hobo Show, Mfengu Day, music concerts, fêtes, ballroom and other dancing competitions, and sports tournaments. Rugby was the main sports activity and there were many teams, such as Swallows RFC, Winter Roses, Black Lions, Storm Breakers, Bushbucks, Tembu United, Early Roses, Busy Bees and the Boiling Waters (*Ayabila*), each with its own following. Great excitement marked meetings of rival teams.

The cultural exchanges and interactions at these events were critical to the way East London's cosmopolitan styles were made. Other spaces outside the township, such as the beach, the city centre, the West Bank racetrack, also became focal points for socializing and style-making, with the swimwear displayed at fashion shows and beauty pageants in the locations being paraded there in public. As Mrs Majavu explained:

> The thing that made the beach such a wonderful place for us was that it was out of the location. It was not cramped. There was open space, clean air and the sea all around. The beach was especially popular on Sundays after church, when we used to pack a picnic and go down there for the day. It was really great fun. It gave the young guys a chance to check out the girls and for people to meet old friends and socialize. ... You can imagine what a shock it was when the apartheid signs went up: 'Whites Only – *Net Blankes*'.[12]

Analysing such events, Arjun Appadurai (1986) coined the term 'tournaments of value'. Using the classic anthropological example of exchanges of prestige goods in the Trobriand *kula* rings, Appadurai suggests that 'tournaments of value' be seen as 'complex periodic events that are removed in some culturally defined way from the routines of economic life' (ibid.: 21). He argues that they contain a 'cultural diacritic of their own' and are involved not only with the quest for status, rank, fame and reputation among different actors, but also the disposition of the central tokens of value in a given society (ibid.). This is seemingly how the sports, dance, music, beach or cinematic events were constituted in East Bank during the 1950s. They created an air of expectation and exhilaration. Moreover, as new styles and influences came into circulation in the dance-hall, for example, so they found their way onto the streets through imitation and alteration.

For example, the Havana Hotshots emerged out of a jazz group called The Cotton Planters Band, which had been established in the early 1930s. They were said to be the first major jazz band in East London locations. In March 1947, 'The Hotshots' played at a beachfront hotel as part of the festivities set up in the city to welcome King George VI, Queen Elizabeth, Princesses Elizabeth and Margaret to East London. In the 1950s, 'The Hotshots' renamed themselves 'The Havanna Hotshots' in order to emphasize their connection with the international 'dance craze' and Cuban music. The latter also influenced African ballroom dancing. In the late 1950s, the Havana Hotshots added the rumba and the chachacha to their repertoire and were one of a number of groups, such as the Cuban Stars from North End, who drew inspiration from political and musical developments in Cuba.

Appadurai uses the concept 'diversions' to explore the ways that the politics of value is domesticated, appropriated and altered to carve its way along different paths of value and meaning. This concept is useful for trying to make sense of how the dance-hall, the beach and sports stadiums were connected and re-connected to the street and the house. It again invokes Hannerz's notion of creolization as a complex marriage of cultural flows and transactions between various spatially defined sites of cultural production, as well as between locations and wider cultural processes (Hannerz 1992).

In terms of an understanding based on the application of these ideas, the 1950s emergence of cosmopolitan styles in East Bank was clearly more than a simple imitation of Western cultural forms. It necessarily involved an active process of cultural appropriation and reworking. As new fashions, styles and cultural forms went on display at these 'tournaments of value', so they were absorbed, appropriated and reworked to create new constellations of value and meaning for the streets (cf. Hansen 2000). The cultural circuits created between the streets and the dance-hall enabled a constant process of appropriation, re-appropriation and transformation, as cultural forms and styles moved back and forth, blending cosmopolitan and local elements along the way. One example of this was the way in which the *tsotsi* youth would focus their attention on the villains rather than the heroes they encountered in B-grade American movies and imitate and add to their styles on the streets. As Pule Twaku explained:

> We were always watching out for something new, where the style was going. Like when the Vikings came first to the Peacock Hall in their gangster style. Suddenly, everyone was checking them out and it was not long before other youths on the streets were trying to imitate them. The same happened with the Panama hats ... it was a fashion for a time, then people got tired of it and looked for something new.[13]

Conclusion

In the above discussion I have tried to highlight local engagement with cosmopolitan styles and cultural forms in East London's African locations during the 1950s. I have argued that the failure of the *Xhosa in Town* Trilogy to acknowledge and reflect on the intensity of this engagement is one of the major weaknesses of this project. However, unlike others who have commented on this work, I have not focused here on the political and theoretical motives of the authors as much as their methodological orientation. I have suggested that the studies comprising the Trilogy were all essentially constructed as 'home-made ethnographies' in the sense that the bulk of the fieldwork and interviews took place inside or around the space of the home. Philip Mayer clearly believed that a strong focus on the domestic domain would provide key insights into the cultural dynamics of urbanization in East London. What the Mayers failed to explore was that the space of the house, the rented room and yard figured differently in the social lives and cultural experiences of different categories of urban dwellers in East Bank. In the case of migrants, especially the frugal Reds, the space of the rented room and the yards formed a primary node of socializing, drinking and relaxation.

If the rented room and backyard were critical to migrant social lives in the city, this was certainly not the case for the majority of urban-born youth and men, who preferred to socialize on the verandah, on street corners, in local shebeens, dance-halls and tea rooms. Given the social profile of the 'borners' and the location of their preferred leisure activities, it is surprising that Pauw decided to use household surveys and family histories as the basis of his account of the cultural orientation of the so-called 'second generation'. Compared with the rich and detailed ethnography of migrant lives found in *Townsmen or Tribesmen*, Pauw's work appears ethnographically thin and unconvincing. The problem for Pauw was that so much of what he needed to see and experience in order to develop a fuller analysis of urban cultural life was simply not visible to him. In order to tap into the dynamics of non-migrant lifestyles and identities, offering the same level of ethnographic detail and insight as *Townsmen and Tribesmen*, he would have had to adopt a very different fieldwork strategy: one that engaged with extra-domestic spaces. I have also suggested that had Pauw and Mayer adopted a less domestically focused approach they might have arrived at different conclusions, especially in relation to the power and influence of cosmopolitan cultural styles in the location.

At a more general level, it is useful to consider Marcus's (1998) concept of multi-sited ethnographic research and especially his notion of *juxtaposition* as a fieldwork and analytic strategy. Marcus formulated the notion of multi-sited ethnography as part of a general evaluation of the way in which anthropologists might re-think method and theory in the context of globalization. He advocated that those studying complex global processes might do fieldwork in different localities, connected to the processes that interested them, but not necessarily in obvious and straight-forward ways. In particular, he highlights the importance of 'juxtaposing' different perspectives based on fieldwork in different sites to reveal the empirical complexity of processes and unravel new layers of understanding. In developing my argument, I have suggested above that the primary juxtaposition in the work of the Trilogy – as with that of the RLI anthropologists – was the contrast between town and countryside. The salience of this opposition was also informed by the fact that many of the anthropologists involved in urban research in the 1950s and 1960s had previously worked in rural communities. The capacity of this generation of urban anthropologists to explore the complex social and cultural connections between town and countryside remains a lasting legacy of their work, which has recently been recognized as a foundational contribution to the field of post-colonial urban studies (cf. Robinson 2005).

But, while I would like to add my voice to those who celebrate the quality of this early work, we also need to be aware of its limitations. My argument here is that not enough attention was given to juxtapositions within the city itself, and that, had the researchers focused more attention on the multiple sites of cultural production within this urban context, their work would have been greatly enriched. However, in seeking to engage more actively with the public spaces of cultural production, it is important that urban anthropologists do not lose sight of their own 'homemade traditions'.

Notes

This chapter is a based on a revised version of a chapter in my recent Ph.D., entitled 'The Xhosa in Town Revisited: From Urban Anthropology to the Anthropology of Urbanism' (University of Cape Town, 2002). I would like to thank the participants at the 2004 Durham ASA conference for useful comments on my verbal presentation of this paper. I also thank my brother Andrew Bank for comments and editorial assistance, and my colleagues at the University of Fort

Hare – Gary Minkley, Mcebisi Qamarwana and Anne King – for their support. The usual disclaimers apply.

1. Khan (2001) makes a distinction between the 'high or *avant garde* modernism' associated with sophisticated aesthetic and intellectual élites – the educated middle classes – and what he calls the 'popular modernism' embraced by ordinary people, which is mediated through the entertainment industry and modern social movements. Khan highlights the mass appeal of 'popular modernism', but insists that this should not be mistaken for a lack of critical content.

2. Mayer used the term 'incapsulation' to refer to the process by which Red migrants maintained their rural home ties in the city by restricting their fields of social interaction to an all-Red circle in town, comprised mainly of close kin and *abakhaya* (home-mates). These patterns of social interaction allowed Red migrants to keep up an unbroken nexus with the rural home and to restrict their social interactions in the city (ibid.: 91–110).

3. Walter Benson Rubusana was born in Mnanadi in the Somerset East district in 1858. He attended Lovedale College and in 1884 was ordained in the Congregational Church and became a minister in the East Bank location. Rubusana played a significant role in the early politics of the African National Congress and remained active in ministry and politics until his death in East London in 1936 (*Daily Dispatch*, 10 June 2001).

4. Kenny Jegels, interview, East London, 20 March 2000.

5. Interview, East London, 28 January 1999.

6. This is, of course, not to suggest that Red and School were not fundamental categories in the classificatory schemes of migrants and urban residents in East London in the 1950s. See also Fay (1996).

7. Mitchell expressed his dislike for door-to-door urban fieldwork when he said that, unlike in the villages, where access to people's domestic spaces could easily be negotiated through the headman, in the towns 'each visit to a hut means the same battle – the same suspicion, etc. The refusal rate is high' (quoted in Schumaker 2001: 177).

8. Interview, East London, 10 September 2000; also see Crouch (1998: 145–67).

9. Cieraad argues that the emergence of window prostitution in Holland was a product of women asserting their agency through the space of the window to solicit men outside.

10. Group interview, East London, 30 May 2001.

11. Mr Foster, interview, East London, 20 October 2000.

12. Interview, East London, 18 November 1999.

13. Group interview, East London, 14 May 2001.

References

Appadurai, A. (1986), 'Introduction', in A. Appadurai (ed.), *The Social Life of Things*, Cambridge: Cambridge University Press.

Asad, T. (ed.) (1973), *Anthropology and the Colonial Encounter*, London: Ithaca.

Bank, L. (1999), 'Men with Cookers: Transformations in Migrant Culture, Domesticity and Identity in Duncan Village, East London', *Journal of Southern African Studies* 25 (3): 393–416.

Bank, L. (2002), 'The Xhosa in Town Revisited: From Urban Anthropology to the Anthropology of Urbanism', Ph.D. thesis, University of Cape Town.

Bank, L. and Maqasho, L. (2000), 'West Bank Restitution Claim: A Social History Report', ISER Research Report 7, Grahamstown: Rhodes University.

Bank, L. and Maqasho, L. (2001), 'East Bank Restitution Claim: A Social History Report', ISER Research Report 9, Grahamstown: Rhodes University.

Beinart, W. (1991), 'Speaking for Themselves', in A. Spiegel and P. McAllister (eds), *Tradition and Transition in Southern Africa*, Johannesburg: Witwatersrand University Press.

Brown, R. (1973), 'Anthropology and Colonial Rule: Godfrey Wilson and the Rhodes–Livingstone Institute, Northern Rhodesia', in T. Asad (ed.), *Anthropology and the Colonial Encounter*, London: Ithaca.

Chapman, M. (2001), *The Drum Decade: Stories from the 1950s*, Pietermaritzburg: University of Natal Press.

Cieraad, I. (1999), 'The Dutch Window', in I. Cieraad (ed.), *At Home: An Anthropology of Domestic Space*, Syracuse, NY: Syracuse University Press.

Clifford, J. (1997), *Routes: Travel and Translation in the Late Twentieth Century*, Cambridge, MA: Harvard University Press.

Coplan, D.B. (1985), *In Township Tonight: South Africa's Black City Music and Theatre*, Johannesburg: Ravan.

Crouch, D. (1998), 'The Street in the Making of Popular Geographical Knowledge', in N. Fyfe (ed.), *Images of the Street*. London: Routledge.

Eriksen, T.H. (2003), 'Introduction', in T.H. Eriksen (ed.), *Globalisation: Studies in Anthropology*, London: Pluto Press.

Eriksen, T.H. and Nielsen, F. (2001), *A History of Anthropology*. London: Pluto.

Fay, D. (1996), 'A Place Where Cattle Get Lost: Rural and Urban Transformation and the Salience of the Red/School Division among Xhosa in East London in the 1950s', unpublished paper, Boston University.

Ferguson, J. (1999), *Expectations of Modernity: Myths and Meanings of Urban Life on the Zambian Copperbelt*, Berkeley: University of California Press.

Glaser, C. (2000), *Bo-Tsotsi: The Youth Gangs of Soweto, 1935–1976*, Cape Town: David Philip.

Gluckman, M. (1960), 'Tribalism in Modern British Central Africa', *Cahiers d'Études Africaines* 55 (1): 634–54.

Gupta, A. and Ferguson, J. (1997), 'Discipline and Practice: "The Field" as Site, Method, and Location in Anthropology', in A. Gupta and J. Ferguson (eds), *Anthropological Locations: Boundaries and Grounds of a Field Science*, Berkeley: University of California Press.

Hannerz, U. (1980), *Exploring the City: Inquiries Toward an Urban Anthropology*, New York: Columbia University Press.

Hannerz, U. (1992), *Cultural Complexity: Studies in the Social Organization of Meaning*, New York: Columbia University Press.

Hannerz, U. (1997), 'Sophiatown: The View from Afar', in K. Barber (ed.), *Readings in African Popular Culture*, London: Routledge.

Hansen, K. (2000), *Salaula: The World of Secondhand Clothing in Zambia*, Chicago: University of Chicago Press.

Hunter, M. (1936), *Reaction to Conquest: Effects of Contact with Europeans on the Pondo of South Africa*, 2nd edition for the International Africa Institute, London: Oxford University Press, 1961.

Khan, J. (2001), *Modernity and Exclusion*, London: Routledge.

Lodge, T. (1987), 'Political Mobilisation during the 1950s: An East London Case Study', in S. Marks and S. Trapido (eds) *The Politics of Race, Class and Nationalism in Twentieth- Century South Africa*, London: Heinemann.

Mafeje, A. (1997), 'Who are the Makers and Objects of Anthropology? A Critical Comment on Sally Falk Moore's "Anthropology and Africa"', *African Sociological Review* 1 (1): 1–24.

Magubane, B. (1971), 'A Critical Look at Indices Used in the Study of Social Change inColonial Africa', *Current Anthropology* 12: 634–53.

Magubane, B. (1973), 'The "Xhosa" in Town, Revisited: Urban Social Anthropology: AFailure of Method and Theory', *American Anthropologist* 75: 1123–41.

Marcus, G. (1998), *Ethnography through Thick and Thin*, Princeton: Princeton University Press.

Mattera, D. (1987), *Memory is the Weapon*, Johannesburg: Ravan.

Mayer, P. (1961), *Townsmen or Tribesmen: Conservatism and the Process of Urbanization in a South African City*, 2nd edition, Cape Town: Oxford University Press, 1971.

Mayer, P. (1963), 'Preface', in B. Pauw, *The Second Generation: A Study of the Family Among Urbanized Bantu in East London*, Cape Town: Oxford University Press.

Mayer, P. (1980), 'The Origins of Two Rural Resistance Ideologies', in P. Mayer (ed.), *Black Villagers in an Industrial Society*, Cape Town: Oxford University Press.

Minkley, G. (1996), ' "I Shall Die Married to Beer": Gender, Family and Space in East London's Locations', *Kronos: The Journal of Cape History* 23: 1–34.

Mitchell, J. (1956), 'The Kalela Dance: Aspects of Social Relationships among Urban Africans in Northern Rhodesia', *Rhodes–Livingstone Paper*, No. 27, Manchester University, Manchester.

Moore, S. Falk (1994), *Anthropology and Africa,* Charlottesville: Virginia University Press.

Nel, E. (1990), 'The Spatial Planning of Racial Residential Segregation in East London, 1948–1973', MA thesis, University of the Witwatersrand, Johannesburg.

Pauw, B.A. (1963), *The Second Generation: A Study of the Family Among Urbanized Bantu in East London*, 2nd edition, Cape Town: Oxford University Press, 1973.

Reader, D. (1960), *The Black Man's Portion: History, Demography and Living Conditions of East London*, Cape Town: Oxford University Press.

Robinson, J. (2005), 'Post-colonial Urbanism', unpublished draft book manuscript.

Rosaldo, R. (1989), *Culture and Truth: The Remaking of Social Analysis*, Boston: Beacon.

Schumaker, L. (2001), *Africanizing Anthropology: Fieldwork, Networks, and the Making of Cultural Knowledge in Central Africa*, Durham, NC: Duke University Press.

Themba, C. (1985), *The World of Can Themba*, Johannesburg: Ravan.

Werbner, R. (1984), 'The Manchester School in South-Central Africa', *Annual Review of Anthropology* 13: 204–44.

Wilson, G. (1941/2), 'An Essay on the Economics of Detribalization in Northern. Rhodesia', Rhodes–Livingstone Paper, No. 5–6, Rhodes–Livingstone Institute, Livingstone.

Wilson, M. and Mafeje, A. (1963), *Langa: A Study of Social Groups in an African Township*, London: Oxford University Press.

Newspapers

Daily Dispatch, East London.

–3–

Fieldwork on Foot:
Perceiving, Routing, Socializing

Jo Lee and Tim Ingold

Walking around is fundamental to the everyday practice of social life. It is also fundamental to much anthropological fieldwork, and we would like to start by recalling a well-known anecdote of walking and (as it turns out) running in the field, from Clifford Geertz (1973: 413–17). He tells of how, at the start of his Balinese fieldwork, he and his wife were apparently ignored by villagers, who simply looked through them as though they were not there. As they wandered around the village, Geertz recalls, they felt as ephemeral and insubstantial as a cloud or a gust of wind. But all that abruptly changed when, during a police raid on a cockfight they had come to watch, they found themselves having to turn and run with the rest of the crowd. The villagers were amazed that their privileged anthropological visitors had not simply identified themselves to the police, but had instead accompanied them in their flight. From then on, Geertz says, their field-work opened out successfully. With the run, it seems, the anthropologists suddenly came down to earth, were able to make their bodily presence felt, and could thenceforth participate with the villagers in the ebb and flow of everyday life.

As this example shows, walking does not, in and of itself, yield an experience of embodiment, nor is it necessarily a technique of participation. Rather, both embodiment and participation presuppose some kind of attunement, such that both the ethnographer's pedestrian movements and those of the people she or he is with are grounded in shared circumstances. This is what happened when Geertz, along with everyone else, ran from the police. All at once he felt embodied, and was able to participate. Or to put it another way, we cannot simply walk into other people's worlds, and expect thereby to participate with them. To participate is not to walk *into* but to walk *with* – where 'with' implies not a face-to-face confrontation, but heading the same way, sharing the same vistas, and perhaps retreating from the same threats behind.

In this chapter we explore in more detail the relationship between practices of walking, the experience of embodiment and forms of sociability, both in everyday life and in the conduct of anthropological fieldwork. The fact that we are focusing on the *relationship* between walking, embodiment and sociability is crucial. That is, we do not assume *a priori* that walking affords an experience of embodiment, or that social life hovers above the road we tread in our material life. Rather, walking affords an experience of embodiment to the extent that it is grounded in an inherently sociable engagement between self and environment.

These ideas are the basis for our research under the title of 'Culture from the Ground: Walking, Movement and Placemaking'.[1] Through ethnographic fieldwork carried out in 2004 and 2005 in the region of Aberdeen and north-east Scotland we have sought to understand the diversity of walking in the area. Fieldwork has involved participant observation, in the form of sharing walks with a variety of people, observation and 'autoethnography' of walking in different environments, twenty-five semi-structured interviews with people interested in the topic, and archival research on the history and material culture of walking. In addition, some walkers compiled walking diaries (recording and commenting on all their outdoor walking over the course of a week), and digital photographing and sound recording of field environments have been carried out. Running through all these techniques has been an idea of mobility in fieldwork, where the journeys people make also make their places and, as a corollary, the ethnographic field itself. Journeys made on foot have particularly social characteristics and, again as a corollary, fieldwork on foot – whilst by no means uncommon in anthropology – is worth considering in its own right.

The chapter is structured around a number of resonances between walking and anthropological fieldwork, through which we draw attention to a dialectic involving fieldwork practice and the content of research. They are resonances in the sense of reinforcing certain meanings within each other. Firstly, the repeated action of putting one foot in front of the other necessitates contact with the ground and, often, a state of being attuned to the environment. Together these bring to mind the detail and directness of ethnography. Accounts of 'being there', in the anthropological field (e.g. Watson 1999), usually result from being metaphorically and literally on the ground. In this way anthropologists can perceive the multi-sensory environment to the fullest, and can claim to be close to whatever is happening in the area.

Another resonance can be felt in the way that the locomotive (or getting around) aspect of walking allows for an understanding of places being created by routes. A place walked through is made by the shifting interaction of person and environment, in which the movement of the whole body is important rather than just an act of vision outwards from a fixed point. In walking we are on the move, seeing and feeling a route ahead of us and creating a path around and after us. We can often explore a new place most fruitfully by walking through and around it. For the anthropologist, this in turn leads to the realization that we have to understand the routes and mobilities of others.

Finally, there is also something distinctive about the sociability that is engendered by walking *with* others. A person walking generates a particular style of movement, pace and direction that can be understood as a 'rhythm' of walking. Sharing or creating a walking rhythm with other people can lead to a very particular closeness and bond between the people involved, as Geertz demonstrated. This physical co-presence, emphasized by common movements, is also important in ethnography as we attempt to live and move as others do. The sociability of walking could be seen to be analogous to the sociability of ethnographers and their subjects.

Perceiving Self and Environment

In Europe and America, and particularly within the Romantic tradition, walking has been associated with a closeness to nature and attention to detail in the environment that are seen to have been otherwise lost in modern life (Wallace 1993). Walking could then be an activity through which modernity can be resisted or re-worked. Nancy Frey (1998) presents contemporary pilgrims to the shrine of St James in Santiago de Compostella in north-west Spain in this light. Those who make the pilgrimage often feel an affinity with those who have walked and ridden the same ways over the last thousand years, frequently along routes of many hundreds of kilometres and taking months to complete. Parallel to this, walking has also been associated with thinking and a philosophical bent to life. Orlet (2004) cites Erasmus, Hobbes, Rousseau and Nietzsche among many others in this regard, but in doing so questions are raised about walking in more ordinary circumstances. To what extent are these rather deep connections between walking pilgrimage and philosophy made in everyday life, for example? Here the focus is on what actually happens during a walk that might lead to particular perceptions of the body, self and environment. The ethnographer, walking along too, has to begin a similar interrogation, and this is the point of entry to our first resonance between walking and anthropological fieldwork.

During interviews and participant observation in our research, walkers described and demonstrated three different 'modes' of interaction with the environment. In interviews they often stressed, on the one hand, the opportunities to look around and, on the other, the time for thinking that walking provides. During walks themselves, a third perspective, that of embodied experience, often came to the fore in conversations and through the events of the walk itself. The walking diaries also seemed to give walkers a certain freedom to express themselves in relation to their experiences. We will discuss each of these themes here.

Firstly, looking around is usually possible in a walk to a much greater extent than in other ways of travelling, and this is a basic but important factor in why people walk. One of the reasons for this is simply the pace of the walk, in the sense of the experience of speed or slowness that it provides. A number of walkers said that walking involves moving slowly in such a way that allows them to notice the details in local environments. One walker tied his experience as a surveyor to his enjoyment of urban areas.

> I mean, certainly, you see a lot more when you're walking. Driving, you look at the road ahead, or should be. And I think there's a lot to be seen: Aberdeen's a very lovely city, and the buildings are absolutely fantastic. And being from a construction background, I tend to look up, wherever I go. Whether it's New York or Sydney, the only way to see is from the ground level: on your feet, wandering around … finding little lanes and places, and things that people who live there won't even see.

Here the walker contrasts his vision with that of the driver. Although both driver and walker are moving, it is the walker who seems to have a real mobility, in terms of the ability to see in different directions and to discover the 'little' things in his or her surroundings. The driver is instead cocooned or encased in his or her vehicle. This quality of walking is similar to that described by Adam Reed (2002) in his ethnography of London tour guides, who found the most significant meaning in the small stories of back streets rather than the more famous tourist sites. In our Aberdeen walker's case, the perspective of looking up 'from the ground' is emphasized, a much wider vista than that of the driver who focuses on the middle distance of the road ahead.

In contrast to this slow-paced, looking-around walk, sometimes walkers feel they are moving quickly, and here walking is understood as an efficient way to get around urban areas in particular. Walking can afford a freedom of passage in a fast walk that cuts through the crowd, which is unavailable to vehicles on busy roads or in traffic jams. Instead of making an absolute measurement of speed, we can see how variations in pace affect the experience of the walk and the environment. Different kinds of attentiveness and walking skills become apparent through the extent to which individual walkers move quickly or slowly, relative to themselves.

Understanding difference over time in the environment is another judgement that depends on the variety of experiences a walker has, rather than being an intrinsic feature of that environment. Frequent repetition of the same route may lead the walker to notice tiny changes in buildings, gardens or fields and to construct an ongoing narrative of place through these experiences. On the other hand, apprehending the place can occur on a larger scale, in which a walk contributes to a different kind of story, with longer-term histories. In Aberdeen the main building material has traditionally been granite, and granite buildings are often recognized and appreciated for their distinctiveness by people who walk around them. During our fieldwork one keen walker ran a series of guided history walks, in which participants were encouraged to notice and share stories about the granite industry. The city was articulated into its region by a network of quarries and building sites, and the labour of those who had worked them. Relating to the granite during a walk can pull the city together as a material entity, with a long coherence over time in its regional setting.

Just as it is possible in a walk to see the world unfolding around oneself, so some walkers also describe a sense of escape from the world, or at least its immediate demands. The 'thinking time' that is available during a walk is often a comment on the busyness of other environments, the demands for immediate attention that prevent what might be seen as a more reflective state. One informant told me that his walks to church by himself were an opportunity for personal reflection. Writing to me on the subject, he later explained that 'This is a time when I have no other calls on my senses or intellect (TV, PC, newspaper, other people), during which I can think about something that needs thinking about.' This might relate to his work or to spiritual matters. He continued: 'The act of walking to church is fortuitous in that it gives me this period of time. I don't walk to church as a way of having this kind of time. It is a by-product of that form of travel.'

People who walk to work in the mornings were also often keen to assert this benefit of walking. Here we can link 'ordinary' walking to that of the philosophers identified by Orlet. It offers the possibility of thinking in a different way, more freely and without distraction or need of distraction from boredom. For our informants, the walk could be a chance to plan the work day before it begins in earnest, or to gradually (in keeping, perhaps, with the pace of walking) turn over problems or issues in the mind. The walk home, however, often varies according to the happenings of the day. One walker discussed this during such a walk:

> It depends really on what sort of day I've had. And like this afternoon was a good day, a good afternoon. Working with the public, they were all nice people. Last week I had someone being really horrible to me, and I was furious – I stormed home. You know, and it was raining, and I was in a foul temper, so I didn't manage to walk out my temper last week.

One beneficial effect of the walk home can be to ameliorate the effects of a bad day, or to walk out one's temper, as this walker puts it. Yet the point is made that while walking can make one feel better, it is not always an escape because the walk will be influenced by one's recent experiences. This is a description of how emotions are realized through walking. Emotions can be channelled through, and even become, the movement of the body. The fury *is* the storming home, a full bodily expression to the self and the world.

During this walk home, our informant described her movements at work as 'running' between objects (such as the desk and photocopier) and people, resulting in a 'bitty' series of movements. She could not get the rhythm of a walk 'like this', she said, as we walked up the street, and would occasionally engineer a short trip out of the office. People who walk at lunchtimes also describe similar experiences.

At Aberdeen beach people often walk alone during lunch breaks from work. The beach is just within reach of the town centre and a brisk walk there can be fitted into a lunch hour. These lunch-time walkers were most likely to mention the 'escape' aspect to the walk, in contrast to 'strollers' who, during conversations about their walk, often brought up the state of the environment at the beach or the kinds of social interaction they have there. From observations, the lunch-time walkers tend to walk more quickly than the strollers, often striding along the flat, obstacle-free promenade, although not necessarily looking around them less than the strollers. Walks to and from work can become a kind of liminal period between what are usually far more structured work or home environments at each end, and the kinds of bodily movement involved seem to be something of a relief from both. This is not to suggest that the body is at all static just because it is indoors, but the rhythms of movement are very different and people draw attention to the specific qualities of the outdoors.

So far, we have described a kind of double awareness in walking. Firstly, walkers can progress outwards to perceive their surroundings in a detailed way, and secondly, they can also turn inwards to the realm of thoughts and the self. In between such outward and inward perceptions, however, there can arise a direct-ness to some of the feelings and experiences generated by walking. One walker used the opportunity of a walking diary to volunteer a list of likes and dislikes about, as she put it, 'walking (in Aberdeen)'. She merged thoughts on walking generally with walking specifically in Aberdeen. Her lengthy list of likes ends with the following:

> Finding objects dropped by others
> Hearing different bird calls, varying through the year, in still quiet places
> The sound of my own footsteps
> The wind in the trees – all strengths
> Crisp, new snow – to be the first to walk in it
> The ever-changing weather, and closeness to nature, make even very familiar walks
> unique every time.

For this walker, the boundaries between the body and the environment are blurred by the movements of both. Indeed, everything seems to be moving. The walker catches both transient and rhythmical sound, imprints herself into snow and is attentive and reactive to both 'objects' and the weather. The wind is in the trees and around the body, and its variations produce reactions in sound and movement everywhere. We could suggest that the walker engages neither in a one-way visual looking out, nor in a turning inwards to the self. Instead we see the co-production of a walking experience between environment and person, both of which are in flux. The eyes, furthermore, seem rather secondary to the feet, ears and skin in terms of how the environment is perceived. This is the case even (or, it could be argued, especially) in these most basic and everyday experiences that the walker describes.

A further small example can illustrate the point. In another diary a walker described her feelings of walking home from work on a sunny day after two days of rain and cloud. The first description of the weather on this day is 'Sunny!', and she comments, again quite simply: 'Beautiful to be out in the sun again.' Here we feel the movement from the enclosing 'in' of a building to the enveloping or immersing 'in' of weather.[2] Perhaps the difference is in the accompanying movement and responsiveness of the outdoor environment, as opposed to the structuring force of indoors. Indoors the body may move, but the freedom of movement outside is usually qualitatively different for the walkers – a feeling of moving at an appropriate pace for the environment.

In discussing the weather, we can return to the articulation of fury through walking described above. With the interjection of 'you know, and it was raining', the walker described her body as resonating with the weather. The state of distress is not an internal reflection of mood, cut off from the environment. Rather, the weather complements and becomes part of the emotion, and each reinforces the other in the production of the walk. The storm is a physical reality both in the weather and in the person, as the walker attunes to the weather rather than 'huddling' or defending herself from it. These examples illustrate how the weather is made real and substantial by the bodily movement in it. Otherwise it is conjectural, how it looks and might feel, rather than something actually felt. The emotionality of weather relates strongly to the body–environment interaction under discussion here, as do other kinds of emotions produced through walking. Fear, in particular, could be usefully explored further from this perspective, where walkers perceive danger in their surroundings and move in a state of fear as a result. In the city this is often, but not always, in relation to the presence of other people in particular circumstances: at night, in quiet or hidden areas, or where alcohol is likely to have been consumed.

These realizations of emotional and environmental conditions through walking are situated somewhere between an external looking-out vision and an internal escape or self-reflective vision. They are processes of lived and embodied experience in which the environment shifts and imprints onto the body, and is at the same time affected by it. The potential for these very real experiences to occur is part of the attraction of walking for many people, and yet there are also circumstances in which the directness of social contact with others is something to be feared.

In summary, we have three ways of conceptualizing the relationships between the bodies and environments of these Aberdeen walkers. The walker may look (or 'sense') around, appropriating the environment around him or her by noticing its details and changes. Alternatively, the walk may be a time to turn inward to the self, to produce a particular state of body or mind. Although by no means cutting themselves off from the environment, these walkers emphasized sensory perception less than the thoughts, memories and stories in the mind. Thirdly, we have processes in which other senses come to the fore, producing an awareness and, sometimes, a crossing of the boundary between body and environment through the embodied and emotional interactions of walkers and their surroundings (including their social surroundings). The skin as a sensory organ is important here.

The description of these modes helps explicate the first resonance between walking and anthropological fieldwork outlined in the introduction, that of the ethnographer's groundedness in his or her research field. The differences between looking out onto a research field, using the presence in the field for personal reflection on the self, and engaging in the embodied experiences and practices of the field hint at alternative modes for the ethnographer that in themselves could be traced through different visions of anthropological fieldwork. In terms simply of methodology books in anthropology, one could read a similar set of contrasts into the differences between, for example, the more positivistic 'looking out' techniques – towards formal or structured forms of data collection – described by Bernard (1988) and to some extent Ellen (1984), the methodological reflexivity of Davies (1999), and Coffey's (1999) encouragement of embodied fieldwork.

Walkers, however, describe these three different types of perception or experience in ways that are not at all in conflict with each other. The looking-around perception, the personal reflection and the category of embodied experience can occur through the course of a few days or even within one walk, although it is also true that a single walk may have more meaning for the walker in one of these modes than in the others. Different techniques or modes often seem to be present and to overlap in walking, much as in fieldwork when different kinds of observation and participation are used. Fieldwork on foot allows for such flexibility, while, it would be hoped, maintaining the overall coherence of the project. At this stage we should consider the course of an entire walk: the journey and the direction the walk takes. In doing so we move away from the details of the interaction between the person and environment at any given point on the walk and towards what the line of the walk means. We encounter the routes and the creativity of place-making, and this is the second of our resonances between walking and anthropological fieldwork.

Routes: The Creation of Place in Walking

We begin this section with more from our fieldwork. During a Monday morning walk to work, a walker told of how he had returned to live in a certain area of town after some years' absence. We talked about our activities and our routes through and around this part of Aberdeen, such as where to get the bus to the supermarket and where certain pubs were, for example. Through these mundane details, the city can be understood from the perspective of a life story, tying a personal biography into the perception of the city environment – in this episode, when a person moves to an area and how life changes as a result. This is much as Finnegan (1998) discusses in the life stories of residents of Milton Keynes in England, who weave together their biographies in relation to the places in which they have lived. From our perspective, such conversations taking place *as* we walk show how temporality in walking can be shifting and unsettled: thinking and perceiving the past, present and future, and combining them in references to routes. From our ethnography again, written by Lee:

> We continued down the road, and then turned off into a back street. I think I must have slowed slightly and looked up at the unfamiliar street, and the change in my posture registered with my fellow-walker. 'A route I discovered yesterday,' he said. 'Well not really discovered.' 'But you tried it,' I suggested.
>
> 'Yes, because it's handy. I have this exploration feeling.'
>
> 'Ah.'
>
> 'Something, try something different. It's crazy, I feel like I can't really afford doing so during weekdays.'
>
> 'Because weekdays is ...'
>
> 'I don't know, weekdays is about other things, I suppose you're always worried about how you do your job, on time.'

For this walker, the weekend is a time for exploration, a walk that tries something different, when the environment is something to be (almost) discovered. During the week, it seems, our jobs rule our lives to the extent that we dare not step out from the known, tried-and-tested route towards the locale of work. We may become familiar with more routes as we test out, wander or search during different times and types of walk, and yet we are careful to avoid such risky behaviour if it might impact on our work lives. It seems that the status of a destination can affect the way we walk towards it. We also need to bear in mind that not all walking will have a specific destination, as Wallace (1993) shows in the development of a 'peripatetic' genre of literature that includes Wordsworth and Coleridge, who walked not to get somewhere in particular, but for the sake of the experience of walking itself.

There are different ways of making and remembering routes, and there is variety in how what might be called the 'aspect' of the body is formed: exploring, wandering, foraging or approaching a goal, for example. Connerton (1989) analyses the body as a site for collective memory, in which habituated bodily actions are the basis for the ability to reproduce a certain social performance. We could perhaps read into the variability of this walker's routes an embodied performance of a work persona in the difference between weekend and weekday walking.

More practically, the 'exploration feeling' is an important quality to some walking that is worth following up here. Lorimer and Lund (2003) describe navigation in mountain hiking as a highly structured and planned process that begins with a visualization of the landscape through the contours of a map and continues with detailed use of a map and compass, or even a hand-held Geographical Positioning System device. While more improvised practices are also present in hill walks, such as responsiveness to weather and the terrain as encountered, participants in our study have expressed through their walks a keenness to explore the city in a relatively unplanned way. To some extent this is related to the predominant construction of risk in mountain environments, which leads walkers, or at least the leaders of hikes, to take every precaution against getting lost. The dangers of getting lost in the city are generally perceived as much less, even though fear of other kinds of situation is undoubtedly present. On the other hand, the positive ways in which urban walkers choose and find routes around their city attest to the importance of creativity in everyday walking.

The skills and habits of wayfinding are therefore open to investigation here. Given the preponderance of the map in modern navigation and the apparent clarity of the city's relationship to the map – where streets equal routes – it is possible to follow up de Certeau's assertion that, owing to the wanderings and networks of its people, 'a migrational, or metaphorical city thus slips into the clear text of the planned and readable city' (1984: 93) As the walker in the previous example showed, by no means do we always use maps to find a route. Yet there is a relationship between the 'map' in a broader sense – the planned and readable city, often thought of as being looked down upon from above, as de Certeau (ibid.: 91) described in his view of Manhattan from the World Trade Center – and the city as lived on the ground, discovered, appropriated or engaged with by people. We can consider the relationship between city (and indeed countryside) planning and the lived experience of people on the ground in a parallel fashion, being open to potential subversions and alternative discourses. It is also not simply a question of 'domination' from above and 'resistance' from below, as de Certeau tended to suggest. The lines and routes of walkers are made through everyday choices and actions.

Elsewhere Ingold (n.d.) contrasts the line that is created as the trace of a free-flowing movement, as a person makes his or her way through an unfolding landscape, with the line that connects predetermined points of arrival and departure, between which the traveller does not move but is rather transported or 'carried across'. Places, in the first case, are actually constituted by the movements to, from and around them. In the city, from the point of view of a walker, the streets form a set of possibilities for routes. Yet the particular path chosen is almost always meaningful for the walker, in denial of the apparent random element in moving through the city. The 'line' created will be rich in the memories and experiences that are formed by moving, by the encounters that occur and the changes in the environment. Hurrying, the walker will seek a direct route. But the road also needs to afford easy passage and to allow crossing at appropriate points if necessary. Seeking quietness, or 'nature', the walker will find routes that avoid busy roads or are flanked by pleasant gardens, parks or waterways. The walker quoted at the beginning of this chapter often seeks architectural pleasure, the 'little lanes and places', or a feeling of being off the beaten track. A keen rural walker, similarly, showed how he enjoys seeking out old country roads and paths that have often fallen into disuse. There are also many examples in our research of short, oft-repeated walks to shops, bus-stops, other houses and circuits around the city that, in their repetition, come to represent what might be seen as 'thick lines' of un-thought-of but nevertheless important and meaningful place-making. Before starting this research, Lee reflected on one of his regular routes:

> I enjoy crossing the road over to Spar in the morning to buy groceries. The walk is about 100 yards. Crossing the road releases me from the constriction of the pavement. It allows me to admire the architecture of the street buildings, otherwise hidden from view by perspective. I see the sky and the road – horizons open. I like being able to cross the street without waiting for some minutes for a gap in the traffic, or for the authority of the traffic lights to tell me when to cross: I live in a relatively quiet city. I like looking in the shop windows as I pass. The cheeriness of Sandra the shop assistant. I like feeling I have the time to enjoy it. I cross the street diagonally, looking up or down it, walking along the street, not just across it.

Lee now feels rather strongly the partiality of this walk, as elsewhere in the city there is busyness, stressed commuting and indeed fear, as already noted, in addition to the partiality of his own situation in writing this (having a shop close by and the time and money to spend there). It is in these ways, however, that walkers come to know the city and its surroundings. Walking for many is an act they make real, moving through and thereby creating particular places – although socially grounded, as we have argued, the walker figures as a subject in a specific environment, as opposed to being just a member of a larger social grouping. By creating routes, walkers inscribe their own lives into the city, if only for the transient moments when they pass along. The meaning of the place is constituted by their bodily presence, and although the specific intent or emotional state of the walker may be hidden to a greater or lesser degree, the route is actually made real by the walker. It is the presence of people that makes what is sometimes thought of as the 'living street'.[3] Repeated walks produce a thicker association of the route with the walker. From this emerges a distinctive relationship of place, in the interaction between the walker and the meaningful environment.

We can also contrast route-making in urban areas with countryside or mountain walking. Our fieldwork has also taken us to the agricultural regions around Aberdeen, and to the hills and mountains of north-east Scotland beyond. In these environments, there is an even greater directness in the relationship between the routes of walkers and their environments. Each footstep may leave a mark, plants pushed out of the way, and trodden earth and stones leaving a record of the linear movement over and through them. The route becomes embedded into the landscape in a way that is usually not possible in urban areas, where pavements and road surfaces are virtually impervious to the effects of walkers, if not to heavier traffic. This is partly why in the city the bodily presence of the walker counts for so much. The route is made by and as the person walks. It disappears as soon as the person moves on, although over time it may produce other traces: pedestrian crossings built at popular crossing points, or shops opened to catch passing trade. An exception, of course, is when a fresh snowfall in the city provides the opportunity physically to imprint one's own route and to see and feel the routes of others. We see the busy places and the quiet. The pleasure of walking in newly fallen snow – and in looking behind us to see our footprints – is related to the creation of a visible route, as well as the tactility of the foot and snow.

Our second resonance between walking and anthropological fieldwork therefore calls attention to the specificities of the route. Understanding the routes taken and being formed by the participants in research is important because it grounds them within trajectories of movement. This could be extended to life-course and biography, or, more literally, to way of life. A way of life is rarely mapped out clearly in advance, but is rather produced along the way, 'continually worked out anew' (Ingold 2000: 242), and thus betokens the active participation of the person who makes it. Much as we have followed and taken part in the everyday walking routes of our informants, so we have had insights into their wider ways of life: their biographies of home, work, leisure and movement.

We can make a comparison here with James Clifford's writing on routes. He explores routes through the 'specific histories, tactics, everyday practices of dwelling and traveling: traveling-in-dwelling, dwelling-in-traveling' (1997: 36). Dwelling is indeed central to route-making, in that immersion in a lifeworld must be a precondition for finding one's way through it. However, Clifford's routes are mostly international and indeed intercontinental movements of people and goods, in the context mainly of museums and diasporic communities. The focus is on how identity and meaning are formed through these processes. The examples amassed by Clifford of distinctive spatialities, or concepts of spatial relations, underline the importance of knowing where and how such movement occurs. But 'everyday practices' also need to include the ways that the very places between which Clifford sees movement as happening are themselves being formed by movement – there is no simple inside and outside, perhaps, to these places. People not only move between places, but also form them by movement itself. By the interweaving of routes over time or concurrently, a place is made.

The Sociability of Walking

John Urry (2002, 2003) has noted the continuing need for physical 'co-presence' in the functioning of social life, where people need to travel in order to meet each other face-to-face, to visit certain places or fulfil various obligations in person, despite the often geographically distant locations from which they start and the availability of modern communications technologies. Urry also describes the disruption of the pleasures and usefulness of walking by 'fast' means of mechanized transport, by 'the speed and rush of much modern life' (2000: 55), and this is clearly the case in many circumstances. However, walkers in Aberdeen have emphasized that the quality of co-presence in walking is still ubiquitous in everyday circumstances. It is a particularly sociable kind of movement, and this is the basis for our third resonance between walking and anthropological fieldwork. The potential for shared understanding through movement, through walking together, is part of the richness of fieldwork on foot.

Urry's argument about the importance of face-to-face meetings is based on the fact that people are able to look at each other, and this allows them to communicate with far more precision and subtlety than they otherwise could. Urry draws on the work of Georg Simmel (1997 [1907]) who, as part of a concern with social interaction on the level of individuals, wrote about the meanings that sensory perception has for social life. Simmel suggested that the eye has a pre-eminent significance amongst the senses because of the 'extremely lively interaction' with which it weaves people together. Moreover, 'this connection is so strong and delicate that it can only be supported by the shortest line – the straight line between the eyes' (ibid.: 112). The 'line' in this instance is a point-to-point connection between people's heads.

To elaborate, this model of social interaction is of two people standing or, most likely, sitting still, and giving each other their full attention. But walking was often described by our informants as an excellent way of being *with* other people, a very rich way of socializing, to the extent that there seems to be something distinctive about the sociability of walking together. During a shared walk, people very often talk to each other, yet the talking usually involves very little direct eye contact. They are already doing a multitude of other things at the same time, many of which have been discussed in this chapter: observing through all the senses what is going on around them; co-ordinating their bodily movements along a particular route; and often dealing with other paraphernalia such as bags, clothing or mobile phones. To respond to a fellow walker on top of all this might seem difficult, or at least to result in a far weaker social interaction than would be the case in the ideal model of the isolated and immobile dyad, described above.

However, the idea that social interaction in walking occurs 'on top' of all these activities is incorrect. Rather, it is *through* the shared bodily engagement with the environment, the shared rhythm of walking, that social interaction takes place. People communicate through their posture in movement, involving their whole bodies. Crucially, walking side by side means that participants share virtually the same visual field. We could say that I see what you see as we go along together. In that sense I am with you in my movements, and probably in my thoughts as well. We can talk within and around our shared vista and the other things we are doing along the line of the walk. Participants take it in turns to carry the conversation on, and when not actually speaking one is nevertheless listening, participating silently in the ongoing flow. Thus:

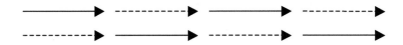

Face-to-face interaction of the kind Simmel describes, on the other hand, is much more confrontational and less companionable, for while one sees the other person's eyes, one does not see what he or she sees. A shared point of view is harder to come by. The conversation that goes on in this context (two people sitting and facing one another) is more like an interview, in which points are batted back and forth:

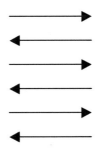

To return briefly to our introductory remarks, when Geertz was wandering around the village before the cockfight, he would confront villagers face-to-face (and the latter would do their best to avert their gaze). But when he turned to run from the police, he was heading the same way as everyone else. Although Geertz could not have seen into the eyes of the people he was running with (until he sat down to tea), he felt that he formed an immediate social bond with them. By the same token, he felt embodied.

These suggestions may be illustrated from our ethnography. Firstly, the bodily orientations of people walking together can be observed. Generally, each walker is of course facing in the direction being walked. During conversation the head periodically moves slightly towards the fellow walker but not so much as to look at him or her directly. This is presumably to project the voice more clearly towards the other person. However, inclining the head also allows the walker to see the gestures of the body and contributes to the creation of the walking rhythm. The gestures of arms and hands in particular can also be much more open during walking because of the space available around the body. The rhythm, though, is set by more than just the arms and hands. There are usually similarities in the whole aspect of the bodies of people walking together. As an example, the following observations were made on Union Street (the main street of the city) in the late afternoon. Two people in their twenties were walking up the street, talking to each other. Lee noted the following:

> They're walking on the backs of their knees. Not really striding but keeping a straight legged walk. And, they're really wandering. Their pace seems to go in a slightly sort of, it's not a regular stride. One of them comes in front of the other and the other one moves out a bit. ... I think they're talking about work.

These two walkers shared a very loose-limbed, wandering gait, with one arm each holding a bag and the other swinging. They did not always walk precisely next to each other, but moved slightly to the side and ahead of each other, and back again, as the walk continued. Their heads inclined towards each other as they spoke. One then turned off Union Street down a side street. For about ten paces, the walk of the person remaining on Union Street stayed the same, moving around the pavement laterally, with a short stride. But then the stride became more regular and straighter. She put earphones in, her head straightened, and she continued up the street.

This small episode is meant to illustrate how social interaction during walking is a full bodily experience. The rhythm when the walkers were together was very strong and distinctive in its looseness of the stride and movement across as well as up the pavement. We are not interested at this stage in the content of the talk, or the gender of the walkers, so much as in the means by which the walkers shared these distinctive bodily orientations. Closeness was produced not simply through the conversation but by sharing the rhythm of walking. When the pair split up, the rhythm continued in the Union Street walker for a short time, and in a sense the interaction seemed to go on for a few seconds after the parting. Then the walker assumed a different rhythm, one much more standard for solo town walkers, with a regular, longer, stride, straight head and straight line on the pavement. This kind of variation lends an additional layer of complexity to the interactionist perspective of Erving Goffman (1971). Goffman described the strategies used to walk in a street in order to avoid collisions and maintain visual awareness. There is still a gap, however, in understanding the personhood that emerges through such activity. This requires that we understand the interactions produced through specific bodily techniques of stepping and movement, rather than just the visual surveillance of other people, or Simmel's lines between the eyes.

Walkers were sometimes quite explicit about the particular kinds of social interaction that could be experienced by walking with someone. During a walk along
Aberdeen's beach front, one reflected (unprompted) that 'walking is a very nice
rhythm in order to chat and do nice things, to focus on each other as people, rather
than get distracted as you would at home'. This is a neat rejoinder to the 'stability'
model of social interaction. Walking gives the opportunity to be together, where
sharing a rhythm of movement is the basis for shared understanding of each other
in a holistic rather than ocularcentric manner: fellow walkers are aware of each
other's bodies but rarely actually look *at* each other. In this we see similarities
between shared walking and, amongst other activities, some forms of dancing (S.
Reed 1998: 520) and martial arts (Kohn 2001). In walking, particularly, people
look *with* each other, as we describe above.

The sociability of walking also came through strongly during participant observation with some of the many walking clubs and groups in Aberdeen. Only some
of these groups are regarded as 'traditional' hill-walking or mountaineering clubs
like the Cairngorm Club or the Scottish Mountaineering Club. Many others
operate in workplaces, churches or simply and less formally, amongst regular
social groups of friends and families. There are also many walking groups for
older people. While these latter were 'officially' for exercise and health benefits,
everyone Lee spoke to either volunteered or agreed with the suggestion that the
social element was just as important, and, indeed, could not readily be separated
from the health aspect. This is also the case for the other groups, including the
more traditional hill-walkers.

The idea here is that walkers have a particular way of being together that is more
than just co-presence, because it has sociability as the basis for bodily movement.
Manifested as a shared rhythm of footsteps and bodily aspect, there is a distinctive
sociality in which the togetherness of the walkers has meaning for themselves and
for people around them. This overall sociality is central to how and why people
walk. It also allows us to expand on our third resonance of walking with anthropological fieldwork. In describing the conjunction of corporeal movement and
sociability, an investigation of walking also demonstrates how ethnographic technique emerges from certain alignments of the body and the person. These foundational embodiments are central to the progress of ethnographic research, as Coffey
(1999) notes. She writes of the 'physicality' of ethnography, a bodily presence that
has to be negotiated during fieldwork. Others have also begun to be aware of the
methodological possibilities of sociability in walking as a research technique, particularly from a phenomenological standpoint. Kusenbach (2003) coins the 'go-
along' as an *in situ* method, which involves accompanying informants in Los
Angeles on their daily street outings and holding a kind of informal interview.
'Talking whilst walking' is also encouraged by Anderson (2004), based on an
investigation of environmental activism in southern England. Through shared

walking, we can see and feel what is really a learning process of being together, in adjusting one's body and one's speech to the rhythms of others, and of sharing (or at least coming to see) a point of view. Combining this with an awareness of routes – trajectories of movement and their meaning – results in fieldwork sensitive to the richness and reality of people's mobility in the world.

Culture Over the Shoulders or On Foot?

We end by returning one last time to Geertz's flight from the police. He tells us that it was only after having been propelled into the same situation as everyone else, by force of circumstance, that he gained a sense of embodied presence and could begin to participate in the social life of the village. But he then proceeds to treat the whole of that social life as though it were just as disembodied – just as much up in the symbolic clouds – as he himself felt to begin with. That is, social life is refigured in his analysis as a 'text', which he is endeavouring to read. He imagines himself reading such social and cultural texts 'over the shoulders of those to whom they properly belong' (Geertz 1973: 452). 'Reading over the shoulders' is more or less the antithesis of 'walking together', insofar as both the anthropologist and the culture he or she is trying to grasp seem to be floating in thin air. This disembodied stance is reiterated in Geertz's well-known essay on thick description, with its image of humanity 'suspended in webs of significance'. Although he does admit (in deference to Wittgenstein) that ethnographic research is fundamentally about 'finding our feet' (1973: 13), metaphors of support rapidly give way to metaphors of suspension. The ethnographer's job, Geertz claims, is to fix the 'curve of social discourse'. Culture, it seems, is blowing in the wind, just as Geertz felt himself to be blowing in the wind until, forced to run from the police, he found his feet (see also Ingold 1997: 238).

What we can offer, then, is a reversal of Geertzian hyper-suspension. We show how people generally, and ethnographers in particular, literally find their feet by walking with others, and not by reading over their shoulders. We show how the 'webs of significance' in which people are undoubtedly caught up are comprised of trails that are trodden on the ground, not spun in the symbolic ether, as people make their way about. And we show how walking itself can consequently become a practice of understanding, so that the record of the walk, and of the experience it affords, is just as important – and just as valid a source of field material – as the record of the 'discourse' that might have accompanied it. Paying close attention to walking and its ways (both *of* walking and *along* which people walk) may be one of the things that would distinguish a phenomenologically inspired fieldwork practice from the more traditional forms of ethnography primarily designed to support symbolic analysis of the Geertzian kind.

Notes

1. Economic and Social Research Council award RES-000-23-0312, from 2004 to 2006. We gratefully acknowledge the support of the ESRC in funding the research. We also thank Katrin Lund, the editors of this volume, the participants in the 2004 ASA Conference, and members of the Social Anthropology, Ethnology and Cultural History Seminar at the University of Aberdeen for their helpful comments on earlier versions.

2. Given that the preposition 'in' normally implies containment – and hence closure – the phrase 'out in the sun' seems almost self-contradictory. Merleau-Ponty wrote on this. His point was that to be in the open is not to be 'set over against' the space one inhabits, but to merge with it. One does not *see* sunlight but *is* sunlight; what one sees is *in* the light (Merleau-Ponty, 1962: 214; see also Ingold, 2005: 101–2).

3. Thus activists of the 'Living Streets' campaign of the UK Pedestrian Authority see themselves as the 'champions of streets and public spaces for people on foot' (Living Streets 2005).

References

Anderson, J. (2004), 'Talking Whilst Walking: A Geographical Archaeology of Knowledge', *Area* 36: 254–61.

Bernard, H. (1988), *Research Methods in Cultural Anthropology*, Beverly Hills, CA: Sage Publications.

Certeau, M. de (1984), *The Practice of Everyday Life*, trans. S. Rendall, Berkeley: University of California Press.

Clifford, J. (1997), *Routes: Travel and Translation in the Late Twentieth Century*, Cambridge, Mass.: Harvard University Press.

Coffey, A. (1999), *The Ethnographic Self*, London: Sage.

Connerton, J. (1989), *How Societies Remember*, Cambridge: Cambridge University Press.

Davies, C. (1999), *Reflexive Ethnography: A Guide to Researching Self and Others*, London: Routledge.

Ellen, R. (1984), *Ethnographic Research: A Guide to General Conduct*, London: Academic.

Finnegan, R. (1998), *Tales of the City: A Study of Narrative and Urban Life*, Cambridge: Cambridge University Press.

Frey, N. (1998), *Pilgrim Stories: On and Off the Road to Santiago*, Berkeley: University of California Press.

Geertz. C. (1973), *The Interpretation of Cultures*, New York: Basic Books.

Goffman, E. (1971), *Relations in Public: Microstudies of the Public Order*,

London: Allen Lane.

Ingold, T. (1997), 'Life Beyond the Edge of Nature? Or, The Mirage of Society', in J. Greenwood (ed.), *The Mark of the Social*, Lanham, MD: Rowman and Littlefield.

Ingold, T. (2000), *The Perception of the Environment: Essays on Livelihood, Dwelling and Skill*, London: Routledge.

Ingold, T. (2005), 'The Eye of the Storm: Visual Perception and the Weather', *Visual Studies* 20: 99–104.

Ingold, T. (n.d.), 'Up, Across and Along', unpublished manuscript.

Kohn, T. (2001), 'Don't Talk – Blend': Ideas About Body and Communication in Aikido Practice', in J. Hendry and B. Watson (eds), *An Anthropology of Indirect Communication*, London: Routledge.

Kusenbach, M. (2003), 'Street Phenomenology. The Go-Along as Ethnographic Tool', *Ethnography* 4: 455–85.

Living Streets (2005) http://www.livingstreets.org.uk/. Accessed 1 September 2005.

Lorimer, H. and Lund, K. (2003), 'Performing Facts: Finding a Way Over Scotland's Mountains', in B. Szerszynski, W. Heim and C. Waterton (eds), *Nature Performed: Environment, Culture and Performance*, The Sociological Review Monographs, Oxford: Blackwell Publishing.

Merleau-Ponty, M. (1962), *Phenomenology of Perception* (trans. C. Smith), London: Routledge & Kegan Paul.

Orlet, C. (2004), 'The Gymnasiums of the Mind', *Philosophy Now* 44: 28–9.

Reed, A. (2002), 'City of Details: Interpreting the Personality of London', *Journal of the Royal Anthropological Institute* (NS) 8: 127–41.

Reed, S. (1998), 'The Politics and Poetics of Dance' *Annual Review of Anthropology* 27: 503–32.

Simmel, G. (1997 [1907]), 'Sociology of the Senses', in D. Frisby and M. Featherstone (eds), *Simmel on Culture*, London: Sage.

Urry, J. (2000), *Sociology Beyond Societies*, London: Routledge.

Urry, J. (2002), 'Mobility and Proximity', *Sociology* 36: 255–74.

Urry, J. (2003), 'Social Networks, Travel and Talk', *British Journal of Sociology* 54: 155–75.

Wallace, A. (1993), *Walking, Literature and English Culture: The Origins and Uses of Peripatetic in the Nineteenth Century*, Oxford: Clarendon Press.

Watson, C. (1999), *Being There: Fieldwork in Anthropology*, London: Pluto.

–4–

Rendering and Gendering[1] Mobile Subjects in a Globalized World of Mountaineering: Between Localizing Ethnography and Global Spaces

Susan Frohlick

Introduction

The question of mobilities – movements of people, objects, images and information that are transforming society – is of importance in social and cultural theory these days (Urry 2000). Linked to theory, the methodology of studying mobilities is also a central concern. This has become a significant issue in anthropology in general, and within anthropological studies of tourism in particular (see Bruner 1995). In this chapter I challenge the notion that ethnography is not suitable for studying global processes and mobile people and, moreover, that a globalized methodology compromises central anthropological modes of knowledge production, namely immersion. I argue, however, as others have suggested (Amit 2000; Clifford 1997; Trouillot 2003), that ethnography must move out of a localizing mode in order to grasp the complexities of mobility.

The linked theoretical and methodological issue of mobility has arisen in part out of the recognition that 'the native' no longer remains stationary, if that was ever the case. Much has been written about the shift in conceptualization of culture as static and rooted to a notion of culture that has come to resemble 'as much a site of travel encounters as of residence' (Clifford 1997: 28). The era of globalization in which we now conduct fieldwork requires us to rethink methods originally devised for what were seen as localized, bounded geographic locales and social groups, where anthropologists could see the entire village from the front of their tent or front porch. Globalization produces phenomena and a 'world of moving populations' 'too large, too quick, too all-encompassing to succumb to our gaze', argues Appadurai (1997: 115) and thus presents what seems like an insurmountable problem for anthropologists. The people with whom anthropologists study are as likely to be as mobile or more so than the anthropologist (Amit 2000: 12).

Arising from this problem is the issue of what to do when our research participants are not in one place long enough to have a sustained conversation, never mind long enough for constant regular interaction or 'twelve months in a village', as per the Malinowskian archetype of fieldwork (Gupta and Ferguson 1997: 25). In speaking more specifically about tourists as anthropological subjects, Bruner states the problem this way: 'A key difficulty in studying tourists is methodological: the tourists move so fast through the sites it hard to keep up with them' (1995: 225). I see the problem not so much as the fact that 'the native' keeps moving (so that we must devise ways to keep up with him or her) as the fact that we appear to continue to see 'their' mobility as separate from 'ours' and, thus, to problematically shore up local–global, travel–location dichotomies.

Marcus (1998) has posed one of the key solutions for studying global processes. His rearticulation of single-site ethnography to multi-sited reflects a wider shift in anthropology from notions of local subjects 'easily located in a world system perspective' to notions of subjects as multiply situated in contingent and diffuse social relations (ibid.: x). In his postulation of multi-local ethnography he calls for mobile methodological strategies that involve 'quite literally' following connections, associations, people, things and stories, in order for ethnographers to capture the gaps between people's lifeworlds and 'the world system' (ibid.). In the post-world-system, ethnography becomes a technique of mapping cultural formations, meanings and identities that now circulate in diffuse time-space through the ethnographer's calculated emplacements in various sites.

All this movement opens up a new set of problems. Notably, there is considerable anxiety over the loss of 'long-term and thorough immersion' as a key technique of anthropological data collection and comprehension (Amit 2000: 1). Drawing on feminist critiques of globalization (e.g. Freeman 2001; Kaplan 2002), I suggest that, rather than provoking anxieties about the loss of immersion, the tensions between localizing ethnography and the global worlds we all occupy can be productive.

I flesh out my argument by way of example from my multi-sited ethnographic research carried out in Canada and Nepal between 1999 and 2001 on the transnationality of Himalayan mountaineering spaces and subjectivities. Nepali citizens, mostly Sherpa men, have participated in Himalayan mountaineering since its beginnings in the nineteenth century. Contrary to how they are represented both in Western mountaineering literature and in Nepali media as localized, racialized and nationally and regionally bound, Nepali Sherpas participate as cosmopolitans through mountaineering in a variety of ways. My own understanding of Nepali Sherpas as relatively immobile, rooted (local) subjects in contrast to travelling, cosmopolitan Western (global) mountaineers, as depicted in Western mountaineering literature and media, was challenged through the course of my fieldwork – and became a substantial subject matter of my analyses, including this chapter.[2]

Here, I focus on the 'Nepalese Women Millennium Everest Expedition 2000' (NWMEE), a state-sponsored team of women who attempted to climb Mount Everest, and the ways I struggled to make sense of the various positionings of the Nepali women climbers as local and global subjects.[3] I show how a specific rendering of the Nepali women climbers in the discourse of the new millennium raises questions both about culturally specific mobilities and subjectivities in an era of globalization and about the methodologies required to 'track' these new subjectivities. In view of mountaineering in Nepal as a highly male-dominated practice, it is imperative to cast doubt on the alleged newness of women's mobility claimed by the state-affiliated organization that produced the brochure in which the representation appeared, although I only touch on this issue now. Rather, in this chapter I elaborate on a partial answer to the question of how we make sense of our data and the linkages between theories and methodologies of mobility. Through contingent travels and opportune events in Nepal and Canada, I came to recognize the significance of the Nepali women's expedition in terms of new meanings and histories of mobility emerging in Nepal in the twenty-first century and, more broadly, in terms of how the global and the local play out in different contexts. I use this example to challenge notions of multi-sited methodology as a matter of *systematically* following the circulation of people, objects or practices within globalized worlds (cf. Marcus 1998). Rather, I view the importance of multi-sited ethnography as a way of encountering, often by chance circumstances, the means through which our research subjects 'circulate' in social circuits of their desire, and thus as a method necessary to unravelling the contingencies of a diversity of cosmopolitan subjects in the early twenty-first century. Multi-sited ethnography to some degree involves a loss of immersion but at the same time can assist us in gaining appreciation and first-hand knowledge of how immersion – and location – plays out and matters to the people with whom we do our research.

Rendering Global Subjects: 'New Millennium Women'

Mountaineering generally has historical linkages to nationalism (Hansen 2000; Morin et al. 2001) and as a mode of international adventure travel is embedded within the global political economy. In Nepal, in the twenty-first century, mountaineering is a cornerstone in the international tourism industry and, marketed as a 'world' adventure travel sport, is salient to the ongoing project of nation building and modernity. With eight of the world's highest mountains located within the national borders of Nepal, the country's national identity is constructed in part through its association with mountaineering as a global sporting and adventure travel arena.[4]

As a source of employment as well as of recreation and travel for some Nepalis, mountaineering provides a way into cultural and economic globalization, through its symbolic association both with 'the West' and with modernity and a range of practices, technologies and social relations constitutive of mountaineering today, such as corporate sponsorship, commercialization and media communications. Traditionally, Sherpa men have been involved in mountaineering mostly as load-carrying low-altitude porters and cooks employed by foreign expeditions. In the latter part of the twentieth century, some Sherpas made their way up the ranks to high-altitude porters and guides and eventually as owners of the plethora of mountaineering agencies in Kathmandu that continue to service the needs of foreign expeditions and adventure sport tourists. The state has a complex involvement with mountaineering. It is clear that the government works hard to construct Himalayan mountaineering on a global scale in terms of imagery and political economy, often against the grain of a popular imaginary in Nepali media of Nepali climbers as nation-bound, amateurish and unworldly climbers (see Thapa 1995, 2000). This work became evident to me especially in the unfolding of NWMEE, where, as I describe below, Nepali women as a group are rendered global, mobile subjects by virtue of their association with Mount Everest in spite of the marginalization of Nepali women from the global arenas, international circuits and transnational relations of Himalayan mountaineering.

For a variety of reasons, including the general masculinization of high-altitude mountaineering as a high-risk, high-cost sport, men have dominated mountaineering in the Nepal Himalayas. The involvement of women of any nationality has been relatively limited. By the twenty-first century, while more than 900 men had reached the top of Mount Everest, only fifty-two women had done so. Few Nepali women participate, to a relatively small degree, as cooks and low-altitude porters on expeditions to lower-altitude peaks. In the early 1990s, however, Nepali women entered the realm of high-altitude mountaineering when an expedition headed by Pasang Lhamu Sherpa attempted the first Nepali female ascent of Mount Everest. Pasang Lhamu Sherpa reached the summit but died on the descent. The state mourned her death and made her a national heroine (Adams 1996), although this development was contentious. Part of the public controversy centred on the way in which Pasang had used the media, promoted herself and raised the money to pay her own expedition through corporate sponsorships (see Lieberman 1993) – a radical departure from climbing Everest as a wage labourer. In short, she embodied and enacted in a new way 'a modern climber' (Thapa 1995). Seven years later, after much reluctance on the part of the government to lend their financial support, a second Nepali women's expedition to Mount Everest was formed, initiated by Lhakpa Sherpa, a teen when the stories about Pasang Lhamu were circulating (personal communication, Lhakpa Sherpa, 2000).

I learned about the Nepali women climbers and their expedition by chance and as an event mediated through a particular discourse. I considered myself very lucky that this endeavour came to fruition in 2000 within the temporal-spatial parameters of my 'field'. Before leaving Canada for Nepal, I was unaware of the Nepali women's expedition. In large part my ignorance arose from my location in the West and my information sources (the internet and research contacts from within mountaineering communities in Canada) where news about Nepali climbers is not widely disseminated. When I first arrived in Kathmandu my energies were focused on getting in touch with foreign women mountaineers, some of whom I had been in touch with while in Canada.[5] However, within days of my arrival the news of a Nepali women's expedition to Everest was hard to miss, appearing on the television in the lobby of the guest house and on the front pages of *The Kathmandu News*. When I enquired about the expedition at a local mountaineering agency office, I was handed a glossy, full-colour brochure. Later on, when I visited the NWMEE camp at Everest base camp, the brochure was given to me again. Back in Kathmandu weeks later, I would be handed the brochure once more. My initial understanding of the women's expedition was shaped by this text, clearly of importance given that it had been handed to me on three separate occasions.

In this brochure, the women are framed in terms of the 'new millennium' by the sponsoring organization of the expedition, the Sushma Koirala Fund. The latter describes itself as a non-profit, non-governmental social welfare organization founded by the late Sushma Koirala, the wife of the prime minister at the time. Based in Kathmandu, the Fund took on the organization and sponsorship of the NWMEE, which would have been a costly endeavour. Presided over by Mrs Sujata Koirala, the daughter of the prime minister, a board of eighty-five advisers and numerous sub-committees was struck to oversee the expedition, drawing from an extensive roster of individuals, local business owners, journalists and government representatives as well as foreign medical specialists and technical advisers.

Emblazoned on the front cover is the Nepali flag appearing alongside the image of a towering mountain, with the figures of two women in the foreground – one of the figures is wearing what looks like a cheerleader's outfit and a second figure is dressed in a Western-style business suit. Despite the fact that this is a promotional brochure for a mountain climbing expedition, there are no images of mountaineers – not surprising given that a mountain climber is not a subject with whom many Nepali women would identify themselves. The text on the front reads:

> The NWMEE Spring 2000 [expedition] is being organized by the Sushma Koirala Memorial Trust to celebrate the predominant role Nepali women are expected to play in the coming century. The Nepali women as mountaineers set to conquer the world's highest mountain are a symbol of confidence, courage, strength, and willpower required to face the challenges of the coming century.

Named in the text on the inside fold of the brochure is a select list of women from various nations from a total roster of fifty-two women who by 1999 had successfully climbed Mount Everest. At the end of that list, we read, 'Pasang Lhamu

is the only Nepali woman known to have reached the summit.' Her death thus
appears to open up a spot on the international map of gendered ascents of Mount
Everest where the NWMEE women climbers are meant to insert their names at the
turn of the twenty-first century. The text continues: 'The Nepali Women
Millennium Everest Expedition Spring 2000 hopes to put four more Nepali
women climbers atop Everest. The entire community of women await their success
with bated breath because it heralds the opening of new avenues and horizons for
women, more specifically the Nepali women.' Within this discursive framework,
the members of the NWMEE are situated symbolically on the brink of a new
gateway to mobility enabled through their participation as gendered subjects in the
emergent global political economy of Mount Everest, a global landscape of economic opportunity, i.e. wage labour, and a world adventure sport 'playscape'
(Frohlick 2003).

This expedition was not the only expedition at Everest in 2000 framed within a
millennium discourse. There is much more to say about that. Here, I focus on how
the deployment of this expedition and these particular representations of Nepali
women to promote and imagine Nepali women's entry into the global economy
raises questions about culturally specific gendered mobilities in an era of globalization. Constructed as 'modern women', they are seen as embodying the 'confidence, courage, strength and willpower' required of females to face the challenges
of the coming century. Even though some Nepali women have struggled without
success to gain entry into mountaineering (Ortner 1999), particularly the high-risk,
high-profit, highly masculinized, high-altitude mountaineering, here is the erasure
of this long, difficult history of their marginalization. Instead, women are posed as
highly mobile, universal players moving freely within this landscape of opportunity and gender equality in the emergent global economy in Nepal in the new millennium. What did I make of this particular globalist imaginary? There is much to
be said about the utilization of the women by the state and business élites but here
I focus on the relationship between methodological and interpretive strategies.

Between Local Ethnography and Global Spaces

While the state promotes a globalist imaginary, Himalayan mountaineering also
plays out through 'transnational arrangements of power and cultural exchange'
(Adams 1996) between Nepali and foreigners, who pay a great deal of money to
climb the world's highest mountain peaks and to be guided by Sherpa guides.[6]
The transnational flows and social relations constitutive of mountaineering practices play an integral role in forming Sherpas' cosmopolitan identity (Adams
1996). For many Sherpas, mountaineering tourism has led to close relations with
foreigners, distinct from other Nepali–tourist encounters. The personal interaction between clients and guides and porters afforded by the nature of service work

in mountaineering often results in long-term relationships with foreigners and deeply enmeshes Sherpas in transnational exchanges and identity formations (Adams 1992, 1996). Transnationalism is a key aspect of the lives of many Sherpas in Nepal.

Situated as an ethnographer within this matrix of transnational relations, I do not yet fully understand the implications. My discussion of the significance of the brochure that was handed to me, because I was seen by locals as a foreign journalist and thus someone who might disseminate information outside Nepal, begins to address this question. My reading of this brochure shifted as I began to unravel different scales of social relations and grasp the meaning of 'shifting locations'. Here, I draw out how, in spite of my placement in these transnational arrangements of power, I found it difficult nevertheless to move out from a 'local' mode of ethnography. Besio (2003) explains how her research subjects, women in a village in northern Pakistan, positioned her (a white, Western researcher) as a colonial subject through the very process of participant observation. 'While I read about relations of colonialism in the archives, it was through daily interactions in research circumstances that I came to greater understanding of colonialism's lingering effects on postcolonial interactions,' she writes (ibid.: 25). Her placement in a particular post-colonial subject position circumscribed her mobility within her field-site, shaping her relations with Balti women, European adventure tourists and her movements through the town. I see in retrospect how my mobility within particular circuits of power and exchange in the Nepali mountaineering communities – and thus where I could hang out, where I was invited, what materials were given to me, and so forth (i.e. 'my data') – were shaped by my placement as a visitor in the history of Nepalis' relations with foreigners (see Liechty 1997). While Nepal has never been colonized, its history of isolationist rule and selective exclusion shapes contemporary relations between Nepalis and tourists in a complex way (Liechty 1996, 1997; also Hepburn 2002).

As a first-time visitor to Nepal staying in Thamel, a 'tourist ghetto' and space of translocality (Liechty 1996), and as an English-speaker entering the country on a tourist visa, I was certainly a tourist. Because of my Canadian citizenship and social status as a foreigner, sometimes as a student but more often as a journalist, many if not all of my Nepali contacts positioned me within the cosmopolitan worlds of the foreign mountaineers. Opportunities were presented to me as gestures of hospitality as well as strategically to place me within the same fields of interaction and documentation with Nepalis as the other foreign 'journalists'– inviting me to parties with mountaineers from all over the world, to media events, and granting me interviews with the local mountaineering celebrities. I was presumed to be someone who would promote Nepali mountaineering back home (and was given a stack of brochures to distribute on behalf of a few trekking agencies). The transnationality of Himalayan mountaineering spaces was thus enacted through my own locations and privileges as a researcher/tourist/journalist and as a white, middle-class, Canadian woman connected in a vague way to potential consumers of adventure travel back in Canada. These insights are retrospective and for the most part eluded me while in the field, an archetypically 'local place' (Trouillot 2003).

Thus, I fell unreflexively into a conventional 'local' ethnography while in Nepal, in large part because of the residual legacy of anthropology as a form of colonial gaze and Western travel practice focused on the exoticization of a non-Western Other. As Clifford (1997) has pointed out, a conventional local ethnography is one where the ethnographer is the mobile traveller while the research subject –'native' – remains in a position of dwelling. Bound up with my linked subjectivities as white, Western anthropologist-tourist, the Western mountaineering literature that had informed my research imaginary was replete with images of Nepali Sherpas as local/ethnic/Other (e.g. Carrier 1992; Dubin 2003; also see Adams 1996; Ortner 1998), in spite of the critiques I had read as a student of anthropology in the 1990s. I did not at first see the Nepalis with whom I spoke in their offices in Thamel in terms of their own touristic practices outside of the travel to local mountains necessitated by their employment as porters and guides for wealthy foreign clients. Nor did I view them as particularly cosmopolitan subjects, for that matter, prior to our extensive conversations and my participant observation carried out in Kathmandu and at Everest base camp.[7] As an anthropological category and in the popular Western tourist imaginary, 'Sherpa' carries a naturalized association of space and subjectivity by virtue of Sherpas' historical movements between home villages and mountaineering base camps. In other words, Sherpas embody 'natural' 'travellers' in the sense of being associated with the traversing of established routes in the Himalayas (India, China and Nepal) over the past century. In a local mode of ethnography I did not interrogate this naturalized, localized association until I shifted places to a more global research imaginary.

Processes of localization occurred outside of intellectual categories too, in particular within mountaineering spaces in Nepal where claims to Everest are made. I found that in the glorification of Nepali mountaineers as 'Everest Summiteers', for example, a few Nepali citizens were constructed and marked as local heroes and heroines. The Nepali government hosted post-mountaineering events at the end of mountaineering season, honouring the most recent Everest Summiteers in a formal procession through the streets of Kathmandu. A vernacular term, Everest Summiteer, appeared to signal a kind of social currency in élite communities in Kathmandu much like, as I would recognize later, the linked category 'world-class mountaineer' has exchange value within cosmopolitan, adventure-travel circles in North America.[8] Nepali men showed me their long climbing resumés highlighting their multiple Everest ascents as a means of demonstrating, possibly, their Sherpaness, an identity forged through mimetic relations with foreigners and foreigners' images of what Sherpas should be (Adams 1996: 208).

Within a mode of local ethnography produced through racialized anthropological, touristic and mountaineering discourses and nationalist geographies, Sherpas are rendered 'a timeless people living in remote region of the world' (Carrier 1992: 70). The Nepali media essentially constructed the Nepali women's expedition in 2000 in these terms as well. In an article from a tourist industry newsletter, the women are described as 'simple hill folk with unparalleled mountaineering skills' (Strestha 2000). That Lhakpa Sherpa was 'born in a yak shed' in the 'shadow' of Mount Everest (or Sagarmatha, the Nepali name) is highlighted in other articles. The point I want to emphasize is that in the context of these multiple processes of localization the rendering of the women as global subjects, through the language and imagery on the brochure, stood out as a discrepant representation. I struggled to make sense of the globalist discourse within a localizing framework where the Nepali women were not seen as 'world mountaineers' by virtue of their gender, class and ethnicity (they were 'poor, ethnic women' by all number of accounts) and from what I observed as a lack of participation and marginalization in mountaineering. In a local ethnography I upheld 'global' and 'local' as separate categories rather than as relational and fluid scales of meaning and subject positions.

There are other means by which I comprehended these data, yet my contingent locations and travels as an ethnographer-tourist within particular transnational circuits enabled me to make what I see as critical conceptual linkages between the local and global. As Bamford has pointed out, in framing our accounts in terms of an opposition between 'the global' and 'the local' we 'fail to capture what is meaningful to participants about these processes' (1997: 110). 'What constitutes the global is often made up of conflicting meanings and dialogues: it is the way these divergent flows get negotiated and worked out on the ground that gives these dialogues their particular cultural content' (ibid.). I provide two brief examples here of how and when I was able to grasp what Bamford describes, through what I now see as 'lucky breaks' taking place within overlapping discourses and locales situated at the intersection of a local mode of ethnography and global worlds.

The first example illustrates how, through unforeseen circumstances, I was practically forced to recognize global/local linkages that played out in an event that brought two of my 'fields' together in a rare exchange. That chance encounter also prompted me to reconsider the nature of immersion. As part of my multi-sited research strategy, I planned to study how Himalayan mountaineering spaces and subjectivities were produced at international mountaineering cultural events in Canada through films, books, talks and multi-media presentations, sites of expressly globalizing mountaineering discourses (Frohlick 2003). After returning from Nepal I was aware of the paucity of news about Nepali climbers in Canada, in particular Lhakpa Sherpa but also Babu Chirri Sherpa, a Nepali climber who gained considerable fame in Nepal in 2000 for his speed ascent of Everest. While attending an event at the Banff Centre for Mountain Culture in Canada, I was surprised to see Babu's name on the programme and to bump into him within a space occupied almost exclusively by a white, North American and European, middle-class, outdoorsy, 'adventure traveller' crowd. During our conversation, he told me that he had flown up to Canada while in the United States doing some work with one of his mountaineering expedition sponsors, an American mountaineering equipment company. He was as much a 'globe-trotter' as the rest of the speakers and audience members, many of whom had travelled from elsewhere for this event. In spite of his mobility, as the only Nepali participant in a multi-day event that discussed the universal and fantastic appeal of the Himalayas as a world mountaineering adventure sport destination, he was placed outside of the global discourse. Rather, the dialogue focused on his Everest pursuits while the other panellists (both male, one from Canada and one from Poland) spoke about their 'worldly' climbing experiences on seven continents, a dialogue which effectively circumscribed his subjectivity as a 'local climber' while enabling the other speakers to enact global subject positions. Babu's appearance (which I was told was a late addition) brought about an exchange of meaning over local and global: Western mountaineers were placed on an expansive scale as 'world mountaineers', a Nepali mountaineer was relegated as 'Everest climber' to his native locality, and an interlocutory international audience was, in my view, complicit with these geopolitical economies of scale and mobility.

I was witness to an interlocution that involved someone from my field-site in Nepal showing up in my field-site in Canada, somewhat by chance. With Babu there, I was displaced from a local mode of ethnography and relocated at the fulcrum of two diffuse worlds where the global and local were actively being worked out and enacted. (For example, Babu both resisted and embraced being circumscribed to the local.) What does this have to do with the Nepali women's expedition and 'millennium women' brochure? In seeing how the Nepali climber was framed by the audience and festival organizers in Canada in terms of locality and lack of mobility in relation to the mobile, global, Western climbers, I was able to see clearly the cultural contingencies of discourses of travel and mobility. 'Everest Summiteer', 'new millennium women', 'world mountaineer' – each term was an interconnected but not homogeneous 'globe-making project' (Tsing 2000) as much as a process of localization, and an enactment of culturally bound mobility in place.

Moreover, within this space I came to recognize that 'immersion' is not necessarily achieved through sustained conversation in a single locale but can be realized, however serendipitously, by placing oneself in the overlapping circuits of social relations and exchanges embodied – and strived for – by our research subjects. I build here on critiques such as Amit's, who argues:

> The notion of immersion implies that the 'field' which ethnographers enter exists as an
> independently bounded set of relationships and activities which is autonomous of the

fieldwork through which it is discovered. Yet in a world of infinite interconnections and overlapping contexts, the ethnographic field cannot simply exist, awaiting discovery. It has to be laboriously constructed ... the construction of an ethnographic field involves efforts to accommodate and interweave sets of relationships and engagements developed in one context with those arising in another. (2000: 10)

Therefore, the issue of immersion is not one of how much time to spend in one locale or with one group of people. Rather, the key question asks: how do our research subjects immerse themselves in 'tough transnational spaces' (Stoller 1997: 91) and networks, networks that can be challenging to access for both the ethnographer and his/her research subject in what Appadurai has called 'the ineluctable globalization of experience' (1997: 118)?

My second example picks up on these concerns that we share with our research subjects. I came to this recognition during an interview in Kathmandu with Lhakpa Sherpa, the one woman on the Nepali women's expedition who reached the summit. In this example, the shift was not from one geographical locale to another but, rather, a conceptual shift derived from my research subject's narrative in which she actively constructs herself in explicitly mobile terms. I had bumped into Lhakpa Sherpa at a few events in Kathmandu in the aftermath of her widely successful ascent – she had been invited to numerous speaking engagements and felicitations in her honour, to which I was invited, once again, as a foreign journalist. I saw many of these events as localizing practices and performances of nation building set amidst the global arena of Everest. Her narrative, translated for me by her *sirdar* (head guide), echoed for the most part the localizing discourses I read in the newspapers, which underscored her identity as a 'poor, ethnic woman with little education who grew up driving her father's yaks and listening to her brother's mountaineering stories in the shadow of Everest' (for example, see Strestha 2000). I viewed her as a young Sherpani marginalized by her ethnicity, gender and national identity in an international race to reach the top of Mount Everest against much wealthier (and more 'cosmopolitan') privileged women from the United States, Scotland, Poland and Spain. Near the end of the interview, she recounted to me her recent experience as an airline passenger. She told me that the flight to Kathmandu for a speaking tour immediately following her Everest climb was one of the first times she had been on an aeroplane, and that the height had frightened her. While she was not afraid of climbing Mount Everest, she was nervous about flying, she said, because it was new to her.

Despite the detailing of her history of travel to me, her story of travelling as a young girl in the Himalayan region with her father's yaks and her climbing adventures in Nepal and elsewhere, it was Lhapka's story about embarking on a plane for speaking engagements around Nepal as an Everest Summiteer that registered for me. Air travel is seen as a quintessential contemporary modality of mobility and interconnectedness (Urry 2000: 63). Lhapka's new mode of cosmopolitanism, i.e. plane travel, led me to question the kinds of mobility that were actually made possible and enacted through mountain climbing for Nepali women in the new millennium. Rather than dismiss the rhetoric of the brochure, I now saw it as a mode through which globality is not only defined and authorized but also mobilized as a desire and a dream (recall the language of the brochure, and the image of the cheerleader) as well as a practice.

Moreover, as an interlocutor in a transnational exchange of power, where I was situated as someone who could possibly tell her story to an audience beyond the borders of Nepal, I was caught up in Lhapka's ongoing negotiation of her location within the emergent global economy of Nepal. Like her predecessor, Pasang Lhamu Sherpa, Lhakpa used the press to gain access to networks that could help her realize her ambitions. Her aeroplane narrative led me to reconsider how she might be, following Freeman (2001), 'enacting new modes of globalization'. Rather than a 'third-world woman defined outside of globalization' (through the Nepali media and an interview with an anthropologist), she might be seen instead 'as the very fabric of globalization' (ibid.: 1009). While Lhakpa engaged in older histories of travel as a mountain climber in Nepal, at the same time she embodied radically new travel practices. She climbed Everest not as a paid labourer, as her brothers have done, but as a sponsored recreational climber, thus embodying a small minority and recent subjectivity in Nepal (Thapa 2000). The speaking tours to which she was invited, the parties she attended in Kathmandu along with mountaineers and journalists from all over the world, her air travel from town to town, and her desires to go climbing outside of Nepal (which were realized next year, when she climbed Everest from the Chinese side) are all part of the new travel practices opened up by her successful negotiation within the opportunistic spaces and 'global worlds' of Himalayan mountaineering. Her desires to climb Everest were fuelled by her position within a set of transnational relations and connections, such that meeting Sir Edmund Hillary and crossing paths with foreign women climbers in the course of her life as a yak herder for her father's business provided the imaginary grist for her childhood dreams. Climbing Himalayan mountains is part of the everyday, physical mobility of many Nepalis' lives, especially the men, whereas boarding a plane as a 'tourist' and a globe-trotting sponsored athlete is an entirely new, and not all together anomalous, mode of mobility for Nepali women.[9]

Conclusion: Location and Immersion in Ethnographies of Mobility

Location and immersion thus play an important role in ethnographies of mobility. Just as anthropologists attempt to gate-crash, gain rapport, exchange information to reciprocate favours and negotiate their access to circuits of information and people, so too do research subjects whose lives and mobilities are not so disconnected from our own. In order to be part of a number of necessary circuits, mountain climbers involved in high-altitude mountaineering, where permits alone can cost US $10,000, need to get past gatekeepers. *Sirdars* have considerable power in Nepal, for example, to hire the high- altitude porters and guides, where the most money is to be made (and the most risk taken). Having a *sirdar* for an uncle is one of the most advantageous ways in, but befriending such a person can also help land a job on an expedition to Everest. The media also play a crucial (although complicated) role in garnering sponsorship.

The question posed by ethnographers concerning the mobility of their research subjects, particularly in the area of tourist and tourism studies, is not so much an issue of how to talk to and hang out with tourists and other mobile subjects. Rather, the issue is one of extending our understanding of the emergence of new global subjects and subjectivities by working against the grain of normative, binary categories of travel, such as tourist (mobile) and local (stationary), which come about in part through moving out of a localizing ethnography and finding ourselves where disruptions of these formulations occur. Appadurai has framed this slightly differently: '[G]lobalization is not ultimately a problem of technique, either for anthropologists or for anybody else. It is a challenge to the imagination and to our ethical selves, as we try to speak for and about people who cannot square the experience of globalization with the ineluctable globalization of experience' (1997: 118). I have attempted to explore this issue by asking how this creativity and disruption are achieved methodologically. Kaplan too has posed this question. She states:

> Transnational subjects are produced through location as well as mobility, certainly, as national economies dictate who moves to obtain work and who stays put. ... If there are new consumer subjects, new methodologies are required to understand them. Electronic workers or domestic workers in transit for work purposes do not have to be viewed entirely separate from tourists or other kinds of travelers. ... I am not arguing that the monied tourist is the same subject as the migrant worker or that the phone worker is the same subject as the conference goer. But a theorization of travel as a Foucauldian field with diverse points in tension with one another or even as a continuum with an origin and a discrete itinerary of sites rather than as the older binary of this versus that may engender more plural subjects. (Kaplan 2002: 41)

The quick answer to the question, 'Must we now engage in multi-sited projects that reflect the mobilities and expanded agencies of those whom we study?' is yes.[10] I have come around to answering the question through a complicated explanation. Our own multiple locations and contingent travel practices have always been constitutive of fieldwork (Passaro 1997). Our 'shifting locations' and our mobility, particularly as ethnographer-tourists, can work to our advantage (Gupta and Ferguson 1997). Thinking of how we place ourselves and are placed in our fieldsites, how we embody the fulcrum of overlapping discourses and circuits of information and people (Amit 2000), might be a useful starting place for analyses of global/local processes. Rather than mourn the loss of long-term immersion (as it is no longer tenable, for a variety of reasons), it may be more productive to rethink how immersion is constituted, not only by ourselves as individual fieldworkers but by our research subjects who are also trying to place themselves and negotiate their locations in various overlapping and disparate worlds and circuits. Moving from site to site allowed me to observe and engage with how subjects were placed through local and extra-local processes and practices, including anthropological concepts, and to grasp how it is that 'mobility' is culturally embedded, specific and strived for. I was challenged to think of 'cosmopolitanism' and 'tourist', two weighty terms signalling ethnocentric notions of travel, as diverse, plural subjectivities. In trying to come to terms with 'a world in motion', Amit has argued, 'we cannot disconnect ourselves from our lives to live our fieldwork, just as our subjects cannot disconnect themselves from the world and their pursuits to engage with or to be abandoned by us' (2000: 16). How do our research subjects find 'immersion' in any number of circuits they imagine and desire to be part of? I have found that immersion and location are of importance to the women with whom I did my research. I suggest we think about immersion not only as an issue for anthropologists but also as part of the wider problem of discrepant mobilities. A multi-sited ethnography open to serendipitous encounters, not merely a multiplication of sites (Amit 2000; Trouillot 2003), may be useful if anthropology is to capture some of this difficulty.

Notes

1. I have borrowed 'rendering and gendering' from Weston (1996).
2. I have demonstrated elsewhere how Nepalis negotiate 'the global' through a variety of local practices in Nepal, seeking identification as key players on the global stage of Everest (Frohlick 2003), for example. I have also shown how 'the global' and 'the local' are scales through which different representations of Nepali mountaineers are produced by various media (Frohlick 2004).
3. I use the term 'Nepali' except where 'Nepalese' is used in a direct quote.
4. See the webpage of the state-affiliated Nepal Tourism Board for an example (www.welcomenepal.com).
5. There were women from the United States, Poland, Scotland and Spain, as well as Nepal, climbing Everest in the spring of 2000.
6. See Ortner (1998) for a discussion of how ethnic Sherpas have come to be associated and even conflated with the occupation of mountaineering portering – the term 'Sherpa' has come to mean a Nepali mountain guide.
7. I use 'cosmopolitan' here in the sense of apparent worldliness or demonstrable international mobility or interest in the world at large. I recognize that

others (for example, Breckenridge et al. 2002) deploy the term in a much more nuanced sense, and ultimately my own recognition of plural cosmopolitanisms as multiple embodiments and discourses of worldliness has been helpful to my analyses of the production of mountaineering worlds (see Frohlick 2002).

8. Nepali climbers are celebrated outside of Nepal too, but at the same time they are either rooted to Mount Everest or their accomplishments are downscaled for climbing 'only' Mount Everest. I write about the linked terms 'Everest Summiteer' and 'world-class mountaineer' elsewhere (Frohlick 2003).

9. Lhapka Sherpa has gone on to climb Everest numerous times and has taken up residency in the United States with her American husband.

10. This question is quoted from the ASA 2004 conference abstract written by the conveners, Simon Coleman and Peter Collins.

References

Adams, V. (1992), 'Tourism and Sherpas, Nepal: Reconstruction of Reciprocity', *Annals of Tourism Research* 19 (3): 534—54.

Adams, V. (1996), *Tigers of the Snow and Other Virtual Sherpas: An Ethnography of Himalayan Encounters*, Princeton: Princeton University Press.

Amit, V. (2000), 'Introduction: Constructing the Field', in V. Amit (ed.), *Constructing the Field: Ethnographic Fieldwork in the Contemporary World*, New York: Routledge.

Appadurai, A. (1997), 'Fieldwork in the Era of Globalization', *Anthropology and Humanism* 22 (1): 115–18.

Bamford, S. (1997), 'Beyond the Global: Intimacy and Distance in Contemporary Fieldwork', *Anthropology and Humanism* 22 (1): 110–14.

Besio, K. (2003), 'Steppin' in it: Postcoloniality in Northern Pakistan', *Area* 25 (1): 24-33.

Breckenridge, C., Pollock, S., Bhabha, H. and Chakrabarty, D. (eds) (2002), *Cosmopolitanism*, Durham, NC: Duke University Press.

Bruner, E. (1995), 'The Ethnographer/Tourist in Indonesia', in M.F. Lanfant, J. Allcock and E. Bruner (eds), *International Tourism: Identity and Change*, London: Sage.

Carrier, J. (1992), 'Gatekeepers of the Himalaya', *National Geographic* 182 (6): 70–89.

Clifford, J. (1997), *Routes: Travel and Translation in the Late Twentieth Century*, Cambridge, MA: Harvard University Press.

Dubin, J. (2003), 'Lucky 13', *Outside*, May: 33.

Freeman, C. (2001) 'Is Local:Global as Feminine:Masculine? Rethinking the Gender of Globalization', *Signs: Journal of Women in Culture and Society* 26 (4): 1007–37.

Frohlick, S. (2002), 'A World of Mountaineering: The Transnationality of Mount Everest and Other High Himalayan Spaces', unpublished thesis, York University, Toronto.

Frohlick, S. (2003), 'Negotiating "the Global" within the Global Playscapes of Mount Everest', *The Canadian Review of Sociology and Anthropology* 40 (5): 525–42.

Frohlick, S. (2004), ' "Who is Lhakpa Sherpa?" Circulating Subjectivities within the Local/Global Terrain of Himalayan Mountaineering', *Social and Cultural Geography* 5 (2): 195–212.

Gupta, A. and Ferguson, J. (1997), 'Discipline and Practice: "The Field" as Site, Method, and Location in Anthropology', in A. Gupta and J. Ferguson (eds), *Anthropological Locations: Boundaries and Ground of a Field Science*, Berkeley: University of California Press.

Hansen, P. (2000), 'Confetti of Empire: The Conquest of Everest in Nepal, India, Britain, and New Zealand', *Comparative Study of Society and History* 42: 307–32.

Hepburn, S. (2002), 'Tourist Forms of Life in Nepal', *Annals of Tourism Research* 29 (3): 611–30.

Kaplan, C. (2002), 'Transporting the Subject: Technologies of Mobility and Location in an Era of Globalization', *PMLA* 117 (1): 32–42.

Lieberman, M. (1993), 'Scott, Amundsen, and Pasang Lhamu', *Himal*, July/Aug.: 7.

Liechty, M. (1996), 'Kathmandu as Translocality: Multiple Places in a Nepali Space', in P. Yaeger (ed.), *The Geography of Identity*, Ann Arbor: University of Michigan Press.

Liechty, M. (1997), 'Selective Exclusion: Foreigners, Foreign Goods, and Foreignness in Modern Nepali History', *Studies in Nepali History and Society* 2 (1): 5–68.

Marcus, G. (1998), *Ethnography through Thick and Thin*, Princeton: Princeton University Press.

Morin, K., Longhurst, R. and Johnston, L. (2001), '(Troubling) Spaces of Mountains and Men: New Zealand's Mount Cook and Hermitage Lodge', *Social and Cultural Geography* 2: 117–39.

Ortner, S. (1998), 'The Making and Self-Making of "the Sherpas" in Early Himalayan Mountaineering', *Studies in Nepali History and Society* 3 (1): 1–34.

Ortner, S. (1999), *Life and Death on Mount Everest: Sherpas and Himalayan Mountaineering*, Princeton: Princeton University Press.

Passaro, J. (1997), ' "You Can't Take the Subway to the Field!" "Village" Epistemologies in the Global Village', in A. Gupta and J. Ferguson (eds), *Anthropological Locations: Boundaries and Ground of a Field Science*, Berkeley: University of California Press.

Stoller, P. (1997), 'Globalizing Method: The Problems of Doing Ethnography in Transnational Spaces', *Anthropology and Humanism* 22 (1): 81–94.

Strestha, S. (2000), 'Nepalese Women Successful in Scaling Mt. Everest', *Nepal Travel Trade Reporter* 3 (12): 13.

Thapa, D. (1995), 'Fame Still Eludes Sherpas', *Himal*, Sept.–Oct.: 50–1.

Thapa, D. (2000), 'The Climber is Nepali', *Himal*, Aug.: 20–2.

Trouillot, M. (2003), *Global Transformations: Anthropology and the Modern World*, New York: Palgrave Macmillan.

Tsing, A. (2000), 'The Global Situation', *Cultural Anthropology* 15 (3): 327–60.

Urry, J. (2000), *Sociology Beyond Society: Mobilities for the Twenty-First Century*, New York: Routledge.

Weston, K. (1996), *Render Me, Gender Me: Lesbians Talk Sex, Class, Color, Nation, Studmuffins ...*, New York: Columbia University Press.

–5–

Post-Diasporic Indian Communities: A New Generation

Anjoom Mukadam and Sharmina Mawani

Introduction

This chapter examines the ways in which academics and the media continue to use terminology that acts against the interests of minority ethnic communities in the West. On the one hand there is talk of pluralism, integration, acceptance and tolerance; on the other hand there are antiquated labels imposed on individuals from these communities. For instance, terms such as 'immigrant' and 'diaspora' are still regularly deployed in reference to individuals who have been born and brought up in the West and have made no journey from any supposed 'homeland'. In order to accept fully these individuals into the multi-ethnic societies in which they live, there is an urgent need for this terminology to be dropped and for its significance to be understood. More generally, the question of what the terms 'British' or 'English' mean has been put under scrutiny, especially in light of the events of 11 September 2001 in the United States and 7 July 2005 in Britain.

In order to ground our argument, we explore the shaping of a distinct identity amongst second-generation Nizari Ismaili Muslims of Gujarati ancestry in London and Toronto. The formation of identity amongst individuals from minority ethnic communities is a complex phenomenon, comprising the amalgamation of components which are of the individual's own selection and others over which he or she has no choice, but around which he or she must construct meaning. It is clear in today's multi-ethnic societies that ethnic identity may not be straightforward and that there exist multiple identities, hyphenated identities and maybe even new identities that are evolving with globalization. This chapter will look closely at ethnic self-identification (a label chosen by an individual to express his or her individual ethnic identity) and cultural adaptation strategies (lifestyle choices made by an individual who is living in the West, but who belongs to a minority ethnic community) employed by second-generation Nizari Ismaili Muslims of Gujarati ancestry, in order to make sense of their bilingual and bicultural lives.

Current social processes are changing the ways in which fields are defined, and the locus of ethnography appears to have shifted so as to include those communities that have been party to transnational movements. Traditionally, anthropology has had a methodological focus on single-site ethnography; however, in light of globalization and increased transnational migration of peoples and cultures, there has been a move towards multi-sited ethnography. 'Locality' has also had to be modified so as to include the multiple sites of those who migrated, as in the case of the South Asian diaspora; but there is now a crisis where locality is concerned for those of the second and subsequent generations who see themselves as the product of the locality in which they were born and raised. We would suggest that ethnography has an important role to play in the study of 'new' single-sited localities which have been created by emerging and evolving communities that are now located in new fixed geographic locations.

Our own studies of the Nizari Ismaili Muslim communities in both London and Toronto involved the use of quantitative and qualitative research tools. It is argued that qualitative research is closely related to ethnography, which involves detailed study based on observation of a particular community (Marsh 2000). There has been much debate as to the place of 'insiders' in conducting research on their own communities (Bhatti 1999; Brah 1996; Hussain 2000; Mukadam 2003). In agreement with Brah (1996), we would posit that there are in fact benefits to this type of insider research owing to the insiders' own first-hand knowledge through direct experience. Neuman explains the way in which the process of participant observation requires the researcher to climb up a series of rungs on an access ladder, ultimately permitting access to otherwise closed spaces:

> A researcher begins at the bottom rung, where access is easy and where he or she is an outsider looking for public information. The next rung requires increased access. Once close on-site observation begins, he or she becomes a passive observer. … With time in the field, the researcher observes specific activities that are potentially sensitive or seeks clarification of what he or she sees or hears. Reaching this access rung is more difficult. Finally, the researcher may try to shape interaction so that it reveals specific information, or he or she may want to see highly sensitive material. This highest rung of the access ladder is rarely attained and requires deep trust. (2003: 373)

In the case of insiders the highest rung of access is in most cases almost immediately attainable due to their longstanding social networks with members of the community being researched. In addition, there is tacit knowledge relating to the rites and rituals which are particularly pertinent when conducting ethnography (Mawani 2006). Conventional methods of fieldwork need to be more flexible and allow for insider perspectives in order to gain access to closed communities, which may otherwise remain under-researched.

Trials and Tribulations

The presence of 'others' in the West can be traced back over generations, resulting in the diversity that forms the mosaic of today's plural societies. Mass migration took place at the end of the Second World War and the most pronounced labour shortages were to be found in areas where the work was low-paid, had low status, unsocial working hours and offered poor working conditions. Brah and Shaw indicate that the position of the migrants to Britain, for example, was very different to that of the local population: 'During the economic boom of the 1950s and 1960s, it was comparatively easy for the white workers to secure better paid jobs or obtain places on skilled apprenticeships and training schemes' (1992: 8). The myth that migrant workers had taken away jobs from the indigenous population can therefore be dispelled. Racial exclusionism and intense hostility were to haunt the lives of many South Asians who had left their homeland in search of a brighter future. These individuals were economic migrants who had secured temporary employment with no long-term plans to stay in the country once their objectives had been met. However, as the years passed the number of immigrants of South Asian origin increased and they began forming their own communities, retaining unity through their regional culture, language and kinship ties (Desai 1963). For the majority there was never a question of putting down roots and creating a new home. This sentiment is exemplified in a recent article by Lord Parekh: 'I came to Britain expecting to return to India in about three years time. I could not have been more wrong' (Parekh 2005: 9). The migrants' image of the homeland was one of nostalgia and idealism, and as the years progressed and communication with their past diminished, so did the 'myth of return' (Anwar 1979). No longer sojourners, they began to form roots in the West. Their children who were born and/or brought up in the West are now facing profound changes in terms of their ethnicity. No longer 'outsiders', they are undergoing a process of change and adaptation, culturally, linguistically and in terms of their identity.

The first generation came to the West as immigrants and were treated as such, their country of origin being India or East Africa. Rushdie in his book *Imaginary Homelands* writes about his own position in Britain as a first-generation Indian: 'Our identity is at once plural and partial. Sometimes we feel that we straddle two cultures; at other times, that we fall between two stools' (1992: 15). It is these very phrases that have been used, and in our opinion, wrongly, to describe the second generation. They have been categorized as being 'between two cultures' (Anwar 1975; Watson 1977) and, more inappropriately, as 'the half-way generation' (Taylor 1976) which subscribes to the 'melting pot' ideal of assimilation formulated by Glazer and Moynihan (1970) in the United States, predicting that the third generation will be completely assimilated. We would conclude that this is not the case; there in fact appears to be a fusion of East and West, which supports the view of Nielsen that 'young people who are living in and with both cultures ... are beginning to create a functional synthesis of both' (2000: 116).

Outdated Terminology

Historically, outsiders were more often than not classified in relation to the majority as the minority or ethnic minority, and to distinguish them further they were commonly described as 'coloured'. It would seem that this terminology was considered, at that time, appropriate by the majority community. Migrants can be conceptualized in a variety of ways: they can be described as foreigners, aliens, immigrants, by their national or ethnic origins, religious affiliation and many other attributes. The terminology used is largely dependent on the political and cultural traditions of the country in which they are living, and later on whether these individuals accept or reject such labelling. They are termed *Ausländer* in Germany, *immigrés* in France and ethnic minorities or *etnische minderheden* in Britain and the Netherlands, respectively (Parekh 2001). The second generation were born and/or brought up in the West and the terminology 'immigrant', 'outsider' and 'foreigner' cannot be used to describe their position in this now permanently multi-cultural society (Anwar 1998). The West is their home, yet they struggle with some of the same issues faced by their parents and compound those with issues of identity and culture conflict. Catherine Ballard tries to give a reason for this conflict: 'While synthesising aspects of both Asian and British culture some Asians seem to be reacting to the rejection they experience from British society by taking renewed pride in their separate cultural identity' (1979: 127). Second-generation Indians in the West have been pigeon-holed by some academics into this ambiguous position of being neither here nor there, confused and maybe even lost. South Asian communities in the West are frequently referred to as a 'diaspora', a population that is considered 'deterritorialized' or 'transnational', whose cultural origins are in another land (Vertovec 2000). Mukadam questions the use of terminology that is commonly used in discourse relating to the second and third generation:

> It appears that the word 'diaspora', like the word 'immigrant', is no longer being used to refer to the first generation and continues to be used when making reference to the second generation and beyond. If the word 'diaspora' refers to those whose cultural origins are in a different land, then how far back do these communities have to go before they are recognised as belonging to the new homeland or will academics and others always refer to them in relation to a past with which many, at best, have symbolic links? (2003: 96)

Rex (2002), amongst others, argues that the term 'diaspora' is misleading and prefers to use the term 'transnational'. The term is another way of focusing on difference as opposed to commonality. Beverley McLachlin, Chief Justice of Canada, asked in the fourth annual LaFontaine-Baldwin lecture in March 2003, 'Why, despite our manifest commonality, do our differences, real and perceived, tend to define our world and dominate our discourse and our conduct?' (McLachlin 2003). These individuals whose ancestry lies in the Indian subcontinent are still commonly referred to as members of the South Asian diaspora (Hanlon and Withington 1999; Younge 2000) or, worse still, as second-generation immigrants (Wainwright 2002). These labels are unacceptable as they are simply a means of reinforcing difference and go against the vision of full participation and acceptance of all individuals in society irrespective of their ancestry.

Following the launch of the journal *Diaspora,* Safran's (1991) characterization of diasporic communities has cemented the meaning of this term. Safran's definition of 'diaspora' consists of five main features: first, dispersal of a community from an original centre to at least two further locations; second, maintenance of a myth in relation to their homeland; third, belief of alienation and lack of acceptance in the country to which they migrated; fourth, ability to envisage returning to their homeland at some future point in time; and, fifth, dedication to a continuing relationship with this homeland. It appears that Safran's intention was to provide a descriptive definition for first-generation individuals of minority ethnic communities whose trajectories are very different from their children and grandchildren. However, many academics continue to use the term 'diaspora' in a heuristic manner (Fortier 2000; Gilroy 1993), thus ignoring Clifford's (1994) warning against the universalization of the term. For the purposes of our research on second-generation Nizari Ismaili Muslims of Gujarati ancestry in London and Toronto we are in favour of a descriptive definition so as to clearly delineate between those who participated in the process of migration and those who have not undertaken any form of migration. Second and subsequent generations have been born into two cultures, that of their ancestors and the majority culture in which they reside, be it London or Toronto. Our findings will highlight the manner in which these individuals are exhibiting varying patterns of ethnic self-identification and acculturation.

If Safran's (1991) criteria are used to establish whether or not second-generation Nizari Ismaili Muslims of Gujarati ancestry born and brought up in the West are members of a 'diaspora', then it is quite clear that they do not share these features. In fact, we would posit that by positioning them as members of a diasporic community, academics are in fact jeopardizing their full integration into their only homeland, the one in which they were born. We propose five defining characteristics of post-diasporic individuals: first, they have not participated in any form of voluntary or forced migration leading to permanent settlement outside country of birth; second, they consider their country of birth as their homeland; third, they hold the conviction that they are full and equal citizens in their country of birth;

fourth, they do not envisage migration to and permanent settlement in an ancestral homeland; and, finally, they show loyalty to and are active participants in their country of birth. We shall use the term 'post-diasporic' to refer to second-generation Indians as they have not themselves participated in any form of migration and are the offspring of those who made the journey. In an interview with Mukadam, Lord Parekh discussed multiculturalism and the pathways open to the South Asian community living in Britain:

> *Lord Parekh*: Everyone knows we are here to stay … the question is not of throwing [the South Asian Community] out but the question rather is of having them as controlled outsiders within society … or brought in on terms set by the mainstream society – in other words, either total assimilation or controlled ghettoization. They are the only two options. Expelling them is not an option, they have nowhere to go and in any case the British wouldn't accept it … the wealth of public opinion wouldn't accept it.
>
> *Mukadam*: So basically those are our two options? Either we assimilate …
>
> *Lord Parekh*: Either we assimilate or we are ghettoized or we persuade the society that there is a third option.
>
> *Mukadam*: So there is a third option?
>
> *Lord Parekh*: From [the South Asian community's] point of view 'No!', but we have to create a space for the third option and I think … we will develop a common culture which is based on the language which we share … we would create a composite culture which is born out of the long British historical experience of the world as we know it. Just as one talks about defining British identity in non-Greek terms, non-English, non-White manner, one would also talk about defining a British culture in a manner which is good for us – I have written a great deal about this in my book *Re-thinking Multiculturalism*. What you need is a multiculturally constituted common culture. Likewise, if you look at the United States – the culture they have created has a Jewish contribution, the Irish contribution, the Black contribution and from all that you create the kind of culture … which is not merely the lowest common denominator, but one which is very complex with its own different idioms and strands. In other words, it's an orchestra where you have to play upon many instruments simultaneously to be part of the whole … we have to open up this society so that there is a third alternative. (Mukadam 2003: 6–7)

We will show through further discussion that the maintenance of aspects of Indian culture by second-generation Nizari Ismaili Muslims of Gujarati ancestry is in fact an appreciation of their rich heritage which does not amount to a diasporic imagination; rather, it is the formation of a 'new ethnicity' that incorporates aspects of the culture of their ancestors, combined with that of the land in which they were born – a hybrid culture and identity that is their defining characteristic.

Troubled Times

Until recently, the religion of Islam was not an issue of very great concern to the general public residing in the West. However, most were aware that it was a religion whose foundations were based in the Middle East and its adherents prayed five times a day in mosques, identifiable by tall pillar-like structures known as minarets. Media coverage of Islam was minimal, yet reports of the annual *hajj* (pilgrimage) to Mecca, with photos highlighting the rituals performed around the *Kaaba*,[1] found their way into living rooms around the world. Those unfamiliar with Islam were at least able to name celebrity Muslims, like Cassius Clay, better known as Muhammad Ali, or Cat Stevens, now Yusuf Islam. Nevertheless, Muslims, like members of other minority ethnic and religious communities, faced discrimination in all walks of life – not because of their religion, but because of the colour of their skin (Mukadam and Mawani 2005b). Sabrina, Rashida and Shafik, second-generation British Nizari Ismaili Muslims of Gujarati descent, illustrate the various forms of discrimination they encountered:

> *Sabrina* (Female Respondent, London): There's a lot of it [discrimination] now, very hidden but apparent. ... Even though I work in an equal opportunities environment, it's very evident that I am looked upon as a stranger. ... I can feel there are opportunities at the moment that I am going for ... and there are other white British going for those as well and they're given much more of a lead and clues ... and much more help, whereas I have to struggle, I have to find the information out myself.
>
> *Rashida* (Female Respondent, London): It was a kid, I was an Indian teacher, so he called me a 'Paki' just to see if he could irritate me.
>
> *Shafik* (Male Respondent, London): I don't know, maybe you're standing in a group or whatever and somebody comes along and you know speaks to everyone in the group apart from you. Which could either be random or you think, 'why didn't you speak to me?' (Mukadam 2003:148–9)

The events of 11 September 2001 propelled discrimination to new heights, which were predominantly based on religious grounds. Muslims, or anyone whose appearance suggested they could be Muslim, were deemed as terrorists who saw the West as Satan and were eager to become suicide bombers in order to demolish it. Infamous personalities like Osama bin Laden and Saddam Hussein came to be seen as official Islamic leaders, and the global Muslim community was falsely accused of condoning their actions and complying with their commands. *Hijab*-adorned women were seen as oppressed victims of physical, emotional and verbal abuse – actions that some in the West claimed were promoted by the religion of Islam (Chandarana 2001; Mukadam and Mawani 2005b). The media played an important role in portraying a negative image of Muslims, with public figures like Robert Kilroy-Silk (2004) justifying hatred towards Arab Muslims:

We are told by some of the more hysterical critics of the war on terror that 'it is destroying the Arab world'. So? ... Few of them [Arab countries] make much contribution to the welfare of the rest of the world. Indeed, apart from oil – which was discovered, is produced and paid for by the West – what do they contribute? Can you think of anything? Anything really useful? Anything really valuable? Something we really need, could not do without? No, nor can I.

Meanwhile, Pat Robertson (2002), a Christian televangelist and host of the Christian news and television talk show *The 700 Club*, disseminated fraudulent Islamic beliefs and practices:

This is worse than the Nazis. Adolf Hitler was bad, but what the Muslims want to do to the Jews is worse ... the so-called 'doves' in America will criticize anybody who says anything against Islam, including me, if I say something that Islam is an erroneous religion, I get criticized by the Anti-Defamation League ... when are you guys going to open your eyes and see who your enemy is? Those people want to destroy Jews. The Koran teaches that the end of the world will not come until every Jew is killed by the Muslims. The Muslims must eliminate every single Jew before there will be a final conclusion of this world and the next kingdom comes into being. That is taught in the Koran, plus the fact, they are like apes and pigs. This is not exactly conducive to peace and brotherhood.

Rabiah Ahmed, a spokeswoman for the Council on American–Islamic Relations (CAIR), expressed the way in which these stereotypical views of Muslims were being propagated by the media: 'There aren't any positive or even neutral portrayals of Muslims on TV; whenever Muslims or Arabs are portrayed it is always in a stereotypical way' (*Journal of Turkish Weekly* 2005).

A small minority of politicians and citizens have taken it upon themselves to attempt to educate the public about the various interpretations of Islam. On a visit to the Ottawa Central Mosque on 21 September 2001, former Canadian Prime Minister Jean Chrétien sympathized with Canadian Muslims and confirmed his support for Muslims and the religion of Islam:

I know that the days since September 11, 2001 have been ones of great sadness and anxiety for Muslims across Canada. Because the cold-blooded killers who committed the atrocities in New York and Washington invoked the name and words of Islam as justification. ... I want to stand by your side today. And to reaffirm with you that Islam has nothing to do with the mass murder that was planned and carried out by the terrorists. ... Like all faiths Islam is about peace. About justice. And about harmony among all people. And I sense your sadness at the way that a great world religion has been unjustly smeared by this evil. Above all I want to stand by your side to condemn the acts of intolerance and hatred that have been committed against your community since the attack. ... As I have said, this is a struggle against terrorism, not against any faith or community. I say today, once again, that we are all Canadians. We stand together as one against this evil. We grieve together as a family. As one nation we defy the twisted philosophy of the terrorists. And shoulder to shoulder we will pursue the struggle for justice. (Chrétien 2001)

British Prime Minister Tony Blair also shared his positive viewpoint on Islam at the Labour Party Conference on 2 October 2001:

When we act to bring to account those that committed the atrocity of September 11, we do so, not out of bloodlust. We do so because it is just. We do not act against Islam. The true followers of Islam are our brothers and sisters in this struggle. Bin Laden is no more obedient to the proper teaching of the Koran than those Crusaders of the 12th century who pillaged and murdered, represented the teaching of the Gospel. It is time the west confronted its ignorance of Islam. Jews, Muslims and Christians are all children of Abraham. This is the moment to bring the faiths closer together in understanding of our common values and heritage, a source of unity and strength. (Blair 2001)

Modernity has brought with it the complexity of citizenship, race and religion, which Cohen (1994) calls 'the fuzzy frontiers of identity' as it includes geopolitical, political, religious, cultural and physical identities (Kershen 1998). In order for Britain and Canada to celebrate their diversity there needs to be a sense of unity, a commonality in the form of common citizenship. America has always been cited as an example of such a society where individuals maintain their cultural identity whilst believing in a common sense of belonging, of being 'American'. Recently, however, there has been a burgeoning of hyphenated identities (Modood 1992). These are what Hall calls 'new ethnicities' (1996: 161). In Canada, multiculturalism was designated as a national symbol which fulfilled the need for a unified and distinct Canadian identity (Esses and Gardner 1996). Britain is a long way away from the ideals set out in the Act for the Preservation and Enhancement of Multiculturalism in Canada (1988), as was shown by the response in the media and by individuals to the Parekh Report in October 2000. The report aimed to take a long-term view as to 'the future of multi-ethnic Britain'. Unfortunately and ironically, the press took the word 'racial' to mean 'racist', and instead of focusing on the findings of the report, Lord Parekh and his team were hounded by the issue of what it means to be British. The report states that: 'Whiteness nowhere features as an explicit condition of being British, but it is widely understood that Englishness and therefore by extension Britishness is racially coded' (Burrell 2000a). The issue of Britishness found itself into the daily newspapers: 'Straw launches scathing attack on "unpatriotic" political left' (Burrell 2000b); 'Celebrate, don't tolerate, minorities' (Younge 2000).

The issue of what it means to be British has become particularly significant since the Parekh Report in 2000. Based on their research, academics have concluded that the term 'British' is being used by those of South Asian ancestry to refer to their nationality – sometimes as a hybrid term to denote their ethnic or religious identity alongside their nationality: for instance, British Asian or British Muslim: 'their British identities express a hybridity of universality and difference: a universality of equal rights as British citizens, with the right to be different within Britain, and a recognition of the difference of Islam' (Hussain and Bagguley 2005: 407). Respondents in our research also indicated that the term 'British' was predominantly one which reflected their nationality and was therefore applicable to all residents of Britain, regardless of ethnic background or religious affiliation. In addition, some respondents felt that being British did not require one to give up one's ancestral heritage; rather, one was able to participate in the British way of life while maintaining aspects of one's ethnic and religious identities.

> *Rashida* (Female Respondent, London): The term British involves a huge range of ethnic groupings. The term British is belonging to a country irrespective of your colour or your identity or your cultural background. It's a question of nationality. (Mukadam 2003: 215)

Regardless of the respondents' strong sense of citizenship and continuous attempts to acculturate into mainstream society, they faced acts of discrimination while growing up and living in Britain and Canada. Following the Oldham riots in 2001 and attacks on the United States on 11 September 2001 the terms 'Asian', 'Pakistani' and 'Muslim' were the ones favoured by the media when referring to second-generation British Muslim youth of South Asian ancestry: '500-strong crowd of *Asian youths*' (*Guardian* 2001); '[the spokesman for the World Council of Hindus] pinned the blame for the unruly behaviour of *Pakistani youth* partly on the mosques' (Roy 2001); 'government plans to broadcast direct appeals to *Muslims in Britain*' (Gregoriadis and White 2002).

Following the 7 July 2005 suicide bombings in London, Muslim communities in particular have become targets of unprecedented hatred and resentment. According to Scotland Yard the total number of faith-related attacks reported across London rose from 40 in the same three and a half week period in 2004 to 269, showing an increase of almost 600 per cent (*BBC News* 2005). Interestingly, the media have given these individuals a new status since 7 July 2005 – they are now *British* Muslims! Were they not British before?: 'the four *British Muslims* who blew up three underground trains and a double-decker bus' (Gray 2005); 'She [a representative from Fox News] asked how *British Muslims* could have turned on their own country' (Rumbelow 2005). We fear that the term 'British' as used here symbolizes a lack of loyalty to the country and is therefore used as a means of showing inclusion which is then rejected in favour of terrorism against one's own country and its people. How did a handful of individuals come to represent a community of peace-loving, law-abiding, loyal British subjects who follow the faith of Islam (Mukadam and Mawani 2005a)?

In the summer of 2005, in the aftermath of the 7 July 2005 bombings, there has been extensive debate in relation to labels and, in the words of the British Home Office Minister, Hazel Blears, 'rebranding'. Blears suggested that introducing hyphenated identities would be a way of giving individuals pride in both their ethnicity and nationality: 'In America they do seem to have this idea that you are Italian-American, or Irish-American … we don't do that here' (Ford and Rumbelow 2005). Far from being a new idea, this concept is one which individuals from minority ethnic communities have operationalized of their own volition (see Figures 5.2 and 5.3). Mukadam (2003) offers a way in which the multiple and fluid identities of these individuals can be graphically represented (Figure 5.1). If we are accepting of Britain as a multi-ethnic society and our rights as equal citizens, then our over-arching identity is one as British nationals – we then have the ethnic group that we belong to, ethnic sub-group, regional ethnic group, religious group and religious sect.

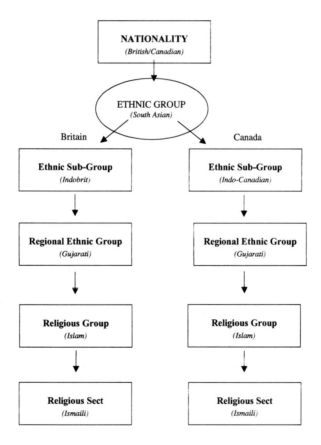

Figure 5.1 Post-diasporic identity model as applied to second-generation Nizari Ismaili Muslims of Gujarati ancestry in Britain and Canada (*Source*: Adapted from Mukadam 2003: 235).

The 'New Generation' in London and Toronto

Having outlined the current socio-political situation in which the second-generation Nizari Ismaili Muslims reside we will focus on the participants' responses to
issues of ethnic self-identification and cultural adaptation strategies. This section
draws on research conducted on sixty-three post-diasporic Nizari Ismaili Muslims
of Gujarati descent (age 18 to 45) in London and Toronto using theoretical models
contained in the Saeed et al.'s (1999) study on identity and ethnic orientation of
Pakistani teenagers in Glasgow. Using the research methodology of McPartland
and Kuhn (1954), Hutnik (1985) and Phinney (1992), Mukadam (2003) incorporated linguistic and religious questions in order to ascertain language use and religious affiliation amongst post-diasporic Gujaratis in London and its environs. This
was further developed by Mawani (2006) to include more specific questions
related to religious practices and participation.

The aim of our research is to generate a clearer picture as to the views of post-
diasporic Indians of Gujarati descent who had been born and/or brought up in the
West in relation to their language, culture and identity. This research aimed to
explore the issues raised by Hutnik (1985), in which she questions the relationship
between ethnic self-identification (the label chosen by an individual to express his or
her individual ethnic identity) and cultural adaptation strategy (lifestyle choices
made by an individual who is living in the West, but who belongs to a minority ethnic
community). Several researchers, including Hutnik (1985), Roger Ballard (1994),
Brah (1996), Anwar (1998) and Bhatti (1999), point to a changing identity amongst
this group, and Bhatti argues: 'Asian children are not completely like their parents,
nor completely like their white peers. They are British Asians. They belong on the
whole to a growing number of young people who are in the process of carving out a
separate identity for themselves' (1999: 238). Hutnik stresses that 'self-categorisa-
tions may be relatively independent of styles of cultural adaptation and that eventually they may acquire functional autonomy. The notion of the functional autonomy
of self-categorisation from cultural adaptation suggests that the ethnic minority individual may feel strongly Indian (say) but be very British in his/her behaviour and
other attitudes' (1991: 159). To date no studies have explored the changing realities
of post-diasporic Indians born in Britain or Canada in relation to their ethnic identity and cultural adaptation to life in two cultures and two languages.

This study was carried out in two stages using quantitative research analysis in
the form of a questionnaire as well as qualitative research in the form of semi-
structured interviews to 'illuminate' the results found in the quantitative analysis.
The participants selected for this study were second-generation Ismailis of
Gujarati descent born in London or Toronto from Gujarati/Kachchi-speaking
family backgrounds, aged between 18 and 45. Blaxter et al. (1996: 79) explain the
types of sampling used in this study as: quota sampling: convenience sampling

within groups in the population; purposive sampling: hand-picking supposedly typical or interesting cases; and snowball sampling: building up a sample through informants. A question that is often asked regarding ethnography is whether a few informants are capable of providing adequate information about a culture. Bernard (1995: 165) is of the opinion that the answer to that question is 'Yes', but that it is dependent on two factors: choosing good informants, by which he means those who are selected for their competence as well as their representativeness; and asking respondents questions about things they know about.[2]

> We conducted forty-three semi-structured interviews which enabled us to focus on lives lived through a period of uncertainty, a time of conflict and racism, a time of change leading to a new vision of acceptance of pluralism and diversity. These are their stories, and their comments matter, because they helped to shape and bring about change to the societies in which they reside. Many of our respondents are now successful business people who fled East Africa with their families and utilized the education given to them in British schools to achieve the kind of status that they have in today's society. Many of the working respondents are professionals: dentists, lawyers, IT specialists, doctors, entrepreneurs and teachers. This is not an unlikely set of second-generation Ismailis in today's society, where parents who ran corner shops sent their children to the 'best' schools (for many parents private education was perceived as being superior) and urged them to pursue higher education. It must be remembered at this stage that the Ismaili community is upwardly mobile and predominantly professional or business-oriented.

The respondents are all Nizari Ismaili Muslims of Gujarati descent who were born and/or brought up in Toronto or London. The Nizari Ismaili Muslims, otherwise known as the Shia Imami Ismaili Muslims, are a small minority within the global Muslim faith who recognize His Highness Prince Karim Aga Khan IV as their *Imam* (spiritual leader). The *Imam*'s presence is crucial in contextualizing Islam for his followers during changing times and circumstances (Israel 1999; Mamiya 1996; Nanji 1996; Picklay n.d.). This group represents the second largest Shia Muslim community and is to be found in more than twenty-five countries spanning Asia (including India, Pakistan, Iran, Afghanistan, Syria, the former Soviet Union and China), Eastern Africa, Europe and North America (Daftary 1998; Nanji 1986).

We deal specifically with two issues emerging from our data: first, that relating to ethnic self-identification (the label chosen by an individual to express his or her individual ethnic identity); and, second, what may be called 'cultural adaptation strategy' (lifestyle choices made by an individual who is living in the West, but who belongs to a minority ethnic community). Following Phinney (1992) and Saeed et al. (1999), the statement: 'In terms of ethnic group, I consider myself to be ...' was incorporated into the questionnaire so as to ascertain what terms respondents chose when asked specifically about their ethnicity. From Figure 5.2 it is clear that an accultura-tive strategy is prevalent amongst post-diasporic Nizari Ismailis of Gujarati descent in London, with 59 per cent of respondents selecting this form of ethnic identity strategy. These findings are in agreement with Modood et al. (1997: 331), who found the majority of Indians (65 per cent) in their survey employed an acculturative strategy. Interestingly, the term 'British Asian' (a term commonly used to describe second- and third-generation South Asians in Britain) was chosen by 41 per cent of the respondents. The results from the Canadian sample were very similar to that of the British sample, with the majority of respondents (51 per cent) opting for an acculturative strategy where their ethnic self-identification was concerned (Figure 5.3). In Canada there is no generally recognized term for second- and third-genera-tion South Asians: 24 per cent of the Canadian sample identified themselves as Canadian Indian. However, it appears that the term Indo-Canadian is slowly gaining popularity. A striking feature amongst this sample is the range of terms used by the individuals to describe their ethnic identity, incorporating aspects that reflect the tra-jectory of their parents; they are at once Canadian, Indian and East African.

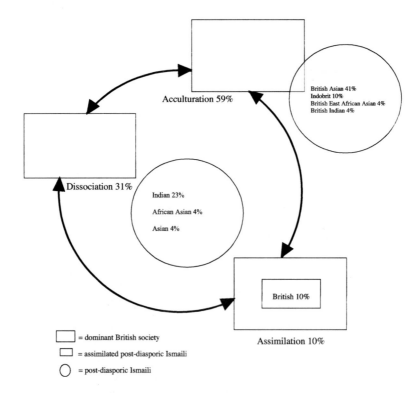

Acculturation 59%

British Asian 41%
Indobrit 10%
British East African Asian 4%
British Indian 4%

Dissociation 31%

Indian 23%

African Asian 4%

Asian 4%

British 10%

Assimilation 10%

☐ = dominant British society
☐ = assimilated post-diasporic Ismaili
◯ = post-diasporic Ismaili

Figure 5.2 Post-diasporic minority ethnic identity formation model as applied to Nizari Ismailis of Gujarati ancestry in London (*Source*: Mukadam and Mawani 2005b).

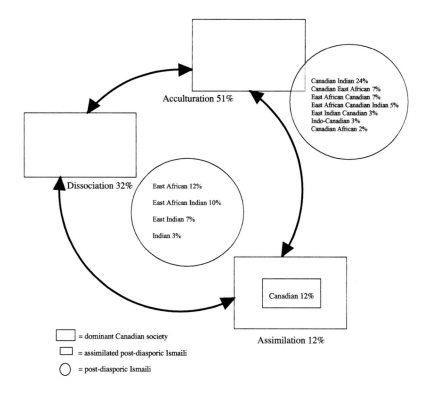

Figure 5.3 in diagram:

Acculturation 51%

Canadian Indian 24%
Canadian East African 7%
East African Canadian 7%
East African Canadian Indian 5%
East Indian Canadian 3%
Indo-Canadian 3%
Canadian African 2%

Dissociation 32%

East African 12%

East African Indian 10%

East Indian 7%

Indian 3%

Canadian 12%

Assimilation 12%

☐ = dominant Canadian society
☐ = assimilated post-diasporic Ismaili
○ = post-diasporic Ismaili

Figure 5.3 Post-diasporic minority ethnic identity formation model as applied to Nizari Ismailis of Gujarati ancestry in Toronto (*Source*: Mukadam and Mawani, 2005b).

Hutnik states that historically there has been an implicit assumption that social behaviour corresponds to labels of self-categorization: 'if a person much prefers aspects of British culture (films, music, food, clothes, etc.) to Indian culture then that person will categorise him/herself in terms of the majority group dimension of his/her identity and will reject the ethnic minority label' (1991: 135). Mukadam's (2003) and Mawani's (2006) studies examine the relationship between cultural adaptation and ethnic self-categorization. Respondents were placed into one of five cultural adaptation types based on their responses to questions relating to: favourite food, favourite movie, favourite clothes, favourite music, celebrations, religious affiliation and minority ethnic language skill (oral or aural). The only section that provided two answers by many respondents was 'celebrations', in which they wrote a Muslim festival as well as a Western celebration, such as Christmas or New Year. Mukadam (2003: 237) formulated five cultural adaptation types. First, *Western* – an individual who shows a preference for Western culture; second, *Symbolic Desi*[3] – an individual who predominantly shows a preference for Western culture, but shows an affinity to a few elements of Indian culture; third,

Balanced Acculturated – an individual who shows no clear preference for Western or Indian culture; fourth, *Symbolic Western* – an individual who predominantly shows a preference for Indian culture, but shows an affinity to a few elements of Western culture; and, finally, *Desi* – an individual who shows a preference for Indian culture.

The responses were then inserted into a bar graph to show the cultural adaptation strategy employed (Figures 5.4 and 5.5). Figures 5.4 and 5.5 clearly show that all of the respondents in this study selected an acculturative cultural adaptation strategy. There appears to be a range of acculturation from those who have integrated to a greater degree down to those who have maintained a greater affinity with the culture of India. Interestingly, *all* respondents included two aspects of Indian culture as part of their overall acculturative strategy, religion and language. These results indicate that within the acculturative framework all the respondents showed a 'glass ceiling' where Western culture was concerned.

Two of the seven aspects of culture that reflected Indian culture were the respondents' religious affiliation and their ability to speak/understand Gujarati/Kacchi. It should be pointed out at this stage that there were significant age differences between the London and Toronto groups – those in London being between the ages of 22 and 45 and those in Toronto being between the ages of 18 and 25. Both groups are second generation; however, there was a marked age difference between these two sets of respondents. Figure 5.4 shows the similarity in cultural adaptation strategy amongst both male and female respondents in London, with the exception of the *Desi* category, which only constituted female respondents. Unlike the London group, those in Toronto, who are in a younger age bracket, showed marked gender differences where cultural adaptation strategy was concerned. Amongst the Toronto sample, the Symbolic *Desi* category was composed mainly of male respondents, which shows a greater move towards Western culture and integration. The female respondents showed a much more varied cultural adaptation strategy, which was fairly evenly distributed amongst four of the five main types of acculturation, none being present in the Western category. From these results it appears that the younger male respondents in Toronto are acculturating at a faster rate than females of the same age group. However, in the older group of second-generation respondents in London, there was a more equal distribution based on gender, with the majority of both male and female respondents in the Symbolic Western category. Against expectations very few respondents from both the London and Toronto groups were found in the Balanced Acculturated category: they were predominantly found either side of this mark, showing either an affinity towards Indian culture or a move towards greater integration and Western culture.

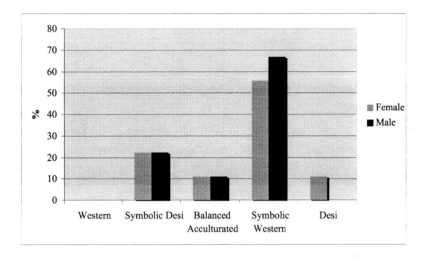

Figure 5.4 Five main types of acculturation amongst post-diasporic Ismailis in London.

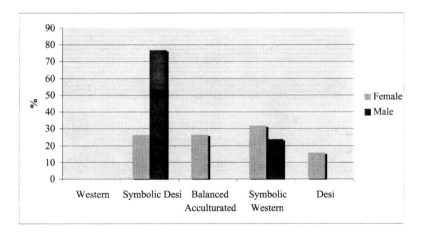

Figure 5.5 Five main types of acculturation amongst post-diasporic Ismailis in Toronto.

Conclusion

In an era of globalization, during which the question of identity has taken on greater significance than before, there are now increasingly complex debates relating to the ways in which certain communities are located, regarding both their allegiance to the nation states in which they reside and the character of their links to the land of their ancestors. We have provided an overview of the current situation facing young second-generation Muslims as they struggle to locate their complex identities in their country of birth. Our investigation of multiple identities of post-diasporic Ismailis in London and Toronto suggests that dominant, essentialist conceptions of 'between two cultures' and 'the half-way generation' can usefully be replaced by a view that encompasses the fluidity and complexity of two cultures co-existing in an evolving environment. From the results of this study it appears that post-diasporic Nizari Ismaili Muslims in London and Toronto are selecting an *acculturative strategy* as far as their ethnic self-identification and cultural adaptation are concerned. This strategy acknowledges a positive image and sense of integrated ethnic and national identity. In addition, the selection of an acculturative strategy reflects commonalities with the 'host' culture in terms of cultural preferences to food, dress, music, and so on, alongside what are perceived to be integral aspects of their Indian culture, such as religion and language. There is a clear indication that the tension between these two factors will play an increasingly important role in the lives of post-diasporic Ismailis living in the West. These individuals are the fortunate ones who live in multi-ethnic Western societies that are generally more interested in their inclusion than exclusion. However, equally significant are the strong cultural, linguistic and religious links that tie them to the land of their ancestors. These individuals comprise a new generation who are learning to manoeuvre between the diverse facets of their identity. At a time when contemporary anthropology is coming to terms with changes in the ways in which communities are researched, there is a need to acknowledge the existence of new fields which comprise second and subsequent generations of people who are products of the locality in which they were born and raised. Far from being on its deathbed, ethnography is critical in the study of these 'new' single-sited localities, and the role of insiders has never been more important in gaining access to and shedding light on otherwise closed communities.

> Be the change you wish to see in the world.
> Mahatma Gandhi

Notes

1. This is the cube-like structure located in the centre of the mosque at Mecca and covered with a black silk cloth.

2. The questionnaire was formulated using Mukadam's (1994) quantitative research tool, as well as incorporating the work of Phinney (1992) and Saeed et al (1999); the statement: 'In terms of ethnic group, I consider myself to be....' was included in the questionnaire so as to ascertain what terms respondents chose when asked specifically about their ethnicity. Mukadam and Mawani further developed the questionnaire to include more specific questions related to Ismailism. Section 2 of the questionnaire asked the respondents questions about their likes

and dislikes in terms of food, clothes, music, films, celebrations, and so on. This was then used in conjunction with the participants' response for their religious affiliation as well as their self-evaluated proficiency in speaking and understanding Gujarati/Kacchi. Questionnaires were submitted to individuals by various means, including hand delivery, postal delivery, internet attachment, via a friend and through the website http://www.communities.msn.co.uk/Indobrits.

The semi-structured interviews lasted approximately 45 minutes to an hour and the main difficulty encountered during this phase of the research was actually getting hold of the respondents; appointments were made and then cancelled, rescheduled and cancelled until finally we did actually manage to complete the task. Many of the interviews were held at respondents' places of work, at their homes, by telephone or over dinner in restaurants – all areas in which the individual(s) concerned would be in a relaxed frame of mind. For many the interview was an emotional experience bringing back memories of an exodus from Africa, racism on their arrival and the scars of a life in a new land. For others it was a time of reflection, one of achievement and pride embodied within an evolving plural society. As interviewers from within the community, we were privileged to be allowed access to the most private thoughts of those who had been kind enough to share their experiences with us. The respondents' honesty and tenacity was moving and it would appear that our position as 'insiders' had positioned us so that we were trusted with information that is normally kept within the individual's private sphere.

3. The term *desi* is a Hindi word meaning 'of the homeland'.

References

Anwar, M. (1975), *Between Two Cultures*, London: Community Relations Commission.

Anwar, M. (1979), *The Myth of Return*, London: Heinemann.

Anwar, M. (1998), *Between Cultures: Continuity and Change in the Lives of Young Asians*, London: Routledge.

Ballard, C. (1979), 'Conflict, Continuity and Change: "Second Generation Asians"', in V.S. Khan (ed.), *Minority Families in Britain*, London: Macmillan.

Ballard, R. (ed.) (1994), *Desh Pardesh: The South Asian Presence in Britain*, London: Hurst & Co.

Ballard, R. (2002), 'Race, Ethnicity and Culture', in M. Holborn (ed.), *New Directions in Sociology*, Ormskirk:Causeway, http://www.art.man.ac.uk/CASAS/pdfpapers/racecult.pdf (accessed 09.01.03).

BBC News (2005), 'Hate Crimes Soar After Bombings', *BBC News*, 3 Aug.

Bernard, H.R. (1995), *Research Methods in Anthropology,* London: AltaMira.

Bhatti, G. (1999), *Asian Children at Home and at School*, London: Routledge.

Blair, T. (2001) 'Tony Blair: Address at the Labour Party Conference', 2 Oct., http://www.americanrhetoric.com/speeches/tblair10-02-01.htm   (accessed 19.01.05).

Blaxter, L., Hughes, C. and Tight, M. (1996), *How to Research*, Buckingham: Open University Press.

Brah, A. (1996), *Cartographies of Diaspora*, London: Routledge.

Brah, A. and Shaw, S. (1992), 'Working Choices: South Asian Young Muslim Women and the Labour Market', *Research Paper No. 91,* London: Department of Employment.

Burrell, I. (2000a), '"Britishness" is Not a Racist Idea in a Multicultural Nation, Insists Straw', *The Independent*, 12 Oct.

Burrell, I. (2000b), 'Straw Launches Scathing Attack on "Unpatriotic" Political Left', *The Independent*, 12 Oct.

Chandarana, R. (2001), 'Teaching Tolerance', *The Toronto Star*, 27 Dec.

Chrétien, J. (2001), 'Speech by Prime Minister Jean Chrétien, Visiting the Ottawa Central Mosque', 21 Sept.,http://www.patriotresource. com/wtc/intl/0921/ canada.html (accessed 19.01.05).

Clifford, J. (1994), 'Diasporas', *Cultural Anthropology* 9 (3): 302–38.

Cohen, R. (1994), *The Fuzzy Frontiers of Identity*, London: Longman.

Daftary, F. (1998), *A Short History of the Ismailis*, Edinburgh: Edinburgh University Press.

Desai, R. (1963), *Indian Immigrants in Britain*, London: Oxford University Press.

Esses, V.M. and Gardner, R.C. (1996), 'Multiculturalism in Canada: Context and Current Status', *Canadian Journal of Behavioural Science* 28 (3): 145–52.

Ford, R. and Rumbelow, H. (2005), 'Britain to Rebrand Ethnic Minorities', *The Times*, 8 Aug.

Fortier, A. (2000), *Migrant Belongings: Memory, Space, Identity*, London: Berg.

Gilroy, P. (1993), *The Black Atlantic: Modernity and Double Consciousness*, London: Verso.

Glazer, N. and Moynihan, D. (1970), *Beyond the Melting Pot,* Cambridge, MA: MIT Press.

Gray, A. (2005), 'Livingstone Says West Fuelled Islamic Radicalism', *Reuters*, 20 July.

Gregoriadis, L. and White, M. (2002), 'Straw to Seek Muslim Support Over Iraq', *The Guardian*, 27 Nov.

Guardian (2001), 'Fears Over Race Violence in Oldham and Aylesbury', 28 May.

Hall, S. (1996), 'New Ethnicities', in J. Hutchinson and A. Smith (eds), *Ethnicity*, Oxford: Oxford University Press.

Hanlon, A. and Withington, T. (1999), 'Sent from Coventry', *Guardian*, 26 Jan.

Hussain, Y. (2000), 'Identity and British South Asian Women: Gender, Race and Ethnicity – Theoretical and Imaginative Perspectives', unpublished Ph.D. dissertation, University of Bradford.

Hussain, Y. and Bagguley, P. (2005), 'Citizenship, Ethnicity and Identity: British Pakistanis After the 2001 "Riots"', *Sociology* 39 (3): 407–25.

Hutnik, N. (1985), 'Ethnic Minority Identity: The Case of Second-Generation South Asians in Britain', unpublished Ph.D. thesis, Wolfson College.

Hutnik, N. (1991), *Ethnic Minority Identity: A Social Psychological Perspective*, Oxford: Oxford Science Publications.

Israel, M. (1999), 'Ismailis', in P.R. Magocsi (ed.), *Encyclopedia of Canada's People*, Toronto: University of Toronto Press.

Journal of Turkish Weekly (2005), 'Fox TV Accused of Stereotyping Muslims as Terrorists', 14 Jan., http://www.turkishweekly.net/news.php?id=2063 (accessed 19.01.05).

Kershen, A.J. (1998), 'Introduction: A Question of Identity', in A. Kershen (ed.), *A Question of Identity*, Aldershot: Ashgate.

Kilroy-Silk, R. (2004), 'We Owe Arabs Nothing', *Express on Sunday*, 4 Jan., http://ww.honestreporting.com/a/kilroyarticle.htm (accessed 14.01.05).

McLachlin, B. (2003), 'The Civilization of Difference', *The Globe and Mail*, 7 Mar.

McPartland, T. and Kuhn, M. (1954), 'An Empirical Investigation of Self-Attitudes', *American Sociological Review* 19 (1): 68–76.

Mamiya, L.H. (1996), 'Islam in the Americas', in A.A. Nanji (ed.), *The Muslim Almanac: A Reference Work on the History, Faith, Culture, and Peoples of Islam*, New York: Gale Research.

Marsh, I. (2000), *Sociology: Making Sense of Society*, Harlow: Pearson Education.

Mawani, S. (2002), 'Devotional Songs of the South Asian Nizari Ismailis in Toronto: The Attitudes of the Older Generation', unpublished Master's thesis, London School of Economics and Political Science.

Mawani, S. (2006), 'The Construction of Identities Amongst Young Adult Nizari Ismailis in Toronto and Mumbai', unpublished Ph.D. thesis, SOAS, University of London.

Modood, T. (1992), *Not Easy Being British: Colour, Culture and Citizenship*, London: Runnymede Trust.

Modood, T., Berthoud, R., Lakey, J., Nazroo, J., Smith, P., Virdee, S. and Reishon, S. (1997), *Ethnic Minorities in Britain: Diversity and Disadvantage: The Fourth National Survey of Ethnic Minorities*, London: Policy Studies Institute.

Mukadam, A. (1994), ' "Until Death Do Us Part": Language as a Factor of Group Identity: Gujaratis', unpublished MA thesis, University of Reading.

Mukadam, A. (2003), 'Gujarati Speakers in London: Age, Gender and Religion in the Construction of Identity', unpublished Ph.D. thesis, University of Reading.

Mukadam, A. and Mawani, S. (2005a), 'Pride and Prejudice: Constructing British Muslim Identities', paper given at the Royal Geographic Society/Institute of British Geographers International Conference, London, UK, 31 Aug.– 2 Sept.

Mukadam, A. and Mawani, S. (2005b), 'Towards a Shared Vision: Unity in Diversity', paper given at the 21st Annual International Conference of the Birkbeck Centre for Canadian Studies, London, UK, 11-12 Feb.

Nanji, A. (1986), 'The Ismaili Muslim Identity and Changing Contexts', in V.C. Hayes (ed.), *Identity Issues and World Religions*, Bedford Park, Australia: Australian Association for Study of Religions.

Nanji, A. (1996), 'The Ethical Tradition in Islam', in A. Nanji (ed.), *The Muslim Almanac: A Reference Work on the History, Faith, Culture, and Peoples of Islam*, New York: Gale Research.

Neuman, W.L. (2003), *Social Research Methods: Qualitative and Quantitative Approaches*, Boston: A and B.

Nielsen, J.S. (2000), 'Muslims in Britain: Ethnic Minorities, Community, or Ummah?', in J.R. Hinnells (ed.), *The South Asian Religious Diaspora in Britain, Canada, and the United States*, New York: State University of New York Press.

Parekh, B. (2001), *Integrating Minorities*, London: Institute of Contemporary Arts.

Parekh, B. (2005), 'Agony of Arrival', *British Gujaratis: Trials & Triumphs* (supplement), *Asian Voice*, July.

Phinney, J. (1992), 'The Multigroup Ethnic Identity Measure: A New Scale for Use with Adolescents and Young Adults', *Journal of Adolescent Research* 7: 156–76.

Picklay, A.S. (n.d.), *History of the Ismailis*, Bombay: Popular Printing Press.

Rex, J. (2002), 'Communities, Diasporas, and Multiculturalism', *Migration* 33–5: 51—67.

Robertson, P. (2002), *Nov. 11 Statement by Pat Robertson on The 700 Club*, 14 Nov 14, http://www.patrobertson.com/PressReleases/bushresponse2.asp (accessed 14.01.05).

Roy, A. (2001), 'Muslim Parents and Mosques are to Blame, Says Hindu Leader', *The Telegraph*, 9 July.

Rumbelow, H. (2005), 'Tony's Political Make-up is No More than Skin Deep', *The Times*, 27 July.

Rushdie, S. (1992), *Imaginary Homelands*, London: Penguin.

Saeed, A., Blain, N. and Forbes, D. (1999), 'New Ethnic and National Questions in Scotland: Post-British Identities', *Ethnic and Racial Studies* 22 (5): 821–44.

Safran, W. (1991), 'Diasporas in Modern Societies: Myth of Homeland and Return', *Diaspora* 1: 83–99.

Taylor, P.H. (1976), *The Half-Way Generation*, Windsor: NFER.

Vertovec, S. (2000), *The Hindu Diaspora: Comparative Patterns*, London: Routledge.

Wainwright, M. (2002), 'Asian Ghetto Notion Dispelled by Survey', *Guardian*, 5 Dec.

Watson, J.L. (ed.) (1977), *Between Two Cultures*, Oxford: Basil Blackwell.
Younge, G. (2000), 'Celebrate, Don't Tolerate, Minorities', *Guardian*, 11 Oct.

–6–

The Internet, Cybercafés and the New Social Spaces of Bangalorean Youth

Nicholas Nisbett

Introduction

Bangalore has become something of a poster boy of the 'information age' of late, a city at the centre of the relatively successful Indian IT industry, filled with software companies, call centres and cybercafés; a city populated by the growing and affluent middle classes. Whilst such an image might ignore the great disparities and urban poverty (Benjamin 2000) that accompany Bangalore's role at the heart of the informational economy (Castells 2000: 436; Sassen 1991: 333; 1998), this is undoubtedly a city undergoing rapid social change. Bangalore is at the forefront of a particular constitution of Indian modernity and middle-class ideals of progress, which is increasingly centred on dreams of IT employment and the highly visible expressions of social mobility that such jobs enable.

This chapter, which draws upon my doctoral research in a Bangalore cybercafé, explores social change as experienced by a group of young, middle-class men who are growing up in the new social spaces of Bangalorean modernity. The focus is on the role played by a number of different places – cybercafés, the Internet and a new breed of coffee shops – in the development of gendered identities for Bangalore's middle-class male youth.

The theoretical framework employed here is informed primarily by Doreen Massey's conception of space and place, in which she asserts: 'If ... the spatial is thought of ... as formed out of social interrelations at all scales, then one view of a place is as a particular articulation of those relations, a particular moment in those networks of social relations and understandings' (1994: 5). Following Massey, we can consider social space to be the unshaped social potentiality of a particular location, and place as its fully formed counterpart, bound up in the social relations and multiple identities (ibid.: 121) *of that particular time*. The result is that 'what is to be the dominant image of any place will be a matter of contestation that will change over time' (ibid.: 121).

This leads to a greater understanding of space and place within the rapidly changing socio-cultural environment of Bangalore, where new spaces are being appropriated, created and shaped into place by Bangalorean youth, which in turn create and shape Bangalorean youth and gender identities.

Hanging out at the cybercafé, chatting to 'girls' online and going to the new and trendy coffee shops were a crucial part of the middle-class lifestyle to which these young men aspired. The cybercafé, a predominantly male social space, was thus the place in which they were constructing their masculinity within the context of male friendship (see Paptaxiarchis 1991; Vale de Almeida 1996; Walle 2004). Where gender and status were being constructed offline, in the space of the cyber-café, they were also being formed online through relationships with girls and young women in the spaces of internet chatrooms.[1] When these relationships progressed to actual dates, they would meet in the élite social spaces of the new coffee shops. Gender relations were thus tied up with conspicuous displays of consumption in locations which are emblematic of the young and affluent Bangalore. Whilst all three kinds of place open up new possibilities for interaction between the sexes, they also work to throw into doubt some of the certainties of the middle-class male. In examining the resulting discourses, I explain how gender relations are in transition within the specificities of social and economic change as experienced by the Indian urban middle classes.

The Cybercafé as a Social Space

Cybercafés play an important role in urban India, as although the internet is slowly starting to take off within homes and businesses, such access has so far been restricted to the élite. Bangalore, at the heart of India's IT industry, is especially well served by internet cafés, with access costing as little as 10 rupees per hour in some places, the price of a cheap soft drink. Whilst this is still beyond the reach of many, the huge number of cybercafés and relatively low prices have certainly widened the access to the urban, educated middle classes, such as my young male informants.

The young men who form the focus of this chapter were English-educated Tamil-speakers (all except one were actually Tamil), both Christians and Hindus (from a range of castes) between the ages of 19 and 29, some with degrees in engineering; all of them having reached the tenth standard of the Indian education system (to the age of 16). None were yet married and so all were thus living with their parents in several different parts of Bangalore, from one-room houses in the old rambling Tamil district of Shivaji Nagar, to more spacious abodes in the middle-class developments near to the new ring road. They were linked, then, by their common Tamil identity (barring one), their youth, their residence in Bangalore, but above all by their friendship, their identities as middle-class males and their daily presence in the space of the cybercafé.[2]

The cybercafé, Networld, was owned by the father of one of the friends, David, and was located in an area I call Lakshminagar.[3] Lakshminagar is a suburb of Bangalore forming a border between the old British cantonment and the new areas that have quickly grown up to the north of the city in the post-independence decades. It hosts, among others, a large Anglo-Indian community and a fairly size-able lower-middle-class population, along with a number of small slums. Networld, located down a dusty side road leading to a residential area of one- or two-storey concrete houses, is one of several cybercafés in Lakshminagar, which cater to a mixture of local residents, college students, school children and passing workers.

Arriving at Networld on any afternoon, I would find a group of these young men hanging around outside, engaged in what they called *'timepass'*. For them, *timepass* (a common word in Indian English) meant sitting around on the parked scooters and motorbikes outside the cybercafé, sharing cigarettes, drinking tea from the local tea stall, chatting, gossiping and just generally passing the time. In fact, they were spending more time engaged in *timepass* than they were inside, using the internet itself.

The phenomenon of groups of young men hanging out together and passing time doing nothing in particular is not an unusual one, whether studied in the Indian, UK or American contexts (e.g. Chopra 2004 and Osella and Osella 1998 in India; Corrigan 1979 and Willis 1977 in the UK; or Whyte 1993 in the US). It has been seen as a particularly important part of the construction of identity, where young men are able to make their own rules and explore their masculinity through performances that might otherwise be restricted by 'external structures' such as school, employment or the state (Osella and Osella 1998: 191). As one of the group told me, 'at this age, it is not good to be at home too much', and given that smoking, talking about girls, telling dirty jokes, play fighting and arranging to go *boozing* were not activities that they would be happy to perform in front of their parents, it is hardly surprising that they chose to conduct these activities away from the spaces of the family at home. Whilst David's father was occasion-ally at the cybercafé to check up on some matter, for the large part he left the place in the care of his son and his male friends. Thanks to the continual presence of these young men throughout the day, the cybercafé, therefore, like the tavernas or coffee shops of Mediterranean and southern European ethnography (Cowan 1991; Loizos and Papataxiarchis 1991; Papataxiarchis 1991; Vale de Almeida 1996), was becoming a 'masculine space *par excellence*' (Vale de Almeida 1996: 53).

The Cybercafé as a Place: Young, Middle-Class and Male

In his paper on the geographies of youth Culture in Bangalore, Arun Saldhana (2002) writes of Bangalore's élite youth, who spend their time driving around in expensive cars, listening to Western music and attending 'midday parties' (so timed to avoid evening parental curfews) in the expensive 'resorts' which surround the city. Such young élites will now also be found in the new breed of flash and trendy coffee shops which are dotted around the city centre and its more affluent suburbs. Although I will go on to describe my informants' presence in these new social spaces of Bangalore's coffee shops whilst on dates, they would be beyond the reach of my informants on a daily basis, with coffees costing anything up to 40 rupees.[4]

Unable to afford regular access to the most conspicuous places of the young and affluent, these young men still wished to find a place in which to spend time together, away from the parental gaze.[5] The cybercafé was the ideal place to do this and, having an association with modernity, progress and connectedness to global networks of technology, was itself a site of middle-class status.

Cybercafés in India are primarily male spaces – not only are men in the majority, but one of the main uses of this space (pornography) is for an explicitly male purpose (male sexual arousal/titillation). Spatial configurations of most cybercafés in India are arranged to ensure privacy for the viewer, to the extent that some even offer fully enclosed cabins. The resulting effect; a somewhat seedy, enclosed area of male sexual enjoyment, does not make them welcoming places for women.

Despite this, women are still frequent users of internet cafés in Bangalore. At a rough estimate, they made up between 25 and 30 per cent of users at this particular cybercafé in Lakshminagar, and an even greater percentage in the cybercafés in the centre of Bangalore used by the more élite sections of society, which were generally more open, with PCs arranged around the walls and often staffed by women. Networld was not the enclosed-cabin variety of cybercafé and, although pornography was certainly viewed there, one would be more likely find young men engaged in the internet chat I describe below.

So whilst the inside of Networld was not as seedy as some, and women were indeed frequent visitors, it would still have carried the connotation of masculine space. Likewise, the outside of the café, because of the nearly continual presence of a group of men, was also tied up with this image of the middle-class male.

Women were not barred from the space outside of Networld, but when a woman passed through it, it ceased to be a male place and reverted to a social space, where the norms of society would reassert themselves. The young men's performance was adjusted accordingly to reflect the fact that they were no longer in a male-only space. Behaviour was quieted down, cigarettes would be held at the side of the body and any talk about drinking or girls would cease. Women passing through, however, would not linger in this space outside, which for them remained liminal, with the potential to take on a male role (cf. Chopra 2004).

Meeting Girls Online

Ironically, given the way in which I have written of cybercafés as significantly male places, they are simultaneously acting to open up online social spaces that allow new forms of interaction between the sexes. As one of the Networld friends, Richard, reveals, this had had a great impact on their ability to speak to females: 'Before that they go to bus stand, they roam around females. ... It was very tough before, actually, if you are studying in a boys' college, it is very tough to meet a female. [But] through chatting nowadays, it has become very easy to meet a female.'

These young men would spend hours online chatting using a combination of popular internet relay chat (IRC) programmes – Yahoo or MSN Messenger and MIRC to 'fish for girls'.[6] They tended to use the 'Bangalore' chatroom of MIRC more than others, trawling it first for potential partners and then, if bored, moving on to other, more international rooms, with a range of places from London to Indonesia. Although there are probably thousands of rooms available on Yahoo, MSN or MIRC which are *non-geographical* (i.e. interest groups or various general meeting places like 'the pub', 'the hot tub', etc.), I never saw my informants choosing a room that was not of a geographical nature.[7]

As Richard pointed out, 'in this age we like to meet a female only ... nobody talks to any guy'. More than anything else, my informants were thus going online specifically to meet young women. In order to illustrate the way in which these relationships progressed, I will focus on one of my informants who was the most prolific chatter, Karan, a 26-year-old unemployed engineering graduate. Karan's experience reveals the way in which the internet was enabling the kinds of relationships that he and his friends were finding it difficult to make elsewhere, enabling them, as Karan puts it, to fall in love:

> Every Tom, Dick and Harry likes to chat, Nicholas. It's totally changed the way a guy proposes a girl nowadays. Guys and girls used to meet in college, they used to see face to face and they used to fall in love and now all these things are gone. Now what they do is they get into MIRC or Yahoo Messenger. Yahoo Messenger doesn't allow you to fall in love that much, MIRC does. You can ... chat with a girl, ok? You can convince her and you feel that you can call her up, you can meet her and you find that if the girl is ok calibre, you like that girl and the girl likes you, you can have a happy married life with her. No matter if she's from Bangalore, from Russia or from any other part of the world.

The way Karan and his friends would start up a conversation in one of these chatrooms rarely varied. They would click on what they thought was a female name from the list at the side and then use one of MIRC's set interactions, for example 'hello hello hello' (in bright-coloured text and background) or 'give someone flowers' (which prints a picture of flowers using lines of text). If these were accepted, they would normally type 'ASL please?' (age, sex, location) and then ask their chat partners something about their home countries.[8]

Once they had a partner's interest and confidence, their strategy would be to move them over to a regular chat programme such as Yahoo Messenger. Swapping Yahoo or MSN IDs would allow them to see whenever their partners were online (and logged in), and thus enable them to chat together on a regular basis: 'What you do is totally disconnect her from MIRC and put her in Yahoo Messenger, so it becomes a private chat. No-one disturbs you in between,' said Karan.

During my fieldwork, Karan had two main girlfriends whom he had met on MIRC. One, Oana, was a Romanian girl with whom he had regular email contact. The other, Nikki, was a young Filipina woman with whom he chatted every day, sometimes several times a day, as she was nearly always online. Karan would continue to look for new partners whilst these relationships continued and would often have a chat window open, talking to Nikki, whilst initiating conversations with several other girls and young women in MIRC. Whenever large pauses in conversation led Nikki to suspect that Karan was chatting to others, he would deny it. Similar pauses on her side would indicate that she was probably doing the same.[9]

When Nikki reported she was ill, Karan became further emotionally involved in this relationship and it is clear that he appreciated the emotional outlet that this was giving him: 'At times, Nicholas, this chatting has helped me a lot, so that I felt as though [she was] my own wife and I felt like I have been missing her for a long time. In fact if this chat, this MIRC or Yahoo Messenger wouldn't have been there I wouldn't have met a nice girl like Nikki.'

For Karan, then, this was a chance to express emotions in the context of a relationship that would not have been possible without the internet. For others, it was the internet's accessibility and immediacy over other forms of communication which made it ideal for these kinds of emotional outpourings with friends and family. Aryan, a friend of mine from another cybercafé in Bangalore, described how the internet was the best way for him to share his emotions with his *cousin-sister* (female cousin) in Mumbai: 'If I want to talk, if I want to do some joke or fun or if I want to be angry or something, [these are] emotional feelings which you can share on net.'

Whilst highlighting this ability for the sharing of emotions online, much of the early social research on the internet was more concerned with the potential for identity play, as it was seen that in online space, one is able to construct identity without reference to one's physical body and place (e.g. Donath 1999; Newitz 1995; Stone 1991; Turkle 1995). Karan would generally reveal his own 'embodied' identity whilst participating in his online relationships, but he would sometimes avoid revealing his location when chatting to girls in Europe or other parts of Asia (Singapore or Indonesia, for example), or pretend that he was in London, because, he said, they were 'not interested in talking to an Indian guy'.

Whilst this strategy does reveal that identity play is in operation to various extents, it simultaneously contradicts the claims that computer-mediated communication has a levelling effect (see Kitchin 1998: 11), as there is clearly a hierarchy in place (of place) between Western and non-Western internet users. Karan would rarely manage to maintain a long-term chat with young women from countries such as the UK, the US and Australia as his Indian English and lack of cultural knowledge would soon betray him. He lacked, therefore, the confidence to attempt conversations with women in these rooms more frequently. This shows, perhaps, that although certain norms and shared systems of symbolic communication prevail across internet chatrooms and multi-media networks, regardless of the location of the participants (Castells 2000: 402–3, Velkovska 2002), there are at least some modes of online behaviour that remain place-bound. Karan may find, for example, that women in the London room of MIRC are a lot less interested in the fact that he 'graduated in engineering – in mechanical' than those in the Bangalore room, where it would be a significant display of status.

Meeting Girls 'Offline': The New Social Space of the Bangalore Coffee Shop

Karan could never be sure himself about the young women he was chatting to, or whether they were even female, but with a couple of them, he went to the extent of ringing them up or having a 'voice chat' to confirm that they were indeed young women. Again, Karan does not seem alone in his desire to confirm identities once relationships had progressed beyond the initial stages of random chat. Slater's (2002) study of traders in pornographic pictures and Hardey's (2002) study of online dating show how, after the disembodied beginnings and relative unquestioning of the identity of a chat partner, participants begin to attach increasingly more importance to a user's 'real identity' as the relationship progresses. In Hardey's study, this demand for greater embodiment could only be realized through meeting up in person (ibid.: 579).

Karan, in the later stages of my research, began to follow this progression from the anonymous, random and imminent nature of MIRC, through the more personalized spaces of Yahoo Messenger and email, to the final stages of phone calls and meeting face to face. For Karan and friends, meeting up with chat partners was a fairly recent development, but, increasingly, this was becoming the overriding purpose of going online.

These dates were usually arranged to take place within one of Bangalore's new and trendy coffee shops. Large numbers of 'Café Coffee Days', 'Quicky's Coffee Pubs' and 'Baristas' have sprung up in Bangalore's central and more affluent areas, giving a whole generation of wealthy young people in their teens and twenties (and others) a space to go and hang out with friends.

The arrival of this new style of coffee shop on the Bangalorean scene (and repeated across metropolitan India from Chennai to Mumbai) finds a parallel in Jane Cowan's article on the arrival of the Greek *Kafeteria*. Cowan writes about the 'sophisticated' and 'European' ambience and identity that it created for the students who first frequented them in the cities and, later on when it spread, for townspeople and villagers (Cowan 1991: 190). Perhaps 'American' should be substituted here for 'European', but the overall picture, of young people sitting drinking Frappuccinos whilst listening to Ricky Martin at full volume in Café Coffee Day, or strumming the house guitar in Barrista, is not far from this picture of aspirational 'sophistication' that Cowan discusses. Vale de Almeida's description of new places of consumption for young, mobile people, such as pubs and discos (as opposed to the male domains of the taverna, café and *boite)*, where 'a different masculinity is constructed *in praesentia* of the girls' (1996: 93), also finds resonance here.

As I have already described, my friends at the cybercafé would not normally have the money to frequent the coffee shops or the trendy bars around town.[10] But it was important to display to their dates that not only could they afford to be in these new social spaces, but that they could demonstrate an ease and familiarity with being amongst the upwardly mobile denizens of India's 'silicon valley'.

Initial dates would often take place between groups of friends, with both sides bringing their own friends along for mutual support. I was therefore to go with Karan on a couple of dates with young women he had encountered online; as a Westerner, no doubt I brought him extra dating capital. One of these dates, with a young woman of school age called Bina, I describe here.

Like all his dates, Bina was someone that Karan had met on the Bangalore room of MIRC. She came from an élite girls' school, which Karan explained had a reputation for producing girls 'who would have many boyfriends'. They had arranged to meet at the Café Coffee Day in Malleshwaran, part of a chain which has set out to appeal particularly to the 'college culture' of Bangalore's affluent youth.

Karan was quite nervous in his meeting with Bina and her friends. We arrived early and sat and waited for them to turn up. Karan – increasingly jumpy – was saying 'Look, Nicholas, the effects of IT on me!' This nervousness lasted throughout the meeting, which Karan tried to cover up with an incessant barrage of questions. Schools, colleges and exam results were a main topic of conversation and were one of the key ways in which these young people were able to establish status between them.

An interesting finding to emerge from this meeting was the way in which these young women described how they approached relationships online. When Bina had met Karan she had been alone, but this was unusual as ordinarily she would have been doing the typing whilst her friends decided what to say. Using a proxy to do the typing thus further removes these other young women from the conversation with men online and provides additional opportunity for identity play.

Other research into online chat reveals multiple bodies behind one online presence to be not an uncommon variable of identity play (e.g. Slater 2002: 232), though more common is the one body behind multiple online identities. In this case, the young women's mixed communities – Hindu and Muslim – of Urdu, Kannada and Telegu mother tongues form an interesting hybrid of identity that is representative of the heterogeneity of Bangalore's population.[11]

Identity here is thus revealed to be fixed neither in online nor in offline space. It appears linked, moreover, to power and status. Whilst Karan might have played with details such as telling chat partners that he went to a better engineering college to increase his status, he was generally content to stick to his own (or close to his own) 'embodied' identity – and this appears to have been the case whether online or 'off'. The girls and young women he was meeting, however, were using identity play to protect themselves within a social space where they might otherwise have been disempowered by their gender identity.

Gender Relations and the Performance of Masculinity in Online and Offline Space

Again, given the early internet commentators' feelings that online relationships would be less intense than their 'real life' counterparts,[12] it is significant that Karan's offline encounters did not come close to the intensity of his online relationships. It also suggests that he was still experimenting and playing with the opportunities that meeting girls in this way were giving him, just as were young women such as Bina.

Despite his continual references to marriage, Karan's inability (or reluctance) to sustain a relationship online or off with any of these young women, and the playful way in which he would demonstrate how he 'fished' for them, seems to correspond to the Osellas's (1998) conclusion regarding the temporary nature of flirting and romance relationships amongst Malayali youth in Kerala. Tensions in the nature of the relationship itself, between love and play, are sometimes apparent in the dichotomous discourses that these young men would use in their talk and gossip about girls and women.[13]

According to Karan, girls who entered into chatting relationships were in danger of falling into a trap. The discourse here, a common one, is that a girl runs the risk of becoming damaged goods, her virginity no longer assured, leaving her unmarriageable and thus having no option left but prostitution. As Karan explained:

Chatting is such a place wherein females get cheated a lot in fact, Nicholas. … The guys that chat with a girl, ok, after chatting they meet at a particular point. After that the girls trust a guy saying ok this guy could be a good boyfriend. [But] he uses her in a different way and he plays with her, spoils her life and lastly she has been thrown to the streets, so that may lead into prostitution.

Karan had described Bina, for example, as 'a sick girl, a dirty girl', because she had touched his knee in the café. Another young woman he went on a date with, Leena, was also a 'bad girl', because 'girls you meet online are only after one thing' (i.e. money). When Karan went on the date with Bina, these young women themselves talked about the reputation of girls at their élite girls' college for having several boyfriends.

My informants' description of someone as 'high class' is thus not a complimentary term. It is used more in opposition to their own, middle-class values and is revealing of the moral aspect that middle-class identity has in Indian society. Friends at the cybercafé would often warn me about going to the 'posh', trendy bars in the centre of town, as they would be full of these 'high-class girls' and 'call girls' (prostitutes) – fairly interchangeable terms. Such assumptions reveal the linkages made between gender, class and morality, which were often underlined in the discourse of my informants, especially in this form of non-middle-class girl = bad girl/low morals.

'Call centre girls', whilst coming from similar social backgrounds to the young men (though possibly from slightly wealthier families), were also girls to be wary of. My informants would make a play on the words 'call centre girls' and 'call girls'. Confident, well educated, in employment and ready to indulge in going to pubs and drinking with their new-found work freedom, these young women in many ways break the stereotype of the docile, demure and *homely* Indian girl (see Abraham 2001, 2002). These men from the cybercafé were happy to meet and interact with women in their new data-processing jobs, but when I asked Arjun whether his new girlfriend would go out drinking with him, he was careful to point out that she would not drink; she was not a 'call centre girl', she was working in the 'back office'.

Whilst recognizing that these high-class girls were merely following the fashion to be 'Westernized', Karan complained about the inevitable conflict with family values that this entailed and worried that this 'Westernization' was only a cosmetic occurrence, leaving people vulnerable to rapid change in what was still an environment controlled by the morals of the middle-class Indian family, or, perhaps more to the point, the Indian male, the husband to be:

Yeah, they are Westernized, but not in a proper way, see … people in Western countries they have been brought up from their childhood in a different way. We have been supported by our parents and we are guided by them not to do good and wrong, and suddenly all of a sudden, just because you see some English[-language] movies, you see some English pop songs and all these things, ok, you get Westernized by wearing all these apparels and you make yourself … you speak like a foreigner and you say that you are a foreigner, you try to lose your virginity and you feel as though you have done a great job. ... Because ... they nowadays are trying to convert themselves [to Western practices], quite religiously in fact, and we are exploiting ourselves and girls nowadays, they feel that losing virginity is a fashion and they lose it. Free of cost. But the sufferer is the husband whom will marry her and whom will know what has happened in her in the past.

Karan's comments are revealing of masculine fears of rapid social change and its effects on gender relations. He encapsulates the uncertainty that young men have in responding to changing gender roles. Analysing Karan's discourse more closely, we see the links he draws as such:

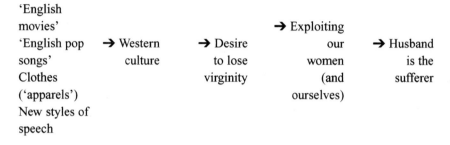

Or to put it more simply, increased exposure to Western media and culture, therefore Westernization, leads to the increased sexualization of Indian women. The Indian male, although exploiting this, will ultimately end up as the victim in his role as the husband.

In explaining this fear, we can look to the rapid social and economic change in the process of occurring, the increased mobility of youth and the availability of new social spaces in which the sexes can interact. Studies both in India and further afield across Asia have linked changes in the way sexuality is lived and perceived to wider social and economic changes, which are the result of increasing exposure to globalization and economic and media liberalization (Abraham 2001; John 1998; Manderson and Rice 2002; Mills 2001; Srivastava 2004). Increased social and spatial mobility thus allow for experimentation and the acquisition of sexual knowledge that would have been hitherto impossible (Manderson and Rice 2002).

The speed of change and the incomprehensibility which results (see Ferguson 1999) is perhaps too great a pressure on these young men from the cybercafé and those like them. Whilst experimenting in their relations with the opposite sex in these new social spaces, they fall back into older discourses and performances which protect their masculinity from the sexual potentiality that these same new spaces may bring to young women. As Jane Cowan has written about the transformations brought about by the new spaces of the Greek *Kafeteria*, these new possibilities can lead to 'a new "structure of feeling" ... confound[ing] neatly commonsensical gender boundaries. As it conceptually irritates seemingly rigid categories of gendered space, the frictions extend to the felt and experienced everyday world' (1991: 29).

In the case of Karan and friends, these new spaces exist not just in the coffee shops, in which, like the Greek *Kafeterias*, they find new ways to interact with girls, but also in the space enabled by their activities online, which frees them from the constraints of parental control over communication. At the same time, these new spaces are somewhat threatening, precisely because of the 'irritation' of the 'rigid categories of gendered space' which Cowan is describing.

Partly because of the irritation of these boundaries, new boundaries are constructed within gender relations and gendered spaces – in this case in the dichotomous discourses discussed above, but also in terms of the gendered space of cybercafés and the internet chatrooms themselves.

Whilst going online was enacted specifically to find a common space for the interaction between the sexes that is not possible in the closely monitored space of everyday life, there is clear evidence of the gendered nature of online space, even to the extent that it may deter some women from participating. This point was apparent when Karan went online and pretended to be a girl, to show me the reaction that girls would get when going online in the Bangalore room of MIRC, as the following passage from my fieldnotes reveals:

> He logged into a different screen, back in the Bangalore room, but this time as a girl. Within seconds, the windows along the bottom of the screen were filling up with responses from males, ranging from 'Heloooo hellllooo helllooo' all over the screen to 'I want to lick your pussy over the phone'. He wasn't able to close the windows faster than they were opening.

Examining the literature concerning women's experiences of the internet confirms that this was not a phenomenon confined to the Bangalore room – 'overall the territories of the on-line world reflect the unreconstructed ideologies of the population of "white male cyberboors"' (Wakeford 1999: 180, citing Winner 1996: 69). Stephanie Brail writes of similar experiences of unsolicited sexual attention for women (or people using women's names) using the AOL chatrooms (1996: 142), whilst Lori Kendall writes how women entering the virtual world of MUDs[14] 'encounter a social environment and behavioural forms formed largely by men' (1996: 211). According to Kendall, 'In some cases, these norms may be disturbing enough to discourage further participation by women' (ibid.). It is not hard to imagine this being the case for an Indian girl or woman encountering the situation described above.

Young Indian woman *do* enter these rooms, however, and despite the harassment they may receive, many continue to use these as social spaces for meeting young men, as Karan's meetings with Bina and her friends attest. In fact, these young women appeared to find this a space where they could choose with whom to interact and in what way, merging their multiple identities into one more powerful online presence. When I asked them how they would deal with being swamped by male attention in the Bangalore room of MIRC, Bina and her friends simply replied that they would chat with anyone with whom they thought they could have an intelligent conversation. A female respondent to my questionnaires at another cybercafé said that she would *only* chat to guys who said that they were (high-status) engineers. Women do thus have strategies for filtering out the unwanted attention of the 'cyberboors' and the fact that they continue to go online to interact in these new social spaces shows that they must at least be partly successful.

Conclusion

In his contribution to this volume, Ulf Hannerz discusses some of the difficulties anthropologists have faced in keeping up with both a changing world and a constantly shifting perception of the ethnographic 'field'. He comments that it may be 'difficult to do an ethnography of any way of life, just about anywhere, without paying at least some attention to media habits, as if everything happened in a face-to-face world'. Whilst the 'life on screen' (Turkle 1995) of my Bangalorean informants would seem to confirm this, it is their life off-screen which provides us with a cautionary note when viewing the internet or the 'virtual' as a separate space or place from the 'real' or 'offline' world.

For some time now, theorists have been criticizing approaches to the internet which try to posit some kind of radical disjuncture between our virtual/real or online/offline lives. Although I have been unable to avoid the latter set of dualisms in describing the spaces enabled by a Bangalore cybercafé, I have attempted to show that the social spaces of the internet are just some of many new spaces which are opening to young people in Bangalore, including the space of the internet café itself (see Miller and Slater 2000; Odero 2003; Wakeford 1999), which are crucial for the formation of their class and gender identities. Ethnographers concerned with the way people are living their lives within the online world must be prepared to document this from the same side of the computer screen as their informants and then to follow them from the computer-mediated spaces and places of the internet to the spaces and places of everyday life, themselves often undergoing rapid changes and transformations for the people who inhabit them.

This chapter thus adds to a growing body of work (e.g. Hardey 2002; Leander and McKim 2003; Miller and Slater 2000) which posits that online identities are rooted in the everyday offline performance of self, and that, even online, hierarchies of place come into operation to restrict this identity play. These young men came to the internet with a clear aim of meeting people from diverse parts of the world, and were therefore attracted to the rooms stressing place over lifestyle.

Their excitement at exploring the world through the mediation of these place-based chatrooms lends support for the centrality of place within our conceptions of the 'online world', confirming Miller and Slater's assertion that 'the internet as a meaningful phenomenon only exists in particular places' (ibid.: 1).

An examination of the performance of gender, both online and off, has also revealed the extent to which these (computer-)literacy practices and new social spaces have led to changes in gender relations (cf. Ahearn 2001). Whilst increased communication between the sexes may lead to a greater knowledge and under-standing of the opposite sex, it seems that masculine performance relating to women remains the same whether occurring in on- or offline social space. Interaction between the sexes taking place both online and off can thus be experienced as both liberating and constraining for the male and female participants, where identity is a strategic tool tied up with gendered relations of both status and power.

Notes

This research was funded by an ESRC Postgraduate Studentship, award no. R42200034532. I am grateful for comments on this and earlier forms of this chapter by Kannan V.; Katy Gardner and Filippo Osella; Peter Collins and Simon Coleman; the participants at the ASA conference panel on 'Communities in Cyberspace'; Shalini Grover and Nicole Blum.

1. In using the terms 'online' and 'offline', I am trying to avoid presenting the classic dichotomy between embodied/'real' and disembodied/'virtual' worlds (see Kitchin 1998: 78–84). As Leander and McKim have remarked: 'the distinction "online" and "offline" is perhaps best seen as an analytic heuristic, a holding place until a more grounded means of understanding and discussing technologically mediated human experiences is formulated' (2003: 223).

2. The reader should be aware that the term 'middle class' within Indian popular parlance is an extremely heterogeneous category (Béteille 2001), and should be understood in its vernacular terms as simply neither rich nor poor, rather than a set of socio-economic characteristics. Educated in English, and many educated to degree level, my informants were certainly falling among the wider definitions of the Indian classes which are linked to education and aspirational values based upon increasing access to consumption (ibid.; Caplan 1987; Das 2002; Varma 1998).

3. A pseudonym. Names of informants employed here are also pseudonyms.

4. Nearly 60p at the then exchange rates.

5. Again, they were not alone in this: young people's lack of alternatives again seems to be a cross-cultural phenomenon when comparing India, the UK and the US (e.g. Chambers et al. 1998: 7; Corrigan 1979; Ruddick 1998: 343).

6. The metaphor of fishing employed here is similar to those used by the Greek men studied by Zinovieff (1991), who chase after foreign tourist women, call themselves *Kamakia* or hunters and try to metaphorically spear as many women as possible before retiring for the winter to boast about their exploits.

7. This is an interesting contrast given the claims surrounding the Death of Distance (Cairncross 1997) or the irrelevance of geography implied by many of the first generation of internet ethnographers (see Dodge and Kitchin 2000: 13–14).

8. As with the participants in other studies of online relationships (e.g. Hardey 2002; Miller and Slater 2000; Slater 2002), they were finding that the norms that have been established for interaction within internet chatrooms allow for the rapid and intense establishment of relationships with young women from around the world (Miller and Slater 2000: 62). Research into chat norms and procedures has shown that 'it is nearly impossible to begin an exchange without conforming to the standard model of opening a conversation' (Velkovska 2002: 205, my translation).

9. Velkovska's analysis also suggests that pauses in replying or replying out of turn are unacceptable in this form of communication because of the need to read text on screen to signify the presence of the other (see also Hardey 2002; Slater 2002). This is why these young men would keep up multiple conversations by often typing only one or two words per turn and using the other user's name to suggest intimacy.

10. Although they did somehow find the money for the more regular visits to the less sumptuous bars and *dhabas* to go drinking with friends. This is discussed in greater detail in my thesis (Nisbett 2005) as another key practice in the formation of their middle-class male identities.

11. Both this mixing of communities and the stress on educational achievement seem to furnish further evidence for Béteille's perception (1991, 2001) that education and occupation have replaced caste as the markers of status amongst the urban middle classes.

12. For a discussion, see Hine (2000: 9), Kitchin (1998:14), Leander and McKim (2003), Wilson and Peterson (2002: 452).

13. The branding of girls and women into such dichotomous categories is, of course, a common discourse for those writing about gender relations, courtship and sexuality or youth, from the South Asian context (Abraham 2001, 2002; Kakar 1990:17 cited in Srivastava 2001: 3; Walle 2004), to that of Greece, Portugal or the UK (Vale de Almeida 1996; Willis 1977; Zinovieff 1991).

14. 'Multiple User Dungeons' – text- or graphics-based virtual environments online, originally based upon role playing games such as Dungeons and Dragons, but now encompassing a much wider set of virtual environments.

References

Abraham, L. (2001), 'Redrawing the Lakshma Rekha: Gender Differences and Cultural Constructions in Youth Sexuality in Urban India', *South Asia* XXIV (Special Issue): 133–56.

Abraham, L. (2002), 'Bhai-behen, True Love, Time Pass: Friendships and Sexual Partnerships Among Youth in an Indian Metropolis', *Culture, Health and Sexuality* 4 (3): 337–53.

Ahearn, L.M. (2001), *Invitations to Love: Literacy, Love Letters and Social Change in Nepal*, Ann Arbor: University of Michigan Press.

Benjamin, S. (2000), 'Governance, Economic Settings and Poverty in Bangalore', *Environment and Urbanization* 12 (1): 35–56.

Béteille, A. (1991), 'The Reproduction of Inequality – Occupation, Caste and Family', *Contributions to Indian Sociology* 25 (1): 3–28.

Béteille, A. (2001), 'The Social Character of the Indian Middle Class', in I. Ahmad and H. Reifeld (eds), *Middle Class Values in India and Western Europe*, New Delhi: Social Science Press.

Brail, S. (1996), 'The Price of Admission : Harrassment and Free Speech in the Wild, Wild, West', in L. Cherny and R. Weise Elizabeth (eds), *Wired Women: Gender and New Realities in Cyberspace*, Seattle: Seal Press.

Cairncross, F. (1997), *The Death of Distance: How the Communications Revolution Will Change Our Lives*, London: Orion Business Books.

Caplan, L. (1987), *Class and Culture in Urban India: Fundamentalism in a Christian Community*, Oxford: Clarendon.

Castells, M. (2000), *The Rise of the Network Society,* Oxford: Blackwell.

Chambers, D., Skelton, T. and Valentine, G. (1998), 'Cool Places: An Introduction to Youth and Youth Cultures', in T. Skelton and G. Valentine (eds), *Cool Places: Geographies of Youth Cultures*, London: Routledge.

Chopra, R. (2004), 'Encountering Masculinity: An Ethnographer's Dilemma', in R. Chopra, C. Osella and F. Osella, F. (eds), *South Asian Masculinities: Context of Change, Sites of Continuity*, New Delhi: Women Unlimited.

Corrigan, P. (1979), *Schooling the Smash Street Kids*, London: Macmillan.

Cowan, J. (1991), 'Going out for a Coffee? Contesting the Grounds of Gendered Pleasures in Everyday Sociability', in P. Loizos and E. Papataxiarchis (eds), *Contested Identities: Gender and Kinship in Modern Greece*, Princeton: Princeton University Press.

Das, G. (2002), *India Unbound*, London: Profile.

Dodge, M. and Kitchin, R. (2000), *Mapping Cyberspace*, New York: Routledge.

Donath, J.S. (1999), 'Identity and Deception in the Virtual Community', in P. Kollock and A.M. Smith (eds), *Communities in Cyberspace*, London: Routledge.

Ferguson, J. (1999), *Expectations of Modernity: Myths and Meanings of Urban Life on the Zambian Copperbelt*, Berkeley: University of California Press.

Hardey, M. (2002), 'Life Beyond the Screen: Embodiment and Identity Through the Internet', *Sociological Review* 50 (4): 570–85.

Hine, C. (2000), *Virtual Ethnography*, London: Sage.

John, M.E. (1998), 'Globalisation, Sexuality and the Visual Field', in J. Nair and M.E. John (eds), *A Question of Silence? The Sexual Economics of Modern India*, New Delhi: Kali for Women.

Kakar, S. (1990), *Intimate Relations: Exploring Indian Sexuality*, Harmondsworth: Penguin.

Kendall, L. (1996), 'MuDder? I hardly know 'Er! Adventures of a Feminist MuDder', in L. Cherny and R. Weise Elizabeth (eds), *Wired Women: Gender and New Realities in Cyberspace,* Seattle: Seal Press.

Kitchin, R. (1998), *Cyberspace: The World in Wires*, Chichester: John Wiley.

Leander, K. and McKim, K. (2003), 'Tracing the Everyday "Sitings" of Adolescents on the Internet: A Strategic Adaptation of Ethnography Across Online and Offline Spaces', *Education, Communication and Information* 3 (2): 211–40.

Loizos, P. and Papataxiarchis, E. (1991), *Contested Identities: Gender and Kinship in Modern Greece*, Princeton: Princeton University Press.

Manderson, L. and Rice, P.L. (eds) (2002), *Coming of Age in South and Southeast Asia: Youth, Courtship and Sexuality,* Richmond, Surrey: Curzon.

Massey, D. (1994), *Space, Place and Gender*, Cambridge: Polity.

Miller, D. and Slater, D. (2000), *The Internet: An Ethnographic Approach*, Oxford: Berg.

Mills, M.B. (2001), 'Auditioning for the Chorus Line: Gender, Rural Youth and the Consumption of Modernity in Thailand', in D.L. Hodgson (ed.), *Gendered Modernities: Ethnographic Perspectives*, New York: Palgrave.

Newitz (1995), 'Surplus Identity On-Line', *Bad Subjects* 18, January, http://bad.eserver.org/issues/1995/18/newitz.html, accessed 09/09/2005.

Nisbett, N.C. (2005), 'Knowledge, Identity, Place and (Cyber)Space: Growing Up Male and Middle Class in Bangalore', Ph.D. thesis, University of Sussex.

Odero, J. (2003), 'Using the Internet Café at Technikon Pretoria in South Africa: Views from Students', University of Bergen: Information and Communication Technologies Education in the South: Beyond Futurological Prophecies and Critical Dystopias, 2–3 October.

Osella, C. and Osella, F. (1998), 'Friendship and Flirting: Micro-Politics in Kerala, South India', *Journal of the Royal Anthropological Institute* (N.S.) 4 (2): 189–206.

Papataxiarchis, E. (1991), 'Friends of the Heart: Male Commensal Solidarity, Gender and Kinship in Aegean Greece', in P. Loizos and E. Papataxiarchis (eds), *Contested Identities: Gender and Kinship in Modern Greece*, Princeton: Princeton University Press.

Ruddick, S. (1998), 'Modernism and Resistance: How "Homeless" Youth Sub-Cultures Make a Difference', in D. Chambers, T. Skelton and G. Valentine(eds), *Cool Places: Geographies of Youth Cultures*, London: Routledge.

Saldanha, A. (2002), 'Music, Space, Identity: Geographies of Youth Culture in Bangalore', *Cultural Studies* 16 (3): 337–50.

Sassen, S. (1991), *The Global City: New York, London, Tokyo*, Princeton: Princeton University Press.

Sassen, S. (1998), *Globalization and its Discontents*, New York: New Press.

Slater, D. (2002), 'Making Things Real – Ethics and Order on the Internet', *Theory Culture & Society* 19(5–6): 227–45.

Srivastava, S. (2001), 'Introduction: Semen, History, Desire and Theory', *South Asia,* XXIV (Special Issue): 1–24.

Srivastava, S. (2004), 'The Masculinity of Dis-location: Commodities, the Metropolis and the Sex-Clinics of Delhi and Mumbai', in R. Chopra, C. Osella and F. Osella (eds), *South Asian Masculinities: Context of Change, Sites of Continuity*, New Delhi: Women Unlimited .

Stone, A.R. (1991), 'Will the Real Body Please Stand Up? Boundary Stories about Virtual Cultures', in M. Benedikt (ed.), *Cyberspace: First Steps*, Cambridge, MA: MIT Press.

Turkle, S. (1995), *Life on the Screen: Identity in the Age of the Internet*, New York: London: Simon & Schuster.

Vale de Almeida, M. (1996), *The Hegemonic Male: Masculinity in a Portuguese Town*, Providence, RI: Berghahn.

Varma, P.K. (1998) *The Great Indian Middle Class*, New York: Viking.

Velkovska, J. (2002), 'L'intimité Anonyme dans les Conversations Électroniques sur les Webchats', *Sociologie du Travail* 44 (2) : 193–213.

Wakeford, N. (1999), 'Gender and the Landscapes of Computing', in M. Crang, P. Crang and J. May (eds), *Virtual Geographies: Bodies, Space and Relations*, London: Routledge.

Walle, T.M. (2004), 'Virginity vs Decency: Continuity and Change in Pakistani Men's Perception of Sexuality and Women', in R. Chopra, C. Osella and F. Osella (eds), *South Asian Masculinities: Context of Change, Sites of Continuity*, New Delhi: Women Unlimited.

Whyte, W.F. (1993), *Street Corner Society: The Social Structure of an Italian Slum*, Chicago: University of Chicago Press.

Willis, P.E. (1977), *Learning to Labour: How Working Class Kids get Working Class Jobs*, Farnborough: Saxon House.

Wilson, S.M. and Peterson, L.C. (2002), 'The Anthropology of Online Communities', *Annual Review of Anthropology* 31: 449–68.

Winner, L. (1996), 'Who Will be in Cyberspace', *The Information Society* 12: 63-71.

Zinovieff, S. (1991), 'Hunters and the Hunted: Kamakia and the Ambiguities of Sexual Predation in a Greek Town', in P. Loizos and E. Papataxiarchis (eds), *Contested Identities: Gender and Kinship in Modern Greece*, Princeton: Princeton University Press.

–7–

Out of Proportion? Anthropological Description of Power, Regeneration and Scale on the Rai Coast of Papua New Guinea

James Leach

Anthropologists are apt to point out that the people with whom they work see the world in different ways. Our descriptions attempt to make the logic of these other visions apparent. Yet the logic of these descriptions, reliant as they often are upon a rational, hierarchical, historical, and so on, integration of elements, have their own scaling (Strathern 1999; Wastell 2001) and organizing (Englund and Leach 2000) effects, one of which is to make the location of 'the field' seem a clearly *geographical* issue. For example, a descriptive and explanatory strategy that outlines how meaning systems are built upon particular social-organizational bases, which themselves rely upon certain material conditions, makes obvious sense to us. We must locate the geographic and material conditions before moving into higher levels of interpretive work. The 'field' of our inquiry is given by the logical demands of such descriptive enterprises. We find explanation convincing because of a hybrid of the obvious (material conditions; possibilities and constraints) and the plausible (social and symbolic analysis, linked to the former). 'Locating the field' happens automatically. It is a terrain to be mapped. Imagination connects elements in a rational sequence. One consequence of this is that aesthetic moments or single images thus nestle in wider social and material domains. But are these the domains that people engaged in their production would recognize? Perhaps locating the field should be less automatic. Perhaps, through reaching out conceptually and descriptively, the 'field' could be constituted (located) in the traffic of ideas and possibilities between people and conceptual terrains.

In this chapter I explore the notion that the appearance of power in people and places on the Rai Coast of Papua New Guinea is difficult to capture with this kind of hierarchical and ready-scaled descriptive apparatus. But this is not a chapter of anthropological angst, nor a critique of the textual practice of social science. I believe that there are analytic vocabularies arising from particular ethnographic engagements with which we can evoke and bring forth a sense of the power, beauty and terror of places for Rai Coast people. It is this positive descriptive endeavour to which I devote my attention. But doing so in this case requires that we 'transcend our grounded and territorial idioms of spatiality' (Corsín-Jiménez 2004). I describe place as a multi-layered process (Bender 1998), one that both is, and produces, entities (Leach 2003:25) that can act, can move, and can have effects.

If such a 'traditional' setting for fieldwork as the Rai Coast of Papua New Guinea (one where locating one's subject population and geographical area is not obviously as problematic as, say, for cyber communities or diasporas), if this setting produces 'places' that are so complex, why should we have ever imagined that the field was a simple physical location? I think that one answer might be because it has allowed us to avoid a certain kind of problem: the problem of meeting the people and thought systems we encounter on genuinely equal terms (Viveiros de Castro 2005).

I begin with a highly rendered outline of the place/knowledge/person nexus on the Rai Coast before moving into an ethnographic description that reveals the scaling effects of some of the principles underlying my descriptions apparent. Description is both means and outcome, for it is through description that we come to know the possibilities and limitations of particular kinds of engagement.

The Rai Coast Person

For Nekgini-speaking villagers on the Rai Coast, the recognition of personhood requires generative productivity. This can be acquired through a lifelong progression in which education, action and effect are central. Power is located in this context: land-based spirits and ancestors *are* the knowledge gained through education, and the means (power) to have an effect on others. Thus education and action relate to specific places. As it is persons themselves that are the most important outcome of any directed action (they embody others' generative work, and thus are constituted by the relations between various powers), persons both contain aspects of (located) power, and can make use of this power as if it were external elements in the land around them. There is a complex spatiality here, with land inside persons as shared substance (as knowledge – see Bamford and Leach forthcoming), as knowledge, and ultimately as power.

Perhaps there is also an unfamiliar temporality here, as 'the past' is made into the present through the regeneration of persons in places. As Basso has written:

> For any sense of place, the pivotal question is not where it comes from or even how it gets formed, but what, so to speak, it is made with. Like a good pot of stew or a complex musical chord, the character of the thing emerges from the qualities of its ingredients ... [yet] always it seems, there is something ineffable about it. (1996: 84)[1]

In what follows, I explore the multi-layered image of the person on the Rai Coast, which necessarily complicates any simple reading of place. Place, like time, is inseparable from the ongoing generation and regeneration of persons. 'Situated-ness' (Leach 2000) in this context, then, is placement in a human, temporal and spatial relational matrix, and is inseparable from particular generative relations between persons and spirits.

One outcome of this complex is the possibility that 'place' can be carried within persons. As knowledge and power, place can be demonstrated anywhere. Persons are places made mobile. If this is a possibility, then the logical 'scaling' of persons *in* places that encompass them must be overturned.

Carving Out Possibilities

I want to relate a narrative given to me by a Nekgini-speaking friend. It is a description of a practical activity (the carving of a small effigy) by a neighbour of mine called Yamui Nombo. Yamui lived in one of the hamlets that makes up Reite Village,[2] was the fourth born of five brothers, and was acknowledged by his kin to be skilled in building houses, making spears and bows, and in carving various forms of decorative design. It will aid readers to follow the description if they know that Nekgini-speaking people, of whom the Reite population (around 350 people) make up around one quarter, actively practise exchange and ceremonial activities reliant upon spirits. Men in this area are initiated, on adolescence, into a male cult (*kaapu* in the Nekgini language), one aspect of which is the musical voices of spirits. Spirits remain hidden from non-initiates, but their evocative and powerful voices allow others to feel their presence and power, and are central to men's attempts to influence others and thus demonstrate their own efficacy.

During certain performances of spirit voice ceremonies, initiated men carry long carved wooden posts. These posts are called *torr* in Nekgini, and usually take the form of planks, two to three meters long, carved with relief images of animals. However, they can also show 'innovations'. On one occasion, a *torr* was made as a cargo ship, and carried by a man who thus made a claim for his connection to the powerful spirits of white people. *Torr* are carried by men by means of an umbrella-like structure, supported on the shoulders and head, which then in turn supports the base of the post. Posts thus rise from a construction (a *mangmang*) harnessed to the man's shoulders, obscure his head entirely, and reach lofty heights above the dancing group (see Leach 2003: 142).

I am going to use Yamui's description as a way into addressing issues of scale. I do so because I notice an analogy between our explanatory and descriptive strate-gies as anthropologists and Yamui's explanation. That is, I am not the first to be struck by how often our descriptions begin with a small element, an object, or an anecdote, and then expand from this into a description of a whole social world

(Strathern 1990). And I cannot help noticing that I am using Yamui's description in this very familiar way. We might think that Yamui, in his description, is also doing this familiar thing. We both focus upon a single, narrow, element, and expand from there. But for me, the expansion is conscious – I add to the singular to make a larger whole by putting it in context (Wagner 1981). Yamui, on the other hand, cannot seem *to prevent* the carving he describes expanding to fill the social world with its own immanence and meaning. There is no conscious making of connection on his part, just the tracing, through description, of connections that were all too apparent in this case.

I am not merely noting a similarity between Yamui's understanding of his specific carving and what turned out to be its huge effect, and how anthropologists routinely use single instances to enter what look like 'larger' contexts. I want to pursue that similarity for what it might yield about scale in our respective positions of anthropologist and carver. Noting similarity, of course, invites differentiation (Strathern 1991), and the 'context' that anthropologists see as potentially expanding, as explanation, from any one moment; and the effect that Yamui understands as a consequence of the process of carving, are not the same kinds of thing. I say this, even though there is a move from the single and bounded to the multiple and expansive in each case. I will suggest that this is because for Yamui there is no natural 'scaling' of the carving and the world it brings forth; they are not 'proportional' to one another in order of magnitude.[3] And this in turn is because of what we might call a non-representational ontology, a recognition of the continuum of language and world (Weiner 1995). A carving does not stand for a power, and thus act as a token event which substitutes for that larger realm of myth and magic. The carving *is* that power, as we will see.

Following this I move to situate this notion of scale and power through elaborating the possibilities of a small event, object or single person that contains a larger reality – an analogy, then, of expansion through (anthropological) textual construction, which partakes of a wholly different kind of expansiveness.

What follows is a translation of some things Yamui said about carving while he was engaged in the activity, and we were together in a spirit place (what Lawrence [1984] calls a 'sacred grove') near to his house. Yamui was carving one of the ceremonial sculptures (*torr*) that are carried by men as part of spirit-voice performances. He said:

> To carve these posts we think about the forms all the time that we are carving. We think of a lizard on the road, or a snake in the bush, how their heads go, how their bodies are, and we follow these memories. If you didn't you couldn't carve them! There are plenty of people here who aren't clear about making *torr* or carving designs – they don't know how these things go. You must also think of how the snake will hold the plank, you must think of it and make it. If not the snake is going to fall off! We used to sit close to Papa and watch his hands carefully, and we were studying these things! We were

watching well – how would they get the head, how the tail. When we were big, we started to try and make all these carvings. We used to see him making them straight [i.e. correctly][4] and now we can make them straight.

This work has a way of learning it. If you are close to the men when they are doing it, you will be able to try. If you did not spend time with them, then you will not have a clue. At one time we saw, Papa used his own thinking and made a design for the *marita masalai*, that is, the spirit of fruit-bearing red *Pandanus*. This spirit does not belong to his people, but he thought of it and carved it. He made a red man, with *marita* fruit above his head, and although he didn't before, while he was making it, he came to know the name of the *marita* spirit.

The time they carried this [*torr*] and danced in Serieng, lots of people became dizzy and collapsed. They all heard the name of the spirit! They asked Papa, and he said 'yes', the name they had heard was indeed the secret and powerful name of marita patuki [story, mythic character]. Many were sick after this. They become short of blood. Plenty went to [the local government centre] Saidor and had blood given to them [at the hospital there]. But a woman who had married into the clan of the marita story died in childbirth from loss of blood. She was not the only one.

Yamui's narrative moves from what appears a fairly straightforward description of apprenticeship, observation of the environment, and imagination, into an incredible story of magic and power. I am just fascinated by how this transition makes sense. My guess is that Yamui did not think there was any transition in what he was describing.

For us, there is a disjuncture: of scale or proportion, we might say. Craft skill, or technical endeavour, seamlessly moves into a description of the mythic and magical – in fact, of the powers of the world-forming mythical ancestors, *patuki*. It appears that these 'scales' are not distinguished by Yamui in his narrative. There is no disjuncture between prosaic carving and the mystical power to cause serious and potentially catastrophic effect. In fact, they are inextricably linked, as the name of *marita patuki* emerged, as it were, from the interaction of observation, imagination and wood. For Yamui, it seems, these things are in proportion.

Although it is an obvious thing to do, I set this off against my view that it is a disproportionate effect: if one thinks of the carving as a shaped piece of wood, that is.[5] But of course it is not the piece of wood that he describes; it is the unfolding of knowledge through making. The question, then, is what kind of knowledge, and how does that relate to the knowledge we make through our descriptive practices?

Yamui's narrative makes sense of the carving's effect through its revelation of a connection with a myth, with ancestral names, and thus with power. These are things that were discovered by the carver in the process of making. The carving expands as a revelation, and it is the magnitude of the revelation (as a revelation of power itself) that is achieved through carving. Carving, then, as Yamui describes it, is a process of discovery that can be revelatory of the world that it engages with. For example, we might say that the exploration of the form of things one sees in one's forest lands, and which lodge in the minds of the carver, is also an exploration of the history of these lands. Through this exploration, powers are revealed and people become more parts of the places and lands they inhabit. That is, they come to know more of those things, as Yamui's father did. The history is not background. It cannot explain the power of the carving. Rather, it is an element of the carving.

What kind of 'landscape' could one inhabit for these kinds of perceptions to be possible? Indeed, how is 'land' or 'material' *scaled* in relation to the person, or to the spiritual, or the powerful, in order that these orders can define one another, encompass one another, and make possible the relations between elements which generate effective interventions by humans as carvers? For this, we have to think about land, persons and places as inhabiting one another as necessary parts.

Education and Knowledge

How does one know a place? How does one demonstrate this knowledge? For Reite people, one comes to know a place through being there (unsurprisingly), because being there allows one to participate in the lives of other animate elements, and have them participate in one's own existence. Children grow up in a particular named hamlet. They eat from the lands adjacent to, and owned by, the adults of that place, and thus continually imbibe the physical substance produced by those adults. In a recognizably Melanesian perception, they also grow because of the 'hard work' of those adults,[6] and this gives them both shared identity through shared substance, and obligation to those who have grown them. This obligation is magnified by the fact that to successfully grow crops which feed children, adults must enter into relationships with land-based spirits and ancestors. It is in fact these entities that *grow* the crops, just as in initiation it is the same entities which transform children into gendered and effective adults. So one is obliged not just through others' labour, but through the fact that their labour was focused upon providing the conditions under which growth (that is, correct and healthy relations with spirits in the landscape) could be formed (Ingold 2000: 132–52; Leach 2003).

Particular spirits in particular areas of land take different forms. These are reflected in the complex and essential form of ritual planting at the centre of a garden, in the different voices that manifest the spirits' presence during gardening and during performances of *kaapu*, in their different names, tunes and, indeed, the form of the carvings of *torr* posts which relate to the lands of particular spirits. One cannot grow up as any-old person; the process of growth is one of engagement with particular people and their spiritual powers, which literally gives the form to the person who is grown.

On initiation, spirits are brought to bear on the bodies of adolescents in order to form them into persons with (re)productive (gendered) potential (Leach 2003: 59–84). It is these same spirits that are used by the initiates subsequently for growing their crops, and indeed children. The model for productivity in subsistence is that of reproduction, so that staple tubers are thought of as children, grown by the same power and thus containing the same substance as people themselves. At the same time, during a period of seclusion, initiates are given advice and education about how to behave correctly. They are given the names and tunes of the spirits relating to growth, change, warfare, sorcery, and so on, from the lands in which they have grown, and in which they will continue to operate as adults in their own right. Thus education (and Reite villagers cite initiation as the main formal education that a person receives) is a process of making connections with, and learning how to manipulate, aspects of the physical/spiritual environment. We might gloss this as 'knowledge'. That is, what people 'learn' are the names of spirits, their tunes, the procedures for ensuring that they are present, the forms of their actions as narratives, and so on. But *unlike* a more familiar version of 'knowledge', 'knowing' is to be put in relation with. One shares knowledge with one's co-residents (and therefore kin) by way of being made, as people, by the same relationships to particular sources of growth and power. Knowledge, then, is to have a relation to another animate entity, not to have an abstract object of thought or understanding located somewhere in one's body (the mind).

Singing the World

If we turn for a moment to what these people say about composition of another kind (than carving), that is, of words that accompany the powerful voices of spirits, then we can perhaps get closer to the understanding of land, place and person as necessarily connected through *substance*, which anthropologists might gloss as knowledge. By this, I mean that what people share when they say they are kin are the constitutive relations to particular generative, land-based, powers. In this sense, 'knowledge' as a relationship to another animate entity is what also connects people to one another. These people are the same because of sharing the same 'knowledge'. What *we* gloss as *knowledge* they translate as the substance of human kinship relations. Sharing particular powers of growth and effect is to take the same form.

Kanining is a word in the Nekgini language which means something like 'singing things with their names' (cf. Basso 1988). Here is Yamui's elder brother, Porer, talking about the power of singing things with names:

> *Kanining* [singing things] is the true purpose of composing songs. There is a tune for planting yams. You hum the tune in your mind and say the powerful name of the yam and plant your yam. When the original yam [who was a man] turned his body into that

of the first yam, he taught his people his name and the tune. You can hum the tune anywhere, but the words must remain hidden. When you plant yam, you '*kanine ing kete
wiynung siri*' – sing the yam and plant it.

It is the combination, then, of name, tune and action that makes successful yam
husbandry possible. For the carver, these connections are played out in a different
order: the action of successful carving reveals the powerful name of a spirit.

Form seems fluid here: whether one knows names and generates form (a yam's
growth demonstrates the correct combination of name and tune), or one generates
form and knows names (carving reveals a powerful connection which is manifest
in 'knowledge' of the secret powerful name), makes little difference. I would
choose to describe it thus: Yamui's understanding of engagement with the land, or
with wood, is *already* an engagement with the social and the relational world in
which it will come to have an effect. The gardener's approach to his earth and seeds
reveals the relations these things already have to the history of generative relations
between people and mythic characters. The carver's approach to his wood reveals
how the forms he has in his mind are already the forms of mythic beings. One does
not have to start with material and then move registers in order to perceive
'meaning'. Meaning is immanent in elements that surround one because they sit
within the matrix of relations that define all.

In Yamui's narrative, he emphasizes spatiality – proximity – in order to have the
relationship which here I am glossing as a Rai Coast form of 'knowing'. It was his
closeness to his father that allows him to carve. It is the proximity of the particular
animal and vegetable forms of particular places that allows one to hold them in the
mind and render them as carved forms. It is no coincidence that Yamui's father
'thought to' carve the *marita patuki*. He had lived in close proximity to the place
of that *patuki*. (Yamui's father was a renowned sorcerer, and, for his own protection, spent much of his life on other people's lands. His own kin feared his power
and there was hostility among them for a time.) This close association put him in
the position of sharing substance (knowledge) with them, which appeared as a revelation of 'things in his mind'. His discovery of the name of the *marita patuki*
accords with the model of the revelation of all knowledge among Nekgini-
speakers in myth, through relationships with powerful beings located at particular
spots (Lawrence 1964).

Place is the term I have chosen in my writings on the Rai Coast to try to capture
this complex. Places are generative, emergent entities that, as whole fields of relations between people, spirits, ancestors and land, situate particular forms.
Participation in the generative process, through what Rai Coast people describe as
'work' (anything relating to and having an effect upon another person), is connection to all its elements. There is no simple scaling or proper proportion to these elements; it is in their combination that power and effect are achieved.

Torr posts are carried in the specific context of performances of spirit voices (*kaapu neng*). As performances, these events incorporate carved designs, vocal and other forms of music, body decoration, perfume and dance. The performances are intended to, and indeed often do, have direct and lasting effects on those who witness them. The effect is not the same, however, as one might expect when viewing paintings or sculptures in an art gallery. If successful, these performances actually re-structure people's relationships to one another. People are so moved by the performances that, not infrequently, they will physically move themselves, and their residence, to be a part of the place that demonstrates such power through their performances.

What is it that these performances draw upon? At their heart are the land-based spirits, who appear through their musical and mysterious voices. These voices are controlled and brought forth by initiated men, they lead the men and women in song, and provide the energy for the night's performances. These spirits are particular to particular places, as we have heard already. And they are in some sense the essence of a place: its power and beauty and dangers and effects all rolled into one. When I say that they are specific to places, this goes quite deep. Indeed, these are people who say that species of their main subsistence crop (the starch, taro) differ because of the land and spirits that grow them. If you take the same species of taro from one people's land to another, then it metamorphizes into a species completely distinct from its parent plant in one generation. This is reported as a simple observable fact by Reite gardeners.

It is the combination of a spirit's name and the tune which brings other things, including carvings, to life. The spirits then animate things, and make them into persons of a kind. The names of spirits, and the tunes in which these names are known, are the magical formulas used in the planting and tending of crops and trees. As I have said, they are also vital for growing adolescents into adulthood. Different spirits and different kinsmen transform a child into a productive adult through initiations. When objects are made with the aid of the spirits, they are animate, have voices of their own, and demand respect (Leach 2002).

Growing crops, then, is just one example of the power of spirits, people and ground combined. Areas are distinct because of the special characteristics of the land and spirits that are there. People partake of this difference also. Eating crops grown by a group of people, and by the powers of the land in which they reside, is a way of becoming 'the same' as the others who live in that land. So people become family to one another – to the extent that they must not marry – by working together, and being grown, on the same lands. In our (or, rather, recent anthropological) terms, they share substance because of being grown together.

Notice that there is a whole complex of relations that define a person. The person is the outcome of the intersecting work and power of many other agents and actors – all of whom are 'kin' in some way. So when people bring the voices of their spirits to a performance, they are very much bringing distinctive and vital powers – not of themselves, not of their land, but powers which reside, if they reside anywhere, in the relationships between people and land. It is tempting to call this 'history', although that requires a rather strange temporal understanding.

A Note on Temporality

It is a temporal paradox that at birth in Nekgini-speaking villages, a body is closest in time to the power of its ancestors. This is true both of the generative force that constitutes the body, and in the simple sense of the progression of time. So the emergence of powerful actors in this context is the re-emergence of power from the past. Time almost flows in reverse, as the lifecycle is a movement towards the ancestral, and to the power of generation.

It would seem that the Rai Coast person is a complex of layers and relations. Children are not automatically recognized as persons just because of descent from their predecessors. They must gain that recognition. Without knowledge, without power, they are the antipathy of the generative, which ancestors embody: they are powerless and dislocated. Through life a person develops a social persona as a regeneration of his or her powerful ancestors. He or she moves forwards in time by doing, while moving backwards into the power of the 'past' in order to achieve that 'doing'. For this reason it seems plausible to describe Rai Coast kinship as focussed upon regeneration (see Leach 2003: 117–18).

Knowledge of how to make effective use of the particular properties and aspects of land is a matter of long-term discovery. Spirits and their powerful names are handed down over generations. Yet they are also being dreamed into existence as time moves on. Myths relate how all the important knowledge in the world – the cultivation of crops, the building of houses, even the separation of genders – was discovered in the landscape somewhere. The powers that gave people knowledge still reside in these places, which stand as sacred groves of trees, or as pools formed by springs. Performances themselves combine carved designs (*torr*) which carry both abstract and representative relief images inspired by the lands that people traverse daily, with smells and colours and body decoration distinct to each place.

I hope you can see why one might want to say that this performance is 'of the land'. It amounts to a presentation of the power of the place, as it is known and controlled by its people, for others to experience. People thus can take land about, can make a presentation of their lands (there are intricate ways of ensuring that spirits follow a dancing group from their home pools), can make clear who they are, by demonstrating the relationships and context of their emergence.

This is hardly a 'representation'; we might call it a 'presentation' of place. Other than people themselves, these performances are the most tangible experience of land possible. The work they involve is the whole work of being in a place: from growing crops to feed the participants, to marshalling spirits, to making designs that illuminate aspects of places. For this reason, I have been tempted to say that they might be described as 'land-made-mobile'. Knowing songs and knowing names of spirits is to claim inclusion in the productive field in which people, crops and songs/designs/ideas themselves emerge.

Locating the Field

Holding stable the elements of any explanation seems to be about getting things in proportion: that is, understanding orders of magnitude, hierarchies of cause and effect, influence and outcome. But Yamui's description blows this apart. The scale of any element is proportional to its effects on other elements. These properties are not given prior to specific relational engagements. It is because a carver is already enmeshed in relations to lands, spirits, mythic characters and other people, and because these relationships are generative as a whole, that any element within them might be an entry into that generative power, while at the same time it may also be capable of encompassing it (as the revealed name did in Serieng).

What is the power of the *marita* carving if it is not the power of entry into a series of relationships that generate people and places: in other words, entry into placed and particular powers? Anthropological description could be seen as a similar enterprise. When we model our explanations on the relational worlds of those we encounter, relations between elements of those worlds come to look for us like the generative working of creative power (Wagner 1981: 142). Through reaching out conceptually and descriptively, the 'field' we might locate is given by the need to adapt our modelling, by the necessary traffic of ideas and possibilities between people and conceptual terrains. The specifics of our explanations too often focus upon hierarchies of cause and effect, of encompassing scales of meaning and reason. It seems too natural for us to place the wood of Yamui's carving at a lower level of influence than the meaning it carries: its representation of a mythic character. But the point of his narrative is the opposite. The carving, far from a representation (something defined as a token leading into a grander scale of significance), is already as wide a scale as it is possible to have. To conceptualize our field as being the point at which we can meet such perceptions is both as old as anthropology and contemporary. It relies upon ethnographic engagement as an entry into a(ny) series of relationships that generate people, places and objects. Description could fulfil the role of making possible that engagement.

On the Rai Coast tiny observations of things in the landscape become encompassing icons of condensed power, and, in having their effect, they reveal that power. The carving scales up and, in a moment, encompasses other people and powerful entities. It does so because it reveals power in the land itself. This power is the complex generative power of relationality. It has no existence outside (does not encompass in scale) the world it appears in and effects. So place, then, is scaleable; it can be singular and contained in a person, or carving, and that is also a containing capacity, or it can encompass others and ultimately act as an image (Wagner 1987) of world generation. To put it bluntly, Yamui's carving is not meaningful because its manufacture situates a piece of wood in a symbolic, cultural context; it is meaningful because in scale it is the same as that context which *we* abstract and call culture – or differently so, as it partakes of an alternative ontology of spirits, persons and Rai Coast places. It is in the meeting of one with the other which I see as the place to locate our field.

Notes

In memory of Yamui Nombo.

Thanks to Alberto Corsín-Jiménez for the initial stimulus and subsequent discussions, to Yamui Nombo, who died while this paper was with the editors and who taught me so much, to Porer Nombo, and to members of King's College Description reading group. This paper was written for the ASA session 'Scalarity and the Cross-Sectional Imagination: Orders of Aperture, Magnitude and Consequentiality in the Organization of Social Relationships' at Durham in 2004. Following the lead of the organizer, Alberto Corsín-Jiménez, I have tried to make something about scale, power and place on the Rai Coast of Papua New Guinea apparent, while at the same time reflecting upon our descriptive strategies.

1. 'As with places, for Nekgini speakers, so with persons' (Leach 2003: 211).
2. 'Villages' in this sense were a product of the colonial organization of dispersed and shifting hamlet sites into larger groups for ease of administration and inspection (Lawrence 1964). Reite people rapidly abandoned them, long before independence, yet the organization of the modern nation state of Papua New Guinea still recognizes 'villages' such as the colonial amalgam 'Reite' as the lowest level of entity with political representation (Leach 2003). They are 'virtual' villages, we might say, yet the presence of a leader for this village who has a say in local affairs makes them 'real' through the journeys of this person, connecting and bringing people together for the purposes of dispute settlement, community work and business development.
3. Following Corsín-Jiménez's (2004) interest in proportion.
4. See Crook (in press) for elaboration on the notion of straightness in another Papua New Guinean setting.
5. As anthropologists we would tend to think of it as a carved piece of wood heavy with symbolic meaning. It is the separation of the mental and material here which I resist, for a number of reasons, not least of which is that Yamui appears not

to make the *same* separation of these things that we would (and see Henare et al. in press).

6. That is, the 'work' of what we call ritual. This is 'hard work' in Reite understanding because of the necessity of eliciting appropriate responses both from other people and from spirits in order to secure a transformation and its recognition.

References

Bamford, S. and Leach, J. (eds) (forthcoming) *Genealogy Beyond Kinship: Sequence, Essence and Transmission in Ethnography and Social Theory*, New York: Berghahn Books.

Basso, K.H. (1988), '"Speaking with Names": Language and Landscape among the Western Apache', *Cultural Anthropology* 3 (2): 99–130.

Basso, K.H. (1996), 'Wisdom Sits in Places: Notes on a Western Apache Landscape', in S. Feld and K.H. Basso (eds), *Senses of Place*, Santa Fe: School of American Research Press.

Bender, B. (1998), *Stonehenge: Making Space*, Oxford: Berg.

Corsín-Jiménez (2004), 'Scalarity and the Cross-Sectional Imagination: Orders of Aperture, Magnitude and Consequentiality in the Organization of Social Relationships', ASA 2004 Panel Abstract.

Crook, T. (forthcoming), *Kim Kuru Kuru: An Anthropological Exchange with Bolivip, Papua New Guinea*, Oxford: British Academy Monographs/Oxford University Press.

Englund, H. and Leach, J. (2000), 'Ethnography and the Meta-Narratives of Modernity', *Current Anthropology* 41 (2): 225–48.

Henare, A., Holbraad, M. and Wastell, S. (in press), *Thinking Through Things*, London: UCL Press.

Ingold, T. (2000), *The Perception of the Environment: Essays in Livelihood, Dwelling and Skill*, London: Routledge.

Lawrence, P. (1964), *Road Belong Cargo: A Study of the Cargo Movement in the Southern Madang District New Guinea*, Manchester: Melbourne University Press/Manchester University Press.

Lawrence, P. (1984), *The Garia: An Ethnography of a Traditional Cosmic System in Papua New Guinea*, Singapore: Melbourne University Press.

Leach, J. (2000), 'Situated Connections: Rights and Intellectual Resources in a Rai Coast Society', *Social Anthropology* 8 (2): 163–79.

Leach, J. (2002), 'Drum and Voice: Aesthetics and Social Process on the Rai Coast of Papua New Guinea', *Journal of the Royal Anthropological Institute* (N.S.) 8 (4): 713–34.

Leach, J. (2003), *Creative Land: Place and Procreation on the Rai Coast of Papua*

New Guinea, Oxford and New York: Berghahn Books.

Strathern, M. (1990), 'Artefacts of History: Events and the Interpretation of Images', in J. Siikala (ed.), *Culture and History in the Pacific*, Helsinki: Transactions of the Finnish Anthropological Society.

Strathern, M. (1991), *Partial Connections*, Savage, MD: Rowman & Littlefield.

Strathern, M. (1999), *Property Substance and Effect*, London: Athlone Press.

Viveiros de Castro, E. (2005), 'Perspectival Anthropology and the Method of Controlled Equivocation', unpublished paper presented at King's College Cambridge Research Centre, June.

Wagner, R. (1981), *The Invention of Culture*, Chicago: University of Chicago Press.

Wagner, R. (1987), 'Figure–Ground Reversal Among the Usen Barok', in L. Lincoln (ed.), *Assemblage of Spirits: Idea and Image in New Ireland*, New York: George Braziller/Mineapolis Institute of Arts.

Wastell, S. (2001), 'Presuming Scale, Making Diversity: On the Mischiefs of Measurement and the Global: Local Metonym in Theories of Law and Culture', *Critique of Anthropology* 21 (2): 185–210.

Weiner, J. (1995), *The Lost Drum: The Myth of Sexuality in Papua New Guinea and Beyond*, Madison: University of Wisconsin Press.

–8–

Far from the Trobriands? Biography as Field

Sigridur Duna Kristmundsdottir

Introduction

As for most anthropologists trained in the Malinowskian tradition of fieldwork, the field hovered on the horizon of my student years as a perfectly magical place, far removed from the mundane realities of life in modern cities and offering untold of opportunities for discovery and intellectual creation. I remember my elation when I landed in my one and only field outside the Western world in 1984.[1] I had finally arrived, I was *there*. I loved that piece of fieldwork, but as circumstances would have it I subsequently did most of my research 'at home', in Iceland; and not only 'at home' but, to an extent bypassing participant observation, on events of the past. For a considerable part of my professional life I have therefore not been *there* in a twofold sense.

Recent interest from anthropology in critically examining the concept of the field and even in relocating the field is therefore doubly welcome, and in this chapter I wish to apply my experience of biographical research to the current discussion. I will begin by outlining the trajectory that led to my doing biographical work and what anthropological reasons I formulated to undertake it. I discuss how biographical research can be defined as 'anthropological', and how it can contribute to the re-definition of the field and the methods of participant observation in anthropology. I examine the situationality of the researcher and how it complements that of the field, and, finally, indicate the importance of reaching across disciplinary boundaries in anthropology. Apart from my experience of biographical research, my discussion is inspired by Gupta and Ferguson's (1997) delineation of the field as location and Braidotti's (2002) discussion of the researcher as location.

Trajectory

One of my research projects in Iceland was to delineate and analyse the history of the women's movement in the country from the 1870s to the 1990s. That I did in terms of several anthropological theoretical precepts, such as Fortesian social structural theory and the concept of the person (Kristmundsdottir 1997). I was careful to keep to the broad sweep of the movements, their ideas and their social and cultural generation, never succumbing to naming individual women activists unless it served the needs of the overall analysis. Yet I knew from my own experiences of feminist activism, which as fieldwork experience contributed considerably to my analysis, that individuals could be pivotal in the generation of a movement and its ideas as well as in its subsequent life. Although the concept of the person proved a useful tool to clarify why women engaged in women's movement activities, the stumbling block continued to be the Durkheimian adage that we study the general and not the idiosyncratic. Was not the individual idiosyncratic?

Then my attention was drawn towards the life and work of an Icelandic woman which seemed to offer rich material for anthropological analysis. She was born in 1874 into an agricultural society which had remained mostly unchanged in Iceland since medieval times. Yet she completed a Ph.D. at the Sorbonne, Paris, in 1926, the first Icelandic woman to attain such an advanced university degree. Her achievement represented an immense leap in cultural time and space. Her life therefore seemed to offer an excellent mirror, reflecting the rapid transition of Icelandic society from its age-old traditional form into the present-day modern, industrial society. Understanding this transition and its effect on contemporary society and culture in the country has been one of the main tasks of the anthropology of Iceland since its inception in the 1970s (see e.g. Durrenberger and Palsson 1989; Hastrup 1998; Kristmundsdottir 1997).

Secondly, this person and her work were at the time virtually unknown in Iceland. In the light of her pioneering status, her life seemed to shed light on the subjects of cultural remembering and forgetting and the role that gender plays in these processes. Thirdly, her voluminous work, which spans the fields of philosophy, psychology, physiology, etymology, nutrition, social issues and literature, was itself interesting and full of ideas that had relevance to anthropological investigations and theorizing. In short, the life and work of Björg C. Thorlaksson seemed to be a goldmine of anthropological subjects waiting to be examined.

Although these seemed excellent anthropological reasons to undertake research into her life, the fact that she was an individual and only an individual remained problematic. Researching and writing biographies of people long dead is perhaps for this reason not prevalent in anthropology. As Langness and Frank (1981) point out, gathering life-stories in the field and using them to supplement other material obtained by observation and interviews has long been practised in anthropology. Several anthropologists have used such life-stories as frames for their analysis of cultural and social formations among the people they study. Salient examples are Oscar Lewis's *The Children of Sánchez* (1961), Marjorie Shostak's *Nisa: The Life and Words of a !Kung Woman* (1981) and Vincent Crapanzano's *Tuhami: Portrait of a Moroccan* (1985). These and similar works are based on interviews and observations in the field as traditionally defined, formed by interaction with the person who is at the centre of the work and supplemented by field data generally. When the biographical subject is dead and the life under exploration lived in a non-observable past, such field methods cannot be employed. In such a case there is no field in the traditional sense. Yet biographical research into lives already lived involves understanding and accounting for social and cultural formations and processes in much the same way as in the above-mentioned works.

Initially I thought I would isolate analytic components from my subject's life and use them to illustrate social and cultural signifiers and their relevance to Icelandic society, past and present. To begin with, a biography was not the object of my research. Yet the chance to present an anthropological analysis in the biographical narrative form became irresistible.[2] What I ended up doing was combining these perspectives into two works: a biography, or an ethnography, of Björg C. Thorlaksson's life, on the one hand, and, on the other, a collection of papers on her work written by scholars in the relevant fields (Kristmundsdottir 2001, 2002).[3]

Biography as Anthropology

Is it possible to understand the life of a person without understanding the social and cultural context that shapes that life and which the person in question in turn takes part in shaping? From an anthropological point of view that is not the case. In order to understand a person's life, the biographer anthropologist has to have a basic understanding of the culture in question in much the same way as we normally do when researching a subject in anthropology. Examining the life itself is therefore not enough; researching the society and culture in question are essential components of the project. In addition, biography can be a vehicle for the description and analysis of certain social and cultural phenomena such as the significance of gender or ideas about productivity, and on that account it also requires a thorough and detailed knowledge of the society and culture in question.

As mentioned above, the life-story has been long and widely used in anthropology as a mirror on the culture in question. When a life-story becomes a full-fledged biography, however, the risk is that the idiosyncrasies of the life will be transposed onto the culture in question, narrowing and even distorting the cultural patterns and social processes in which the life takes place. A sound knowledge of the culture is for that reason also a necessary prerequisite for the researcher. Biographical research hence involves attaining much the same understanding of culture and society as we traditionally hope to achieve in anthropology, and the ability to transmit that understanding.

Biographies where the social and cultural context is a mere backdrop to the story of a life or is simply subsumed into the story and therefore hardly extant are not uncommon. Consider, for instance, how gender is often subsumed in the biographies of men, where this significant social fact and its social and cultural ramifications in their lives is an unexamined given. An example is Roy Jenkins's (2001) biography of Winston Churchill, where the fact that he is male is hardly commented upon, nor is the significance of his gender made into an analytic component. Often such disregard for an important cultural element in a person's life stems from an uncritical acceptance of the culture in question; in the case of gender, being a man is often considered the norm, as Simone de Beauvoir (1972 [1949]) argued over half a century ago, and we need not question the normal. When the subject does not fit the norm, it needs to be explained, and such hidden cultural elements come into view. A case in point is John Campbell's (2000) biography of Margaret Thatcher, another British prime minister, where her gender and the fact that she was a woman in an unconventional social position are explored and discussed at considerable length.

For biography to be anthropology, a critical examination of the culture in question is essential. Anthropology has of course a rich store of theoretical insights and ethnographic knowledge which lend themselves readily and productively to such an undertaking in biographical description and analysis. A case in point is gender, as mentioned above. Anthropology has a plethora of useful insights to offer on this component of a person's life from the early concepts of muted and dominant models to discussions about how a person can be differently gendered according to different social contexts (e.g. Ardener 1975; Lambek and Strathern 1998; Nandy 1999). These insights prompt questions such as: does my subject (according to context) belong to a dominant or a muted social model?; and, whichever is the case at different times, what significance does that have for my subject's life? Or does my subject in spite of her sex have certain male-gendered social characteristics exhibited in certain social contexts, and what does that mean? And what do the answers to these questions tell us about the culture and society in which the subject lived? As a woman, living a life different to that of most Icelandic women at the time, my subject certainly belonged to a muted social model, which insight shed light on why she made the choices she made. The concepts of dominant and muted also helped to explain the failure of her attempts to gain acceptance in the male-dominated world of scholarship in the 1920s and 1930s and how her voice there was constantly muted. And certainly my subject exhibited certain male-gendered characteristics in certain social contexts, such as, in spite of being an ardent feminist, talking down to women or telling them they needed scientific education to be better mothers. Theoretical insights from anthropology helped form the relevant questions and answering them produced an analysis of the life and the society in which it was lived.

Another case in point is the intersection between the domestic and the politico-jural domain in a person's life and how a person negotiates between the private and public spheres in her life (e.g. Fortes 1969; Rosaldo and Lamphere 1974). On occasion, especially in the biographies of men, whose work in the public domain prompts the biography in the first place, discussion of the domestic domain is reduced to a mere statement of the relevant facts and its existence and its effects on what happens in the public domain are not an integral part of the analysis. Understanding the life of my subject, who strove for recognition in the public sphere but was continually defined in terms of the private sphere, was greatly aided by anthropological insights on these issues.

Then there are, for instance, theories about power in anthropology (see e.g. Gledhill 1994). Insights into how power is allocated in a society and how it is transmitted are of course conducive to understanding the ramifications of a person's life. Finally, personhood theory has direct relevance to understanding a person's life. What is it that allows a person to do to become whatever she becomes at different stages in her life? What are the sources of her agency? Which are denied her? How does she employ the ones she has, and how does she by her agency contribute to social and cultural change? Underlying the answers to these and similar questions is the anthropological understanding that society is made up of systems of values and systems of social relationships that intersect and affect each other constantly. Biography is after all about exploring the linkages between individual and society and explaining how values, agency and structure contribute to form a person's life.

These are just a few examples from the rich store of anthropological knowledge that can inform biographical description and analysis. Biography undertaken on these premises is in effect the ethnography of a life and a certain social and cultural context, and hence very much within the boundaries of what we define as anthropology.

The Field

Having established that biography need not be but can be anthropology, what then happens to the field in biographical research? As pointed out above, the field cannot be there in the conventional anthropological sense when the subject is deceased and participant observation cannot be employed. In spite of a recent move towards the historicization of anthropology, the functionalist emphasis on researching what we can actually observe is still very much with us (see e.g. Hastrup 1992). Hinging on participant observation is the field as the place where we do that observation, and hence the centrality of the field to anthropological investigations.

It need not be surprising that the field as the spatial locus of anthropological research, and as geographically and/or culturally removed from the autochthonous context of the researcher, has shown a remarkable tenacity in anthropology in the face of a fast-changing world. As Gupta and Ferguson have pointed out, we have

used the extent to which research is done 'in the field' as 'the single most significant factor determining whether a piece of research will be accepted as (that
magical word) "anthropological"' (1997: 1). The concept of the field has thus
served to distinguish between what anthropologists do and what others do in
related disciplines such as history, sociology or political science. We have, in other
words, used the centrality of the field in anthropological research to draw the line
between 'them' and 'us' in the academic world and hence to define our self-image
and the image of our discipline. Examining critically this identity-loaded concept
and its importance in anthropology is therefore in a sense like invading with dirty
feet the mythical grove of our creation. That may in turn account for the relative
paucity of such examinations in anthropology.[4]

Yet we live in a world that appears vastly different from the one in which the
centrality of the geographically and culturally defined field was formed. That is
reason enough for taking a critical look at our conceptualization of it, but not the
only one. Another reason is to include other traditionally non-anthropological
areas of knowledge in our investigations and to open up the boundary walls we
have built between ourselves and related disciplines. As I have argued, one such
area which seems to have been fenced off from anthropology is biography, because
biographical research can most often not be undertaken in a traditionally defined
field. But does biography have a field? Is that tradition-bound concept useful in
such research, and if so, what can biographical research contribute to the redefin-
ition of the field in anthropology?

The field as a geographical place is very much there in biographical research in
the sense that a life is always lived in certain places that need to be investigated in
the course of the research. As a subject may have lived in a number of different
places, the field may in fact be geographically diverse. Yet these geographical
localities are by no means the actual field of biographical research. In such
research the life of the subject becomes the field constituted by the events of the
life, what happened at different times and in different places, the passions and
sorrows, laughter and tears coursing through the life, the significant, and not so
significant, others in that life, and so on – and of course the life's social and cultural context, as discussed above. Hence the field cannot be a place or locality in
the traditional sense, but rather it becomes a location defined by the life and its
context. The researcher is situated in this location wherever she happens to be; she
carries the field with her wherever she goes or stays during the course of her
research. Contrary to traditional anthropological fieldwork, she may not need to
travel at all away from her home base. She is in the field whenever she is occupied
by her research. Hence in biographical research the locality of the field has shifted
from being a geographical place to being a subjectively defined location.

If gaining access to the field in biographical research may not entail much or any
spatial travelling, it often entails travelling in time, as historical social processes

and cultural ideas have to be researched and investigated in order to make sense of the life. Although we can, along with Lowenthal (1985), define the past as a foreign country, we are not able to move at will in time as we are between countries. This part of the field in biographical research therefore also needs to be subjectively defined as locational rather than as a place. What is still coterminous with the traditional anthropological concept of the field in biographical research is the fact that the researcher has to command an understanding of a specific, usually spatially defined, culture, that of a specific society or that of a specific region. The field thus retains a geographical dimension in biographical research but its main focus has shifted to a subjectively defined location.

As Gupta and Ferguson point out, ethnography has always had a well-developed sense of location, but 'this strength becomes a liability when notions of "here" and "elsewhere" are assumed to be features of geography, rather than sites constructed in fields of unequal power relations'(1997: 35). It is precisely the importance of viewing the field not as a geographical place but primarily as a constructed site or location that surfaces in anthropological biographical research. In the process the field, as traditionally defined, is decentred as 'the one, privileged site of anthropological knowledge' (ibid.: 37). At the same time the boundaries of the field open up, admitting new kinds of research and access to new kinds of knowledge, enabling anthropology to move onwards in a changing world.

This does not mean that the concept of the field has lost its usefulness; quite the contrary. As I found in my biographical research, the concept of the field, as modified above, continued to be useful. It could still define the boundaries of the research, albeit to an extent subjectively, and in that capacity it served to contain it. That is not least important for a researcher working from a home base, as a biographical researcher often does. In such a situation the boundaries between everyday life and research can become blurred and the concept of the field helps to keep them separate and hence contained and manageable. So far from rendering the concept of the field as something to be dispensed with, biographical anthropology points towards the continued usefulness of the concept redefined as location.

Participant Observation

But what happens to participant observation when the field is primarily defined subjectively as location in both time and space, as in biographical research? Obviously in such a field the actors, being dead, can be neither observed nor questioned about their lives or the culture and society they live in.

In this respect I have found the concept of *voices in the field* useful. Traditionally, anthropologists listen to people in the field, and in the modified field I have outlined here there are plenty of voices to listen to. They have a different form: they are spoken only insofar as concerns the reminiscences of people inter-viewed by the anthropologist about the person in question and her times. Most of them are to be found in written documents of various kinds, in personal letters, official statements, printed material about the person and her culture and society, the works of the person herself, and so on. The researcher has to use her eyes rather than her ears to discern most of the voices in the biographical field but it is a field like any other in anthropology, teeming with voices that speak to the anthropolo-gist.

Some of these voices, for instance those contained in private letters, can be con-siderably more personal or private than the voices an anthropologist can expect to hear in the traditional field. But there are also drawbacks. The voices in the biog-raphical field can be more patchy that those in the traditional field. What has been preserved in archives, for example, are most often documents concerning persons deemed to be of note for some reason, and the researcher may have a hard time finding the voices of people who do not fit that eclectic category. It should also be taken into account that often the biographical subject has herself chosen what voices remain for an eventual researcher to work with, since it is not uncommon for people selectively to destroy or preserve documents concerning their life. Still, this need not be very different from the traditional field situation where the anthro-pologist is told what people want her to know or what they think she wants to know; in both instances the fact that informants themselves have a view and an explanation of what is being studied has to be borne in mind.

The anthropologist in the traditional field can use her eyes to observe what are taking place, whereas the anthropologist in the biographical field cannot. Although such an observational element comes into play when the biographical researcher investigates the places where the life was lived, she still has to rely on her knowl-edge and imagination to conjure up the events of the field and to assess what the voices tell her about what happened. Interpretation is therefore unavoidably an integral element in biographical research, and so, consequently, is the situation-ality of the researcher.

The Researcher As Location

Braidotti (2002) has argued that our mapping and understanding of the world are undertaken from a specific position or location, which shapes our understanding. In her view a location is not individualistic but rather 'a collectively shared and constructed, jointly occupied spatio-temporal territory' that we inhabit (ibid.: 12). More often than not we are so familiar with our location that it escapes self-scrutiny. Hence our understanding, our analysis and explanations of social and cultural phenomena lack the necessary critical dimension of self-reflexivity. Braidotti emphasizes that self-reflexivity is not an individual activity but 'an interactive process which relies upon a social network of exchanges'(ibid.: 13). By being aware of our location and hence in a position to engage in this kind of self-reflexivity, we can in effect de-territorialize ourselves in terms of time and space and thus throw an external light on our research subjects. That approach in turn allows us to become accountable for ourselves as locations.

The importance of reflexivity and the awareness that the knowledge we gather in anthropological research is socially generated is not new in anthropology. Braidotti's formulation, however, lends itself very well to my present concerns. I have argued that for biography to be anthropology it needs to critically examine the social and cultural context of the life being investigated and must avoid succumbing to either the familiarity or the otherness of that context. In doing so the researcher must be aware of herself as a location in social and cultural terms and make that awareness active in her research. If, as I have argued, the field is to an important extent subjectively defined in biographical anthropology and involves mental time travel on the part of the researcher, it becomes all the more important that the researcher be aware of herself as a location so as to ensure the accountability or at least the transparency of her interpretations.

To take an example from my research into the life of Björg C. Thorlaksson: I was aware from the beginning that those who had any knowledge of her assumed that she was mentally deranged. Being a feminist, I thought that this was the usual writing off of unusual women who attempted to carve out a place for themselves in social spaces where they were not supposed to be. Such women would of course be considered mad to attempt to do so. My view was vindicated as I proceeded with the research. I found no sign of madness in Björg's writings; they were perfectly lucid and very well argued. Even her letters, where she told of how the German military pursued her in Paris in the 1920s, were utterly convincing, if scary. I knew that she had spent a year in hospital in Paris in 1930 and that she was sick with breast cancer, and assumed that was the reason for her hospitalization. Then one grey November morning I visited the hospital, deceptively named Maison Maternelle, and realized that the institution in which I found myself was a hospital for mentally deranged women. From that moment on my research took a new course. Everything I had done so far had to be rethought in the light of the fact that Björg had been considered mentally deranged by her contemporaries. But most importantly I had to come to terms with myself as location. My feminism had led me to interpret her life according to feminist lights. I, as a location, had influenced the research; it had blinkered my vision and led me to wrong conclusions. I thought I had been aware of myself as a location but was stopped short and proved to be insufficiently so. I subsequently reviewed all my material with that in mind.

That the researcher be sufficiently aware of herself as location is all the more important in biographical research as she usually cannot ask her subject for permission to research the life. The anthropologist in the traditional field, by contrast, can usually ask permission for an interview or, for example, to be present at a certain social event. The biographical researcher may very well be trespassing in some sense or in certain areas of the life but there is very little she can do about this except being aware of it. Besides, the power of biography once published is such that it can define the life in question. A biography is a monograph with a person's face and name on the cover. The accountability of biographical interpretation is therefore exceedingly important.

The concept of the researcher as location and the concept of the field as location reflect each other. As locations, both are to an extent subjectively defined, yet both rely on a common, collectively shared spatio-temporal territory that in turn needs to be de-territorialized to allow for critical evaluation and accountability. The two distinct processes of de-territorialization, that of the field and that of the researcher, mirror each other and become mutually comprehensible or inclusive, placing the researcher and the field in a complementary position.

Disciplinary Boundaries and Multi-sided Anthropological Projects

For most of the twentieth century social anthropologists shied away from history, to which genre biography has usually been seen to belong. This was partly a reaction to nineteenth-century scholarship in anthropology, but equally important was the invention of fieldwork, coupled with the Durkeiminan tradition of analysing social systems as coherent functional entities. These functional entities or wholes were generally conceived of in anthropology as a local culture, something the anthropologist studied in the field as a more or less balanced and tradition-bound social system. As Hastrup (1992) and others have pointed out, this view served to alienate anthropology from history, to such an extent that even when written records of 'other' societies existed they were often ignored. The centrality of the field and work done in the field in defining what anthropology was and was not was instrumental in erecting the boundary between anthropology and history.

Hastrup (ibid.) convincingly argues the case for the 'historicization' of anthropology, where the object of investigation is no longer defined in spatial terms, that is, in terms of the field as a locality, but rather as a synthesis of diachrony and synchrony according to which we are able to allow for there being more than one place or one time in a given social and territorial space. This point is abundantly clear in biographical anthropology if only because the life being investigated contains at any given time all that has previously shaped it in time and space. Yet, as I have argued, the concept of the field, modified as a location, continues to be useful in such research. Examining it critically and applying it to different areas of investigation such as biography is therefore also a move towards reaching across disciplinary boundaries, including those between history and anthropology.

Biography, furthermore, points towards the necessity of curtailing other disciplinary boundaries and the importance of multi-sided projects. To use again my research into the life of Björg C. Thorlaksson as a case in point, neither my knowledge of Icelandic society and culture, based on years of research, nor my anthropological training and understanding met all my needs for analysing the data I had assembled on her life. Quite early on I realized I needed the collaboration of experts in other fields.

On one level, there were the facts of the life itself. Björg's illnesses, mentioned above, are an example of an area where I needed expertise which I did not possess. Illness has multiple effects in a person's life and can shape her personhood to the extent of diminishing or partially denying it. Björg battled breast cancer for twelve years until finally succumbing to its ravages in 1934. Understanding her life during those last twelve years meant understanding the basic facts about this disease, how it develops, its physical effects, and, last but not least, its effects on the person's understanding of herself and her relation to her social environment. For that I sought the collaboration of a cancer specialist who directed me towards reading material and who painstakingly analysed my subject's medical records from different hospitals. Without his collaboration I would not have come to understand how the disease shaped her life and how her unwanted childlessness came to haunt her in her last otherwise productive years.

The same applies to Björg's mental illness. In order to understand it I sought the collaboration of a psychiatrist, who referred me to readings, discussed her symptoms with me, and, because in the case of this illness I did not have access to medical records, precluded some possibilties and indicated others. As Björg was convinced she was being persecuted by the German military, as mentioned above, and about which she told convincing stories, I sought the collaboration of a historian who specialized in this area to try to decide whether her stories could be true in the factual sense. Although it is both difficult and risky to diagnose a person's mental state after the fact, this collaboration led me to the conclusion that she had suffered from a certain kind of delusional disorder. To complement my own insights derived from gender theory as to why she should have suffered from such a disorder, I sought the collaboration of an analyst who discussed with me the various facets of her life, placing the disease in context. What emerged from this collaboration was an analysis not only of the life of my subject but also that of women seeking recognition in the male-dominated world of scholarship in the 1920s and 1930s. Without this collaboration I would not have been able to make more than superficial sense of these data, and for the analysis it was invaluable.

On another level I sought the collaboration of various specialists in order to understand Björg's work. She was a wide-ranging scholar and a prolific writer and wrote on such diverse subjects as philosophy, psychology, physiology, nutrition and etymology. She also published extensively on social issues and wrote and published poems and plays. In order to understand a person's life, it is necessary to understand her thought, of which I had abundant data in the form of her written work. Her work was also interesting in itself and her contribution to the various fields in which she engaged were valuable and deserved to be reassessed and brought to light. Part of my project was thus to make her work accessible to the reading public and to create a place for her in the history of Icelandic scholarship.

For those purposes I sought the collaboration of specialists in Björg's various fields. A philosopher analysed her work in philosophy and evaluated it in the light of current research in the field, as did a psychologist, an etymologist, a physiologist and a nutritionist in their respective fields. An historian of science placed her work within the context of scientific development and a specialist on literature analysed her poems and plays. Since Björg's writings on social issues and the position of women were within my own field of expertise, I analysed her work in this area. As mentioned above, this resulted in a companion volume to the biography published the following year. It combined scholarly articles on her work with excerpts from her own writings, some of which had not previously been published. Without this collaboration I would have been much less successful in bringing to light Björg's thoughts and ideas. At the same time the contribution of these scholars fed into my analysis in the biography, where, as a result, I was able to discuss her work with some confidence and to connect it to what was happening in her life. Had it not been for the multi-sided dimension to the project, the analysis which emerged would have been much the poorer, if not in some aspects downright flawed.

My experience of collaborating with specialists in different fields thus clearly points towards the creative potentiality of such working methods and how they can enrich and enhance what we view as anthropological concerns. At the same time the different fields of knowledge became part of the field, further extending its delineation. So if the concept of the field as traditionally employed in anthropology has to an extent been instrumental in erecting boundaries between disciplines, it can also be used to curtail them by making the field, defined as location, encompass disciplines other than anthropology.

Conclusion

In biographical anthropology the locus of ethnography has shifted. It involves locality only to a limited extent and has instead become a 'location' that in important respects must be subjectively defined. Yet I have found the concept so modified to be of continued usefulness in this untraditional anthropological area of investigation. It still serves to define the boundaries of research and hence to facilitate the differentiation of research from other concerns. We may seem far from the Trobriands in biographical anthropology but that is not really the case.

By deploying the concept of *voices in the field* the method of participant observation can still be applied, albeit subjectively, since in interpreting these voices the researcher has to rely on her imagination to a greater extent than in the traditional field. That points towards the importance of the researcher being aware of herself as a location of the research in order to augment the accountability of her interpretations. In this respect the field as location and the researcher as location complement each other.

I have also pointed out that even if the traditional concept of the field has been instrumental in erecting boundaries between anthropology and related disciplines, it can, modified as a location, serve to curtail these very same boundaries and encompass cross-disciplinary knowledge. At the same time biographical research points towards the importance of multi-sided projects that can deal with the many subjects that a life and its context can raise. Furthermore, as I have argued, there is no doubt that anthropology offers many useful theoretical insights which are excellent analytic tools with which to cut through diverse material such as encountered in biographical research.

Some may fear that by encompassing diverse areas of knowledge we may be exploding anthropology into nothingness or into a shapeless mass of method and knowledge where anything goes. I would rather see this move as one of imploding anthropology, extending its sphere and opportunities for new knowledge and theoretical insights. As long as we retain and develop our major theoretical insights and the discipline's central defining concepts, 'anthropology' will not disappear. The concept of the field occupies such a central defining position. My examination of the concept in the light of biographical research has shown that it is far from redundant in such research. On the contrary, with modification, this identifying concept of anthropology can continue to serve as an important tool in our quest for knowledge and understanding.

Notes

1. This refers to a period of fieldwork in Cape Verde researching the position of women in the island's fishing industry.

2. Perhaps my own cultural formation asserted itself in my choosing the biographical narrative form because the Icelandic sagas, which formed an important part of the early education of my generation of Icelanders, rely on chronological narrative, the telling of a story, and can also be viewed as composite biographies. Indeed two other Icelandic anthropologists have susequently published biographies: Gisli Palsson (2003) and Inga Dora Björnsdottir (2004).

3. The biography (2001) was awarded the National Litertuture Prize for Non-fiction the year of its publication and became a best-seller, whereas the collection of scholarly papers which followed (2002) enjoyed the moderate attention that

scholarly works normally attract in Iceland.

4. Compared, for instance, with the equally central concept of culture in anthropology, which has been and continues to be thoroughly examined.

References

Ardener, S. (ed.) (1975), *Perceiving Women*, London: J.M. Dent and Sons Ltd.
Björnsdottir, I.D. (2004), *Olöf eskimoi*, Reykjavik: Mal og menning.
Braidotti, R. (2002), *Metamorphoses: Towards a Materialist Theory of Becoming*, Cambridge: Polity Press.
Campell, J. (2000), *Margaret Thatcher: The Grocer's Daughter*, London: Jonathan Cape.
Crapanzano, V. (1985), *Tuhami. Portrait of a Moroccan*, Chicago: University of Chicago Press.
de Beauvoir, S. (1972 [1949]), *The Second Sex*, trans. H.M. Parshley, Harmondsworth: Penguin.
Durrenberger, E.P. and Palsson, G. (eds) (1989), *The Anthropology of Iceland*, Iowa City: University of Iowa Press.
Fortes, M. (1969), *Kinship and the Social Order*, Chicago: Aldine Publishing Company.
Gledhill, J. (1994), *Power and Its Disguises: Anthropological Perspectives on Politics*, London: Pluto Press.
Gupta, A. and Ferguson, J. (eds) (1997), *Anthropological Locations*, Berkeley: University of California Press.
Hastrup, K. (ed.) (1992), *Other Histories*, London: Routledge.
Hastrup, K. (1998), *A Place Apart: An Anthropological Study of the Icelandic World*, Oxford: Clarendon Press.
Jenkins, R. (2001), *Churchill*, London: Macmillan.
Kristmundsdottir, S.D. (1997), *Doing and Becoming: Women's Movements and Women's Personhood in Iceland 1870–1990*, Reykjavik: University of Iceland Press.
Kristmundsdottir, S.D. (2001), *Björg: Ævisaga Bjargar C. Thorlaksson*, Reykjavik: JPV utgafa.
Kristmundsdottir, S.D. (ed.) (2002), *Björg: Verk Bjargar C. Thorlaksson*, Reykjavik: JPV utgafa.
Lambek, M. and Strathern, A. (eds) (1998), *Bodies and Persons: Comparative Perspectives from Africa and Melanesia*, Cambridge: Cambridge University Press.
Langness, L.L. and Frank, G. (1981), *Lives: An Anthropological Approach to Biography*, Novato, CA: Chandler and Sharp.
Lewis, O. (1961), *The Children of Sánchez*, Harmondsworth: Penguin Books.

Lowenthal, D. (1985), *The Past is a Foreign Country*, Cambridge: Cambridge University Press.

Nanda, S. (1999), *Neither Man nor Woman: The Hijras of India*, Belmont, CA: Wadsworth.

Palsson, G. (2003), *Frægd og firnindi: Ævisaga Vilhjálms Stefánssonar*, Reykjavik: Mal og menning.

Rosaldo, M.Z. and Lamphere, L. (eds) (1974), *Woman, Culture and Society*, Stanford: Stanford University Press.

Shostak, M. (1981), *Nisa: The Life and Words of a!Kung Woman*, New York: Vintage Books.

Diaspora, Cosmopolis, Global Refuge: Three Voices of the Supranational City

Nigel Rapport

First Voice: Diaspora

Diaspora as Fashion

Is it more than political correctness and the modishness of reversals – deconstructing hierarchies and privileging the margins – that results in the diaspora, the migrant and the pariah being so often seen as central to present-day experience? According to Iain Chambers, for instance, 'To be a stranger in a strange land ... is perhaps a condition typical of contemporary life' (1994: 18).[1] And he goes on:

> The chronicles of diasporas – those of the black Atlantic, of metropolitan Jewry, of mass rural displacement – constitute the ground-swell of modernity. These historical testimonies interrogate and undermine any simple or uncomplicated sense of origins, traditions, and linear movement. ... The migrant's sense of being rootless, of living between worlds, between a lost past and a non-integrated present, is perhaps the most fitting metaphor of this (post)modern condition. (ibid.: 16, 27)

The migrancies of Blacks, Jews and (say) the Irish seemingly become 'typical conditions', 'fitting metaphors' and authentic 'ground-swells'. Nor is this only the view of commentators at the erstwhile centre. The journeymen themselves now consider their experience as 'typical symptoms of a modern condition at once local and universal' (Nkosi 1994: 5). For the African, according to Lewis Nkosi, whether in exile from his continent in the aftermath of colonialism or reconciled with it via the moment of post-coloniality, homelessness abides. There can be no homecoming for anyone in the modern world, indeed, because the 'modern consciousness' is itself 'alienated or marginalized', enduring the radical instability of rupture, abandonment, departure and displacement (ibid.: 5). Hence, the exile of the African is the central motif of modern culture.

Then again, the deracination and reorientation long experienced by the Irish, we are told (Kiberd 1998), moving from remote rurality to the inner cities of Britain and the USA, have come to constitute the central modalities of 'progress' in our time for millions. Far from backward, Declan Kiberd concludes, the Irish have been among the first to deal with 'the modernizing predicament' and, since the mid-nineteenth-century, been one of the most forward-looking and future-oriented of peoples.[2]

Or again, the Czech writer Milan Kundera, in exile from Eastern Europe in Western Europe, would point to 'great Jewish figures' as those who have shown an 'exceptional feeling' for what all of Europe now works towards and esteems: namely, a home polity 'conceived not as territory but as culture' (1990: 157). Exiled from their land of origin and lifted above nationalist passions, the Jews, Kundera contends, serve as exemplars of a possible transnational identity.

Nor have anthropologists been loath to theorize on the normativity of global movement and the consequent hybridity, creolization, synchronicity and compression of multiculturalism. 'Diaspora' has become a key tool in the disciplinary armoury, with studies of the ways in which members of diasporic communities imaginatively preserve and regenerate distinctive identities, and maintain a sense of distinctiveness, even though separated from their 'home' terrains and scattered. Ideal homes are vicariously experienced through myth, through tales of aboriginal practices and exploits retold (ready for some wished-for future return), while social solidarity is achieved by way of complex transnational cultural forms which transmute space continually into place. Indeed, being rootless, at home between worlds, inhabiting a cultural milieu between a lost past and a fluid present – these are now seen as more accurate descriptors of social life than former accounts of socio-cultural stasis and structure (Rapport and Dawson 1998). Life is a journey, consciousness is a journey, thought and writing are journeys, anthropology itself is a journey.

Diaspora as Actual

The dangers and drawbacks in this kind of socio-cultural accounting are as apparent as its fashionableness. The level of generality at which it can be written – the employment of global generalization *per se* – can easily usher in statements which are true only inasmuch as detail and subtleties of appreciation of individual lives are absent. The essentialisms of treating 'Jewish', 'Irish' or 'Black' experiences as uniform, and then as archetypes of a contemporary human condition, run the risk of reiterating the very kinds of fateful, categorial stereotypifications which they were intended to deconstruct – periphery becomes the new centre (and essence), diaspora the new society and culture. The analytical panaceas of migration and transnationality can threaten to euphemize all socio-cultural experience as versions of the same diasporic phenomenon (Amit 2002).

What is called for is an appreciation of the global phenomenon of movement in its multiple and diverse local manifestations. Then a developing of values and of social arrangements whereby the individual particularities of social life, the fluidities and multiplicities of diasporic identities, are not prejudged and may, as far as possible, have their various cultural expressions accommodated. As such, this chapter is a thought-piece on the supranational city.

Second Voice: Cosmopolis

The Cosmopolite as Global Guest

One of the chief crimes with which diasporic movements – in particular 'Jewish' – have commonly been charged by nationalist regimes (by both the Nazis and the Soviets, for instance) is cosmopolitanism: conceiving of themselves as operating in a global space, they will have little attachment or loyalty, it is said, to any particular local one. As the *Oxford English Dictionary* succinctly sums up, in common usage 'cosmopolite' is '[o]ften contrasted with patriot'. This is precisely the contrast that I feel it proper to esteem, however. Cosmopolitanism, I shall suggest, is the habit of mind, the proclivity and the practice which is of vital importance for the inculcating of a global social order which is 'postnational' or, better, 'supranational' – in ethos if not yet in institution. Through the notion of being guests in any particular social milieu – guests, as it were, of the social procedures which make the contracting of mutual guest-hood possible – this is a social order to which all might belong, might feel they belong; a social order which might offer a successful accommodation of an ongoing variety of diasporic practice.

The advent of supranationalism – in the context of institutional arrangements such as the European Union, and disarrangements such as the ethnic nationalisms in the Balkans, the Caucasus and the Middle East – is something which is at once easy to imagine and far-fetched. But then many commentators have linked the two processes of global centripetalism and regional centrifugalism as aspects of one and the same millennial shift: a globalization which renders the nationalisms and patriotisms of the past two centuries obsolete even though, in the medium term, these might be replaced by virulent renascent particularisms. To this extent, we are justified in employing our anthropological imaginations in considering social arrangements for this global, supranational condition. Indeed, according to Ernest Gellner (1993a), we have little choice in the matter. A shared global human condition is a fact of all our lives and to pretend otherwise on the basis of some spurious, culturally relativist or post-colonial perspective is a travesty of reality and a dereliction of our professional duty. Any 'adequate' anthropology must begin from the wholly 'transcultural' nature of the contemporary world – its institutional arrangements and knowledges – and work towards setting up a transcultural morality (ibid.: 54). Of course, this will not be easy, it might be impossibly difficult, but this is precisely our predicament: 'to work out the social options of our affluent and disenchanted condition' (Gellner 1995: 8).

I should like to make a start in this direction by suggesting a location where supranational social order might best be imagined on the ground: the cosmopolis, the 'world-city'. This is the natural setting for a meeting of global, multicultural and transcultural travellers, of diasporic identities, under the aegis of universal procedures and on the basis of contractual associations. The cosmopolis, more exactly the world-city as focus of a regional hinterland, might offer a complex supranational domain. This is a setting for urban amenities in a relatively dispersed space, in which a cultural ethos might flourish where notions and idioms of autochthones and aliens are superseded by parties to local contracts, standing in relations of politico-legal equality, of 'mutual guests' partaking in local exchange.

Hosts and Guests is the title of a well-known collection of articles, edited by Valene Smith, concerning tourists and the sometimes long-suffering inhabitants of the regions which they visit. Smith defines a tourist as 'a temporarily leisured person who voluntarily visits a place away from home for the purpose of experiencing a change' (1989: 1). Perhaps, however, what has most characterized the anthropological appreciation of tourism since Smith wrote has been the central importance of this phenomenon for addressing the contemporary world as such; the 'temporary' experience of 'leisure' by 'persons away from home' has been centralized, theoretically, so that it now touches on the experience, ordinary and out-of-the-ordinary, of many, if not all. Again (as with 'diaspora'), I am attracted by this image and also fearful of its possible essentialist application. 'Travel', moving away from or between homes (moving as home) and 'experiencing change', we can say, is something practised by many and possessing consequences for all – albeit that the actualities of those experiences and consequences are individual and diverse. The outcome, however, may be that it becomes neither easy nor wise to attempt to demarcate or differentiate, in any absolute way, between 'hosts' and 'guests'. A reciprocality and a seriality of the roles of hosts and guests moves us towards an appreciation of that social state where neither party is clearly or absolutely 'at home' in a place, or where one is at home in and through being 'away'. Recognizing, that is, in the context of contemporary global transculturalism and movement – tourism, labour migrancy, pilgrimage, exile – the fluidity of the notions of hosts and guests is also to recognize the way in which one might imagine and promote mutual guesting as being the normative role played out in social space: where who is 'at home' is a matter of the nature and purpose of particular exchanges rather than absolute identities.

Cosmopolitanism and the Urban Imaginary

The above imaging of the cosmopolite as a kind of global guest resonates with a venerable tradition of social theorizing which likewise imaged a possible future of global voluntary association, of belonging deriving from social contracts entered into on a purposive, mutual and serial basis. Both Henry Maine and Ferdinand Toennies plotted a possible transition from locally indexed social orders to ones able to encompass global or cosmopolitan largesse. Moves from 'status' to 'contract' (Maine 1861) and from 'community' to 'association' (Toennies 1963 [1887]) look forward similarly to a time when relations are routinely entered into and regulated on instrumental, impartial and reciprocal terms for the conducting of specified business, and from positions of legally assured voluntarism.

At the same time, contractual association has a distinctly modish ring. 'Stakeholder' polities and economies are government policy on both sides of the Atlantic, and notions of contracts extending into domains previously only vaguely constituted in law, and under more 'traditional' provenance, are proceeding apace. We have the moot cases of contracts between parents and children, between children and schools, between doctors and patients, between suppliers of services and customers, between citizens and their governments.

In the spirit of cosmopolitanism, I find this contractualization of social life generally to be a 'good thing', leaving aside the niceties of whether this or that political party has the more appropriate arrangements for its implementation. At the same time, the echoes of Toennies and Maine remind us that these changes have supposedly been underway for a while, and that it is also a moot point the extent to which nineteenth-century predictions and prescriptions of ideal-typical socio-cultural evolution (including those of Saint-Simon, Marx and Durkheim) are practices one would want to be associated with or seen to be repeating.

I am also aware that claiming the city as a site where global ideology and local practice might meet, where individuals in transit might contract to serve as mutual guests, makes the focus of this future imaging more precise but not perhaps sufficiently so to surpass generality. After all, in the history of the Western imaginary the city can be said to hold a special place; cities have long been 'good to think with', and with a diversity of results. Instantiating the 'totemic' nature of the Western city only briefly, then, would be to recall that the model city-state advocated by Plato (1963) is a decidedly authoritarian milieu, in which a perfect republic is conceived of in terms of a ruling élite schooled in the intellectual apprehension of what is 'good', and governing to ensure the greater 'happiness' of the whole by way of censorship and social differentiation. For Milton, subsequently, looking back to Plato's *polis* means espying the very 'eye of [ancient] Greece': mother of the arts, of eloquence, wit, hospitality and study (1932 [1671]: book iv, lines 240–7). Goethe (1949), meanwhile, would reference the ancient city-state in order to distance it from present times and needs; for while the *polis* prescribes loyalties and exclusivities on the basis of it being a separate and distinct *patria*, 'patriotism' now calls for a constant intercourse between nations such as modern city life was properly suited to providing. For an earlier witness, William Penn (1726), however, the pertinent distinction is not between Classical *polis* and modern conditions but between urban and rural: 'country life is to be preferred, for there we see the works of God, but in cities little else but the works of men'. Similarly, in Dickens's depiction of 'Coketown' (Preston), the city as archetypal industrial agglomeration transmogrifies into a home for all that is essentially unnatural, for confinement, disease and greed:

> that ugly citadel, where Nature was as strongly bricked out as killing airs and gases were bricked in; at the heart of the labyrinth of narrow courts upon courts, and close streets upon streets, which had come into existence piecemeal, every piece in a violent hurry for some one man's purpose, and the whole an unnatural family, shouldering, and trampling, and pressing one another to death. (1971 [1854]: 102)

For founder member of the Chicago school of sociology Robert Park, the idiomatic dichotomization of rural and urban remains apposite but now the ingeniousness and contemporaneity of the latter is to be favoured over the originality and folksiness of the former. Building on the apperceptions of his teacher, Georg Simmel, Park delineates the city as a future-bearing social and moral milieu where very different kinds of people will meet and mingle (albeit without complete mutual understanding), where contact between people will often be transitory, causal, fortuitous and instable, and where status will by and large be a matter of presentation, of manners and fashionableness. Altogether, the modern-day city – *par excellence* Chicago – will come to be designated 'the natural habitat of civilized man', fulfilling the mediaeval proverbial promise that 'city air makes for freedom' (Park 1968: 3). Finally, for human geographer Harvey Cox, in the 'secular city' human beings take responsibility for the spaces that afford pace, variety and orientation to their lives. Urban secularism 'dislodges ancient oppressions and overturns stultifying conventions. It turns man's social and cultural life over to him, demanding a constant expenditure of vision and competence' (Cox 1965: 86).

Besides the intertextual quality of these references, what a brief trawl does illuminate is the malleability of the city as an item of social-philosophical consideration. Park himself observed how cities are wont to take on the characteristics and qualities of their inhabitants and thus be inherently diverse, and more recently Jonathan Raban (1973) has drawn attention to what he calls cities' 'softness'. An urban environment is soft, Raban explains, in that it awaits its consolidation into a certain shape by its inhabitants and observers, while embodying little in and of itself. Cities assume a shape around individual inhabitants according to the choices which the latter make, reflecting back the identity they have imparted to it. The social structures of cities are indeterminate and amorphous, in short, and cities are home to a wide array of lives, embodying a potential for diversity which is at once the stuff of dreams and of nightmares. Plastic by nature, offering few anchors and no hard groundings of their own, the habitation of cities (as with their conceptualization) amounts to an ongoing, creative ordering. For those without continued belief in their creative vision, or without the resources to put that vision into effect, an urban softness can be alienating; it can make the homeless or urban poor, the inhabitants of shanty towns in São Paulo, Cairo or Manila, all but invisible to the well-to-do.

While I would not want to accept an essentialist conception of an urban environment (or any other), and argue for a necessarily 'urban way of life' (Wirth 1938), I do find it useful for my purposes here that cities have been and still are imaginatively constructed in commentary in this way. Granted that here is 'the city' as idiom – posited in relation to the ideal republic, the rural idyll, the civilized dreamscape – and not as essential descriptor of actual spaces, milieux or lives, the urban imaginary is serviceable here too. As soft space, humanly constructed, malleable and contemporary in its conceptualization, 'the city' affords me the possibility of imaging the supranational cosmopole of mutual guest-hood.

The Supranational City

Having dwelt on the vagueness or fuzziness of the city as critically conceptualized (cf. Rapport and Overing 2000), let me offer a vague definition, borrowed from Ulf Hannerz: 'a sizeable, dense settlement in whose more or less common physical space a relatively high level of accessibility between a relatively large number of people obtains' (1980: 243). Hannerz sees the city as expressive of a 'centripetal tendency' in a particular regional setting. And while Britain in the mid nineteenth century was probably the first socio-cultural milieu in which most people lived in towns and cities, it is now estimated that more than half of the world's population is urban. There is no sign of this trend reversing, or of urban populations decreasing; some half a dozen cities can now boast populations of greater than 15 million. Even in those areas of the West where counter-urbanizing movements are reported, the so-called 'rurbanization' of rural locations by ex-urban residents, what eventuates is a dispersing of urban amenities and lifestyles over a wider area.

This is why Hannerz and others have paid modern cities significant attention. They have also granted cities a special place in that international trafficking of meanings (as Hannerz [1987] puts it) which is evidence of (and responsible for the furthering of) a world socio-cultural system or 'global ecumene'. Certain metropoles – London, Miami, Paris – Hannerz would already describe as 'international' milieux *tout court*. Here, entrepreneurs, migrant labourers, students, exiles, tourists, mingle with 'residents' in dialogic exchange. Such cities become social bridgeheads across which cultural practices flow and new creolized forms are taken up. Hannerz describes a new 'metropolitan culture' which pertains to these international cities, and is recognized as diverging from the 'rural' and 'rustic', less 'sophisticated' or 'modern', forms which preceded it. And yet, he resists the urge of treating the urban and the rural, even idiomatically, as two discrete and opposed (types of) social systems, in favour of plotting social relations in terms of one overarching set of global structures, economic, political, aesthetic, moral. One can image a global, creolizing spectrum, Hannerz (ibid.) concludes, linking first-world metropole to third-world village. A conversation flows along this spectrum such that diverse cultural forms engage and merge, comment upon and parody, influence and subvert one another, in an unending intermingling and counterpoint. And from this reciprocal exchange none are left out: 'we are all being creolized' (ibid.: 557). Even more appropriately, in Keith Hart's words: 'everyone is caught between local origins and a cosmopolitan society in which all humanity participates' (1990: 6).

Moreover, if practices and symbols are, in Hannerz's image, continuously trafficked through international cities, becoming transformed and creolized in the process, then this is, partly at least, because people are in continual movement across and within these urban spaces. A diffuse sense of mobility thereby characterizes urban life as inhabitants, in transit across multiple and diverse social worlds (house and work, family and friends, religion and recreation), find connections, avoid relations, meet people, garner experiences, routinize space and escape routine. Cities are 'migrant landscapes', in Chambers's words (1994:14, 94), home to 'shifting, mixing, contaminating, experimenting, revisiting and recomposing': recomposing histories and traditions, shifting centres and peripheries, mixing global tendencies and local distinctions. They are sites of transformations of social reality, of transitory lives, and of cultural movements.

An important element which is also brought to the fore by Hannerz's notion of the international city as a site for a global traffic in meaning is the experiential nature of this milieu, and the necessarily interpretive quality of its anthropological accounting. The city as a 'world-city', the socio-cultural milieu as part of a global ecumene, the movement and exchange as evincing a world-wide network – these are matters of judgement as much as of measurement. They are, furthermore, of vital importance in an anthropological apprehension of contemporary urbanism and what it might become. The meaning of the city to its inhabitants and its observers possesses a quality, a reality, in human life which is as significant as the seeming objectivity and fixity of the city on maps and in statistics, if not more so.

This is especially true in my search for a possible future-image of the supranational in the midst of the contemporary metropolitan-international. What interests and heartens me is less the measurable accuracy of the details of change which Hannerz marshals in his description of modernization via creolization than the place he would give to the cosmopole. For if I am to see in the international city not only a bridgehead to a global ecumene but also a prototype of a culture of cosmopolitanism in a supranational social order, then it is significant that Hannerz and his informants impart certain meanings to the social form. 'The city' is a significant symbol whose use can serve as a route to certain happenings; the discourse of 'international city as global ecumene' can acquire the illocutionary force to create certain social facts: to create the supranational city as an objective reality.

Nevertheless, if my imagining of mutual guests amid the just procedures of the supranational city is to be anything more than a castle in the sky, then the discursive process whereby people employ the symbolic in the negotiation and construction (and reconstruction) of the social-structural must be appreciated. It must be understood, as Cohen (1993) has put it, that people are responsible for investing cities with culture – they enculturate the city – rather than it being passively responded to as a deterministic force. As much as any other, urban milieux are constituted by (not constitutive of) the selves of their individual inhabitants, and their meanings – the meanings of lives lived within them – cannot be generalized. It is wrong to envisage an urban milieu as necessarily massificating and anonymizing individuals (*à la* Wirth), for instance, fracturing them into roles, segmenting them apropos different social worlds, for this merely reduces a city's inhabitants to ciphers of the logic by which an analyst (or administrator) would model urban social life in his or her effort to manage it. Rather, it must be appreciated how 'people shape the city through their everyday resourcefulness' (ibid.: 8), their involvement less a matter of coercive imperative than of purposive transacting, deploying and acquiring of resources (Amit-Talai 1989). In short, it is because the city is a significant symbolic form which people animate and inform through their ongoing experience and use – something individuals supply with meaning in the contexts of their personal circumstances – that the notion of the supranational city may be more than mere wishful thinking.

St John's, Newfoundland: A Phraseological Community

'[T]he crowds, the helter-skelter, and the constant buzz of joking conversation' mean, for Geertz (1960: 49), that urban milieux come to be imbued with a certain elusive quality, well nigh impossible to apprehend systematically. For Hannerz (1980: 200) there is a key, nonetheless, which is to be found in an analysis of the series of networks of urban interaction: cities portrayed as 'networks of networks' in a shifting collage of individuals, roles, cultural domains and social situations of exchange. In an ethnography of the Canadian city of St John's, Newfoundland, I endeavoured to trace the network of links pertaining to the ways in which individuals in different urban settings conversed about 'violence' (Rapport 1987). Analysing the categories, idiosyncrasies and diversities of 'talking violence' – the violence of armed robberies, of the police, in bars, around drugs, against women, and in possible nuclear war – I felt I could apprehend how people variously came together in St John's for the instigation and development of different kinds of relations, before again departing on their personal itineraries across the city and beyond. 'Violence' was a node of communication around which conversation was regularly and conveniently constructed; a catchword which made transient (potentially unsafe) conversational exchanges appear expectable and routine. Speaking of uncertainty in an habitual fashion engendered certainty.

My feeling, amid that urban research, was that the conducting of contemporary social relations was more a matter of verbal exchange than anything else; moreover, of verbal exchange which was more or less routine (even formulaic) in character. For it was words which individuals in global transit across and between socio-cultural milieux could most easily carry with them and look to as sources of stability, as remembrances of relations and times past, as toothing-stones to safe places present. More than this, in the give and take of conversational exchange, of turn-taking, portraying and being portrayed, there resided an intrinsic mutuality and equality. Conversationalists acted as mutual guests to one another's individual and idiosyncratic verbal forays, ploys and summations (Rapport 1990). Individuals were at home in the city by way of a set of habitually repeated, largely conversational practices: 'words, jokes, opinions, gestures, actions, even the way one wears a hat' (Berger 1984: 64).

The picture that emerged in St John's was of a socio-cultural milieu constituted by a fund of common catchwords-in-use, and a host of changing agreements and disagreements over how individuals chose habitually to come together by way of these catchwords and converse. Dipping into this fund as they crossed urban space, individuals would develop relationships of variable verbal-cum-social closeness and complexity, and meet on varying levels of verbal-cum-social inclusivity; here was a shifting sliding-scale of verbal sameness and difference (Rapport 1994a). As a city, St John's comprised a phraseological community: catchwords, clichés and formulas of exchange being its relatively common and stable currency by which a globally transient population might embed itself for the purpose of local exchange.

We have heard Hannerz describe cities such as London, Miami and Paris as 'international' milieux serving as social bridgeheads towards new 'metropolitan cultures' of dialogic exchange. Even in my provincial Canadian capital, I found an urban socio-cultural milieu constituted by a fund of common catchwords put to use by a population in global transit between places and relations. Finally, then, I am led to ask whether the actual practice of diasporic lives in international cities might not offer insights into a possible moral programme of supranational, transcultural social relations.

Third Voice: Global Refuge

Urban Experiment: The Network of Refuge Cities

The International Parliament of Writers (IPW) was inaugurated in 1993 by a group of authors (of both literature and science) concerned, as they put it in one of their first Newsletters (IPW 1994), that writing is today a crime in numerous countries around the world (Algeria, Iran, Nigeria, China ...), and that, in recent years, many individuals have paid with their lives for exercising what is their basic human right to write, and to have others read what they write. One of the major events preceding the setting up of the IPW was the sentence of a fatwah incurred by writer Salman Rushdie in 1989, and the ensuing series of orchestrated riots around the world, book-burnings, and murders of those seen to be furthering the book's dissemination. In the wake of feeble public posturings of the British Parliament, the IPW would represent an institution in defence of writers and artists the world around – their works, their persons and their languages. It would assert the autonomy and sovereignty of litera-ture over and against political, economic and dogmatic institutionalism of all kinds, and promote a new kind of universalism. 'Writing', as Jacques Derrida phrased it, should be seen to include a universal creativity and narrativity: 'The term "writer" concerns all those who express themselves, including those who are threatened in their ability to give testimony by speaking or writing' (1998: 1).

Salman Rushdie penned A Declaration of Independence for the IPW (14 February 1994), which stated:

Writers are citizens of many countries: the finite and frontiered country of observable reality and everyday life, the boundless kingdom of the imagination, the half-lost land of memory, ... and – perhaps the most important of all our habitations – the unfettered republic of the tongue.

It is these countries that our Parliament of Writers can claim, truthfully and with both humility and pride, to represent. Together they comprise a territory far greater than that governed by any worldly power; yet their defences against that power can seem very weak. The art of literature requires, as an essential condition, that the writer be free to move between his many countries as he chooses, needing no passport or visa, making what he will of them and of himself. ... The creative spirit, of its very nature, resists frontiers and limiting points, denies the authority of censors and taboos.

... Today, around the world, literature continues to confront tyranny – not polemically – but by denying its authority, by going its own way, by declaring its independence.

... Our Parliament of Writers exists to fight for oppressed writers and against all those who persecute them and their work, and to renew continually the declaration of independence without which writing is impossible; and not only writing, but dreaming; and not only dreaming, but thought; and not only thought, but liberty itself. (Rushdie 1994: 2)

Salman Rushdie became Honorary President of the new IPW, while Wole Soyinka has been the President, and among the Administrative Councillors (Vice-President, Treasurer, Secretary-General et al.) have been Adonis, Breyten Breytenbach, Hélène Cixous, J.M. Coetzee, Jacques Derrida, Anita Desai, Margaret Drabble, Jörgen Habermas, Émile Habibi, Václav Havel, Toni Morrison and Harold Pinter.

The first action of the IPW was to campaign for a Network of Refuge Cities in Europe: 'A network against intolerance and for the protection of menaced and persecuted writers' (IPW 1995b) – in effect, havens for writers whose right to creation (if not their right to life) was under threat in their home communities. The Network of Refuge Cities was to be a practical means to show solidarity with persecuted writers, and as the embryo of a system though which to reintroduce diversity, otherness and dialogue within and between cultural (legal and economic) exclusivities in the world, and hence to fight a growing sense of extremism in Europe and beyond; not only artists but art itself, the play of imagination and the practice of creativity, was seen to be under threat.

The IPW's Charter for Refuge Cities was adopted by the Congress of Local and Regional Authorities of the Council of Europe on 31 May 1995, on behalf of 400 conurbations within the Council's thirty-six member states; all were asked to participate in the network. On 21 September 1995, the European Parliament also voted through a resolution in support of the Network. The first city formally to sign a treaty with the IPW as a place of artistic 'asylum' was Berlin. Under the terms of the treaty, the Refuge City paid an annual charitable subscription to the IPW (as a contribution to the management of the Network) and also offered an annual grant of residence and accommodation (including travel, social security, child care and other municipal services) to threatened artists whom the IPW proposed and the city accepted. Berlin, in 1995, began to provide a stipend and housing for Taslima Nasreen (hounded out of Bangladesh by religious fundamentalists) and Mohamed Magani (hounded out of Algeria). Besides finances, the city would endeavour to facilitate the artist refugee acquiring legal status not only to reside in the city but also to settle in the host country if desired. For, as the 'Charter of the Cities of Asylum' expounds (IPW 1995b: 5), enshrined in the European Charter of Local Self-Government's emphasis on subsidiarity is the role of local authorities, especially cities, to promote 'local democracy'.

To date, the Network comprises more than twenty cities and a number of urban regions, each hosting one or more artist refugee(s) engaged in creative writing and broadcasting, and giving testimony to abuses of human rights in their past milieux. Included in the Network are: Berlin, Frankfurt, Strasbourg, Basse-Normandie, Amsterdam, Venice, Tuscany, Barcelona, Lleida, Bern, Salzburg, Vienna, Stavanger, Kristiansand, Gothenburg, Oporto and Brussels (where, since 1998, the IPW has been based). Beyond Europe, Nagasaki, Durban, Mexico City, São Paulo, Passo Fundo, Buenos Aires, Ithaca, Gorée and Lamentin are also signed up. An annual Congress of Cities of Asylum maintains communication between these signatory bodies, and there is a website and a journal. The IPW continues to urge its individual members to propose their own home cities as Refuges 'and so redraw the map of exile in the world' (IPW 1995a).

'Members' of the IPW are all those individuals who have paid a (modest) annual subscription towards the running costs of the secretariat of the Parliament (based in Strasbourg), towards the fund for persecuted writers and artists, and towards the publication of the Newsletter *Littératures*, and then a journal, *Autodafé*. The IPW began with an operating budget, from grants, of US$150,000. Ultimately, the aim is financial independence, and towards this end, in 1997, Salman Rushdie suggested the founding of a chain of shareholders across Europe whereby 1,000 donor groups would each contribute $100 per year and so assure the IPW of an annual $100,000. Subscribers to the IPW are assured that their gesture of solidarity 'manifests the living proof of an active network of citizens who can see themselves and their values in the actions of the IPW'; for 'the defence of the right to creation is a matter for everyone' (Rushdie 1997). Here is an international, supranational network which takes as its lodestone the dignity of individual citizens over and against the groups and traditions they happen currently to patronize, and refuses the right of cultural communities and traditions to determine how those individuals might range, imaginatively, in the construction and performance of polyglot and mobile identities.

Voluntary Urban Community and Democracy Reborn

In arguing for an appreciation of what he terms 'personal nationalism', Anthony Cohen (1996) would deny that the logic of national and international political economies need necessarily translate into those who deem themselves members of such entities sharing a homogeneity of identity. To the contrary, the upsurge of often militant collective identities which we have witnessed, in Europe say, over the past few centuries – nationalistic, ethnic, religious, regional, and so on – and continue to witness today (in Europe and beyond) owe their power and conviction to the grass-roots phenomenon that it is these collectivities that individual members, separately and distinctively, feel to be the most advantageous medium for the expression of their whole selves. It is in the community voice that individuals best recognize their own experiences and mentalities, and by way of collective symbols that they think through and express their individual identities. In short, it is through the nation (et cetera) that they accrue 'a compelling formulation of self' (ibid.: 802).

I do not doubt that this 'personal nationalism', the inventing and investing of a collective entity with individual meaning, can be true (Rapport 1994b). But I think it has dangers: the dangers visited on Salman Rushdie, and the conceptual dangers of essentialization and categorization. As argued by Michael Jackson, collective identities and identity-terms always and inexorably reduce and traduce. 'Subjects of experience' are converted into 'objects of knowledge', humanity and individuality alike transmogrified into stereotype. 'Any kind of identity thinking is insidious', Jackson continues (2002: 115). Nation building, in the post-colonial era in particular, has employed a 'cultural fundamentalism' (nostalgic and utopian) which has reduced the world to simplistic, generalized, category oppositions with disastrous consequences: true belongers and true believers versus apostates and outsiders who may (at best) be shunned. We can surely do better than such groupism. As Gellner observed, 'we are all human' and we should not 'take more specific classifications seriously' (1993b: 3). We might aspire to having our societies based on legal recognition of identities which are other than collectivistic or classificatory, which recognize the sovereignty of moving individuals (Amit and Rapport 2002).

In practical terms it is this which the IPW has sought to conceptualize and routinize in its Network of Refuge Cities, it seems to me: the city being deliberately chosen as the social milieu in which a postmodern liberal polity imbued with a personal ethos might hope to be instituted. Refuge Cities with claims to global responsibility model themselves as ideally open spaces, polythetic and multicultural spaces, without minorities or marginals; citizenship is conceptualized not in inward-looking or isolationist terms but inclusively. The city becomes an assemblage of individual life-projects and trajectories; it is envisaged that individuals in physical movement through space and in cognitive movement through their lives may all contract into civil and political rights and duties on the basis of choice and at will. A 'supranational' exchange may then take place between the 'national cultures', the perspectives, constructed by those who are citizens at one time and over time. In the Network of Refuge Cities, in sum, legally constituted, social and physical 'free zones' are appraised in terms of the extents to which they are synonymous with 'free territories of the mind'. The Network, 'an arena for invention, a forum for inventors', offers an escape from that 'obsession with [essentialized] identity' (ethnic, cultural and linguistic) which threatens to render individuality 'speechless' (Salmon 1993: 2; 1995: 4). A particular form of citizenship is here championed, one which sees beyond 'collective manifestations [of identity] based on coercive dogmas' to a recognition that the freedom to write and create individual worlds is the foundation of a vital, democratic society (IPW 1999: 6). Here is a vision which attempts to operationalize a notion of communities as voluntaristic 'worlds of meaning in the minds of their members' (Cohen 1985: 82).

Ancient democracy was born in the *polis*, it is argued in the IPW literature (Lopez 1995: 5), European towns and cities have acted as sanctuaries since the Middle Ages, and it is a 'civic conscience' which might still hold out the best chance of protection to the individual and the free expression of his or her artistry.

If, as Bourdieu put it (1995: 6), the IPW might serve as a research laboratory for new forms of action against international, political and religious tyranny, the unchecked power of money and the media, then the Refuge City serves at least as a trope with which to image a reinvention of democracy. A network of such cities – at the same time decentralized and co-ordinated – can then amount to 'an archipelago of the imagination' (Lopez 1995): a refutation of classificatory limits to migration, legal membership and sentimental belonging, and an effecting of voluntary community amid a world of movement. From the Refuge City as locus and as trope one can imagine democracy reborn – in cities and by cities around the world – possessing the twin features of global movement and local security: from *polis* to cosmos. In the face of the closed and fixed nature of states and the reactionary orientation and institutionalization of censorious opinion, in the face of new persecutions emerging in the gaps between the authority of states – 'arbitrary', terroristic expressions of life-threatening intolerance which the state no longer controls – the Refuge City serves as an actual locus of individual freedom (IPW 1995b: 6).

Envoi: *Supermodernity, Supranationalism*

Anthropologists, according to Marc Augé, traditionally have mistrusted travel – movement, fluidity, flux – to the point of hatred (1995: 86). This is because they, as much as the people they have studied, have promulgated ideologies of 'societies identified with cultures conceived as complete wholes' (ibid.: 41). The nation state has represented this ideological project *par excellence*: the massification of humankind into general categories and classes; a collectivization, typification and essentialization which has issued forth as genocide and 'ethnic cleansing', and lives on in identity politics and fundamentalism. Augé is hopeful that the experience of what he calls 'supermodernity' can help us rid ourselves of such ideology. The rhetoric of 'place', of social relations, identity and history neatly mapping onto one another, the structuralism of society, culture and individual consistently and transparently eliciting one another, are overwhelmed and relativized, Augé contends, by the supermodern 'excess' of population movements, urban agglomerations and non-places. Here we might find an excess of individual subjectivities freeing themselves from ideological constraints and reflexively establishing their own cultural styles, tracing their own social itineraries, entering and leaving places, groups and identities.

But then the relationship between experience – the actuality of excess, of movement, flux and fluidity – on the one hand, and ideology – the rhetoric of classes – on the other, is always a complex one in human life. We seem only ever able to accept so much 'excessive' reality, and we resign ourselves to symbolic classifications which reduce, fix and stereotype; we oscillate, as Nietzsche (1967 [1871]) framed it, between the Dionysian and the Apollonian (cf. Rapport 1995). According to Augé, the notion of closed and self-sufficient classes – societies, cultures, nations, places, ethnicities, genders, religiosities – has always existed as a provisional myth, a semi-fantasy, even for those – natives and ethnologists – who identified with it. No one has ever been finally unaware of the relativity of such totalizing rhetoric. Our problem has been, however, and continues to be, the superlative human capacity of living the illusion, with baleful consequences for 'the open-endedness and ambiguity of lived experiences' (Jackson 2002: 125).

Unable ultimately to escape the ideological – the Apollonian dependence on model, classification and imagery – it would seem to me a capacity, even a duty, of anthropology to offer ideologies as open as possible to accommodating the open-endedness of experience and human 'will to power': to ongoing reinvention and refashioning of identity and self (Rapport 2003). From diaspora through cosmopolis to global refuge, this chapter has suggested three voicings of a possible space I have posited as the 'supranational city'. In a world of movement, the city – more exactly the cosmopolis in a global network of links – may offer a better institutional framework, a more open image, than the nation state for hosting a world of guests. The relative smallness of cities and their numerical profusion may better ensure that here people play the role of guests of social spaces, of procedures and of one another in a common and routine fashion, and thus resist the temptation of an unreflexive absolutism. The global cosmopolis may serve to promote an ironic detachment, which might in turn nurture a generosity of spirit whereby guest-hood becomes an everyday expectation and practice not merely associated with the diasporic, with the overprivileged tourist or the underprivileged refugee. The Network of Refuge Cities of the International Parliament of Writers makes this hope more than merely wishful thinking.

Notes

I am grateful to Peter Collins and Simon Coleman for the opportunity to air these thoughts at the Durham ASA Conference, and for the ensuing discussion chaired by Jeanette Edwards.

1. Or, from John Berger: 'emigration is the quintessential experience of our time' (1984: 55).
2. Not only is the Irish diaspora paradigmatic of modernity, but '"exile" is historically intrinsic to Irishness', preceding nationalism, capitalism, industrialism, colonization; 'to be Irish is to be an exile' (West 2002: 24).

References

Amit-Talai, V. (1989), *Armenians in London*, Manchester: Manchester University Press.

Amit-Talai, V. (2002), 'Armenian and Other Diasporas: Trying to Reconcile the Irreconcilable', in N. Rapport (ed.), *British Subjects*, Oxford: Berg.

Amit, V. and Rapport, N. (2002), *The Trouble with Community: Anthropological Reflections on Movement, Identity and Collectivity*, London, Pluto.

Augé, M. (1995), *Non-places*, London: Verso.

Berger, J. (1984), *And Our Faces, My Heart, Brief as Photos*, London: Writers & Readers.

Bourdieu, P. (1995), 'In Interview', *Littératures*, Autumn: 6.

Chambers, I. (1994), *Migrancy Culture Identity*, London: Routledge.

Cohen, A.P. (1985), *The Symbolic Construction of Community*, London: Routledge.

Cohen, A.P. (1993), 'Introduction', in A.P. Cohen and K. Fukui (eds), *Humanising the City?* Edinburgh: Edinburgh University Press.

Cohen, A.P. (1996), 'Personal Nationalism', *American Ethnologist* 23 (4): 802–15.

Cox, H. (1965), *The Secular City*, Toronto: Macmillan,

Derrida, J. (1998), 'Reaction', *Correspondence of the International Parliament of Writers* 4, Spring: 1.

Dickens, C. (1971 [1854]), *Hard Times*, Harmondsworth: Penguin.

Geertz, C. (1960), *The Religion of Java*, Glencoe, IL: Free Press.

Gellner, E. (1993a), *Postmodernism, Reason and Religion*, London, Routledge,

Gellner, E. (1993b), 'The Mightier Pen? Edward Said and the Double Standards of Inside-Out Colonialism', *Times Literary Supplement*, 19 February: 3–4.

Gellner, E. (1995), 'Anything Goes', *Times Literary Supplement*, 16 June: 6–8.

Goethe, W. (1949), *Wisdom and Experience*, trans. H.J. Weigand, London: Routledge and Kegan Paul.

Hannerz, U. (1980), *Exploring the City*, New York: Columbia University Press.

Hannerz, U. (1987), 'The World in Creolization', *Africa* 57 (4): 546–59.

Hart, K. (1990), 'Swimming into the Human Current', *Cambridge Anthropology* 14 (3): 3–10.

International Parliament of Writers (1994), *Littératures*, October/November.

International Parliament of Writers (1995a), *Littératures*, Autumn.

International Parliament of Writers (1995b), *The Charter of Cities of Asylum*, Strasbourg: International Parliament of Writers,

International Parliament of Writers (1999), *The Correspondence* 5.

International Parliament of Writers (2001), *Autodafé* 1, June.

Jackson, M. (2002), *The Politics of Storytelling*, Copenhagen: Museum Tusculanum Press.

Kiberd, D. (1998), 'Romantic Ireland's Dead and Gone', *Times Literary Supplement*, 19 September: 12–14.

Kundera, M. (1990), *The Art of the Novel*, trans. L. Asher, London: Faber.

Lopez, F. (1995), 'The Cities of the Asylum Charter', *Littératures*, Autumn.

Maine, H. (1861), *Ancient Law*, London: Murray,

Milton, J. (1932), *Paradise Regained*, London: Partridge.

Nietzsche, F. (1967 [1871]), *The Birth of Tragedy*, trans. W. Kaufmann, New York: Random House.

Nkosi, L. (1994), 'Ironies of Exile', *Times Literary Supplement*, 1 April: 5.

Park, R. (1968), 'The City', in R. Park, E. Burgess and R.D. McKenzie (eds), *The City*, Chicago: University of Chicago Press.

Penn, W. (1726), *The Works of William Penn*, London: Sowle.

Plato (1963), *The Republic*, trans. J. Adam, Cambridge: Cambridge University Press.

Raban, J. (1973), *Soft City*, Harmondsworth: Penguin.

Rapport, N. (1987), *Talking Violence: An Anthropological Interpretation of Conversation in the City*, St John's: ISER Press, Memorial University.

Rapport, N. (1990): 'Ritual Speaking in a Canadian Suburb: Anthropology and the Problem of Generalization', *Human Relations* 43 (9): 849–64.

Rapport, N. (1994a), ' "Busted for Hash": Common Catchwords and Individual Identities in a Canadian City', in V. Amit-Talai and H. Lustiger-Thaler (eds), *Urban Lives*, (eds), Toronto: McClelland & Stewart.

Rappport, N. (1994b), 'Trauma and Ego-Syntonic Response: The Holocaust and the "Newfoundland Young Yids", 1985', in S. Heald and A. Duluz (eds), *Anthropology and Psychoanalysis*, London: Routledge.

Rapport, N. (1995), 'Migrant Selves and Stereotypes: Personal Context in a Postmodern World', in S. Pile and N. Thrift (eds), *Mapping the Subject*, London: Routledge.

Rapport, N. (2003), *I am Dynamite: An Alternative Anthropology of Power*, London: Routledge.

Rapport N. and Dawson, A. (eds) (1998), *Migrants of Identity: Perceptions of 'Home' in a World of Movement*, Oxford: Berg.

Rapport N. and J. Overing (2000), *Social and Cultural Anthropology: The Key Concepts*, London: Routledge.

Rushdie, S. (1994), 'A Declaration of Independence', *Littéatures* October/November: 2.

Rushdie, S. (1997), Open letter to the 'friends of the International Parliament of Writers', June, Strasbourg.

Salmon, C. (1993), 'No to Speechlessness', *Littératures*, November: 2.

Salmon, C. (1995), (1995), 'Within the Asylum Cities', *Littératures*, Autumn: 3–4.

Smith, V. (1989), 'Introduction', in V. Smith (ed.), *Hosts and Guests*, Philadelphia: University of Pennsylvania Press.

Toennies, F. (1963 [1887]), *Community and Society*, trans. C.P. Loomis, New York: Harper.

West, P. (2002), 'Out of Ireland', *Times Literary Supplement*, 15 November: 24.

Wirth, L. (1938), 'Urbanism as a Way of Life', *American Journal of Sociology* 44: 1–24.

Index